Faces of the Sea
Stock Island - The Florida Keys

John Van Horn
johnvanhornphoto.net

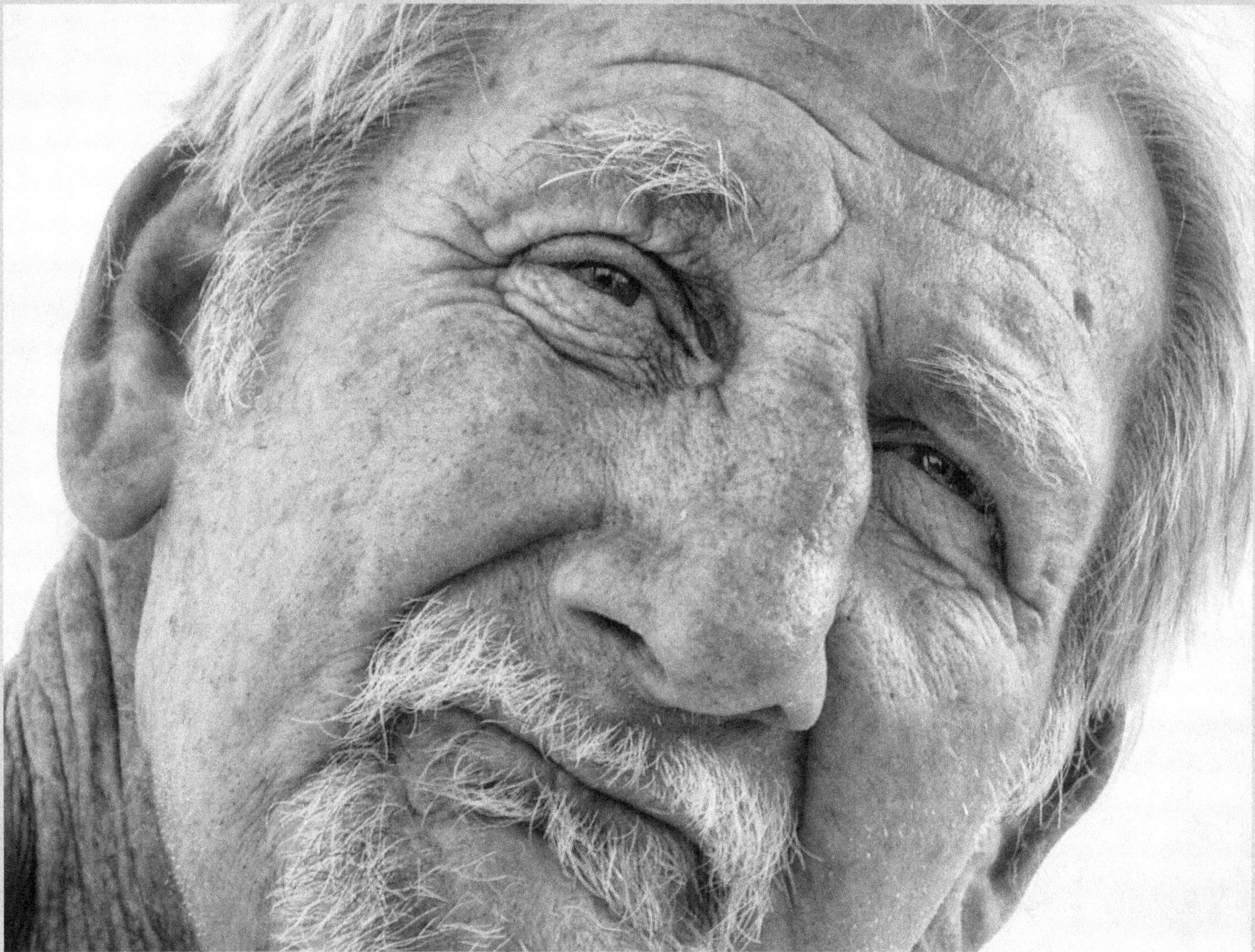

Published by Moosic Mtn. Wild Co.
Honesdale, Pennsylvania
www.moosicpublishing.com

ISBN: 153342652X
ISBN-13: 978-1533426529

All photographs by John Van Horn
Book and Cover Design by John Van Horn

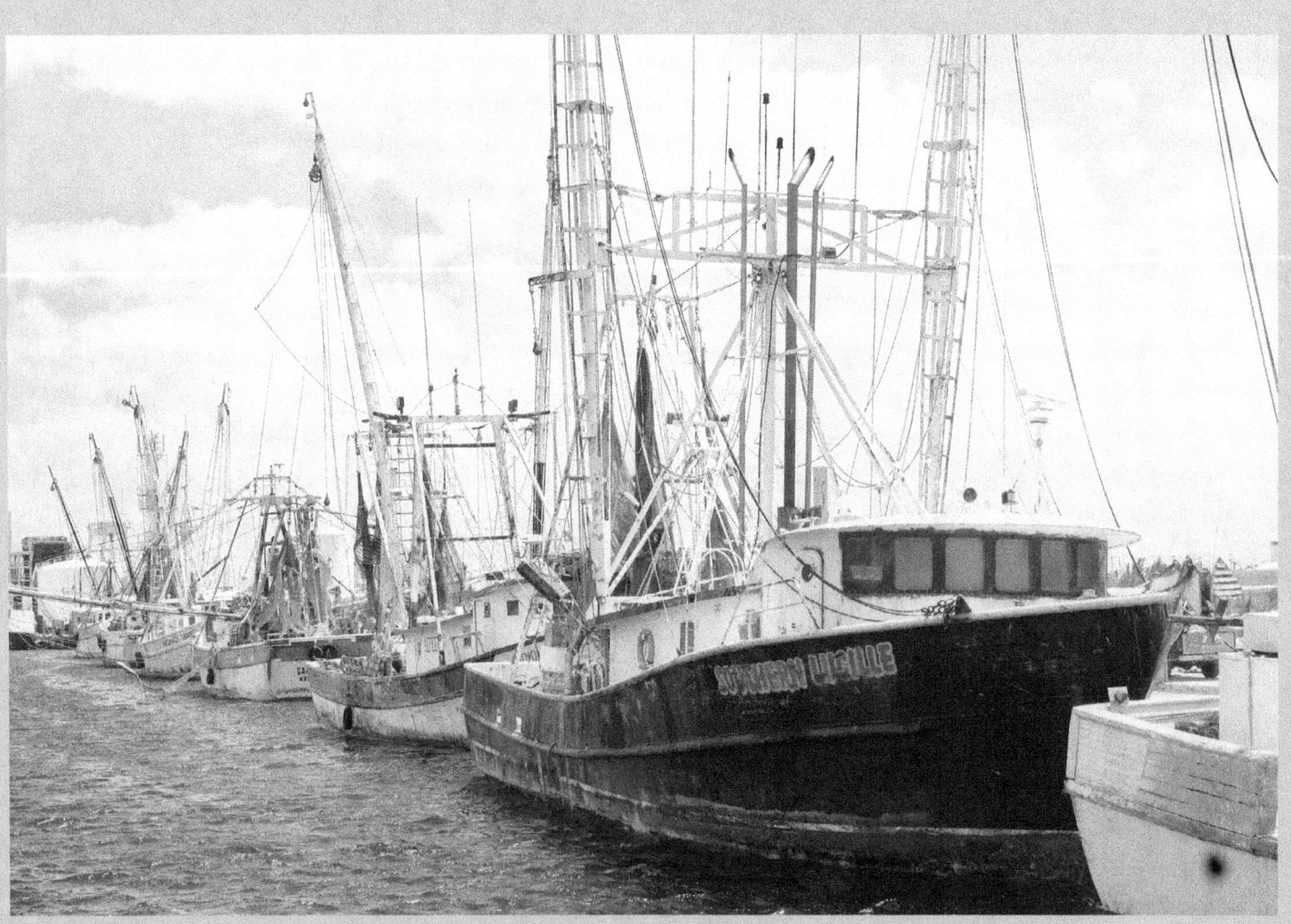

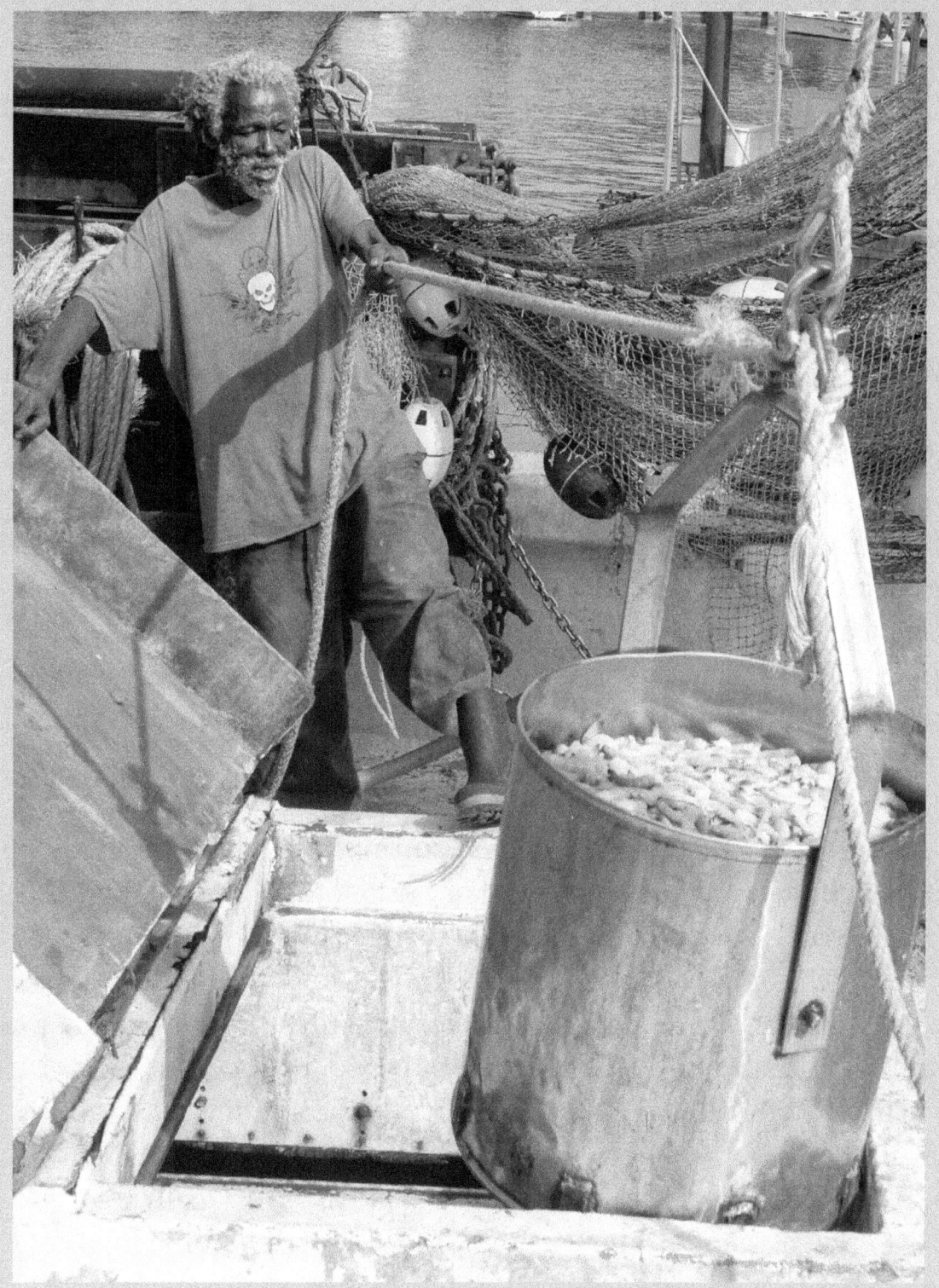

Front Cover: Composite of Faces.
Title Page: James, 2013.
Opposite: Shrimp Road dock, 2007.
Above: Charlie unloading shrimp, 2008.
Back Cover: A conversation with Charlie, 2008.

Introduction

For many years in Key West, Florida, the local economy was dependent on the US Navy base and shrimp boats. Today it is tourism, luxury yachts and cruise ships, the latter often tying up at old Navy docks. There is not one shrimp boat tied up in Key West harbor. Where did they go?

I enjoy taking photos of fishing boats, and I had started to visit the Keys in order to get away from the mountains of northeast Pennsylvania in the middle of winter. One day in 2007, after photographing some of the tourist spots on Key West, I left the island on Route 1 and drove east towards Stock Island. As I glanced to my right, I could see large fishing boat outriggers in the distance. I left the highway and worked my way through a series of side streets until I was on a street called Shrimp Road, and there were the remains of the Key West shrimp fleet. I say "remains" because at one time there were between 150–200 shrimp boats home ported in Key West and neighboring Stock Island. I saw less than a dozen boats that day.

A few days later, I visited this dock again and started to photograph the boats. Gradually I got to know the crews, and began photographing them. For the most part, the crews were older men who had shrimped much of their adult lives. The crews matched the boats—old and weather—beaten. Few local young people were joining the shrinking ranks of shrimpers, and new boats were not being built for shrimp in the Keys. The majority of the boats at the dock were wooden construction, often fiberglassed over. Most of the crewmembers I got to know not only worked on the boats, they lived aboard as well. Some owners had local residences, or at least someplace to crash with a girlfriend, as did a few of the crewmembers. Others just worked away from home for long periods of time.

In 2007 the last shrimp dock on Shrimp Road had been sold and was soon to be gentrified; there was more money in yachts than shrimp boats. When I returned in the winter of 2008 the shrimp boats I had previously photographed had moved to the Fishbusterz dock across the harbor. This was the last dock for this dying industry at the end of the Florida Keys. I decided to make a concerted effort when visiting the area to photograph the boats and crews as much as possible.

This book is dedicated to the crews of the shrimp boats who still work off the shores of the Florida Keys. This photo essay covers six visits to the area beginning in 2007 and ending in 2015. I only photographed boats and crews from whom I obtained permission, and I did not attempt to photograph everyone on the docks. I enjoyed the time I spent there, and the friendships I made. When I returned in 2015 there were three or four boats that could still be considered working from Stock Island. Other boats occasionally stopped in from other ports on the Gulf of Mexico or the Atlantic Coast, but the shrimping fleet of the Keys had all but disappeared.

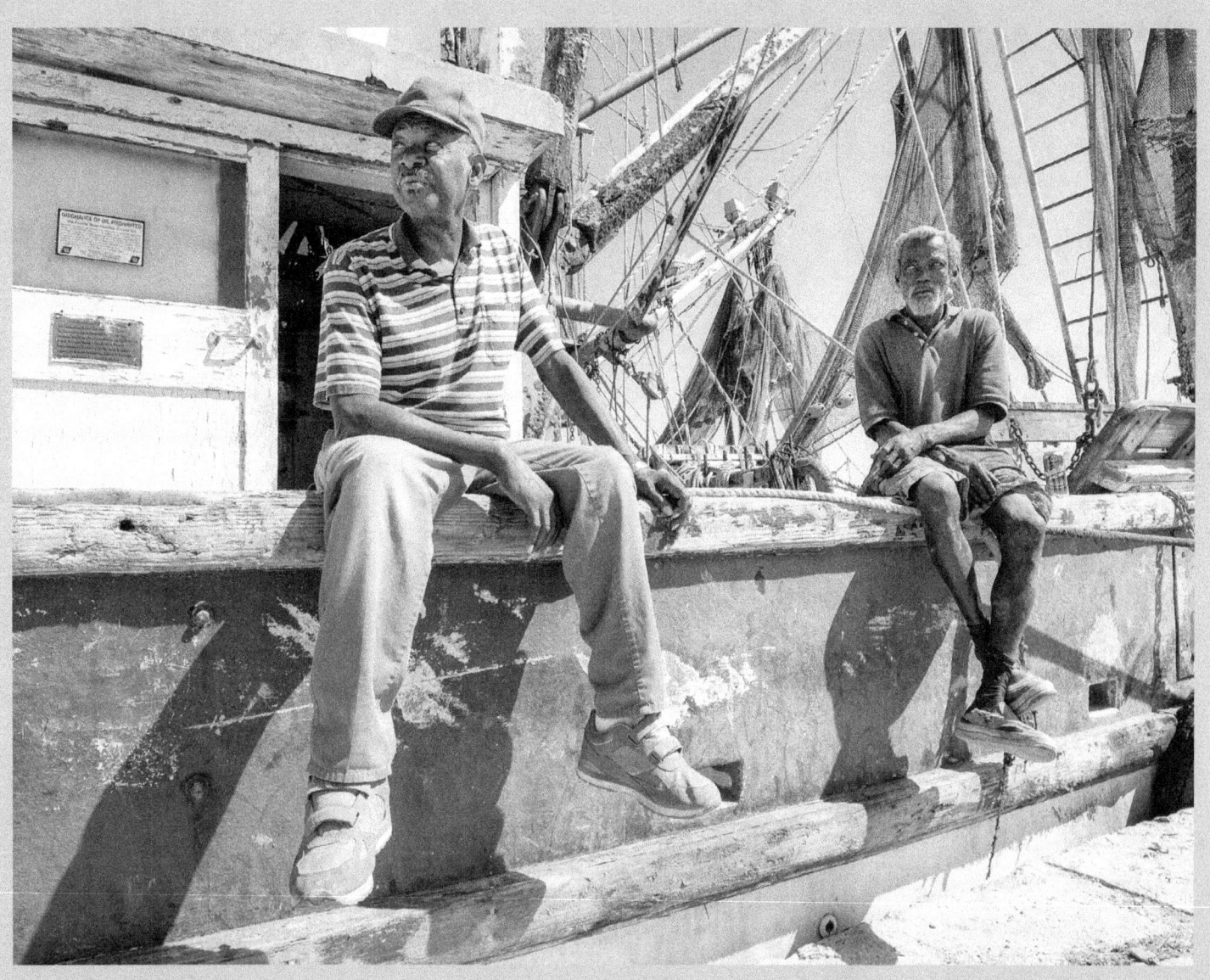

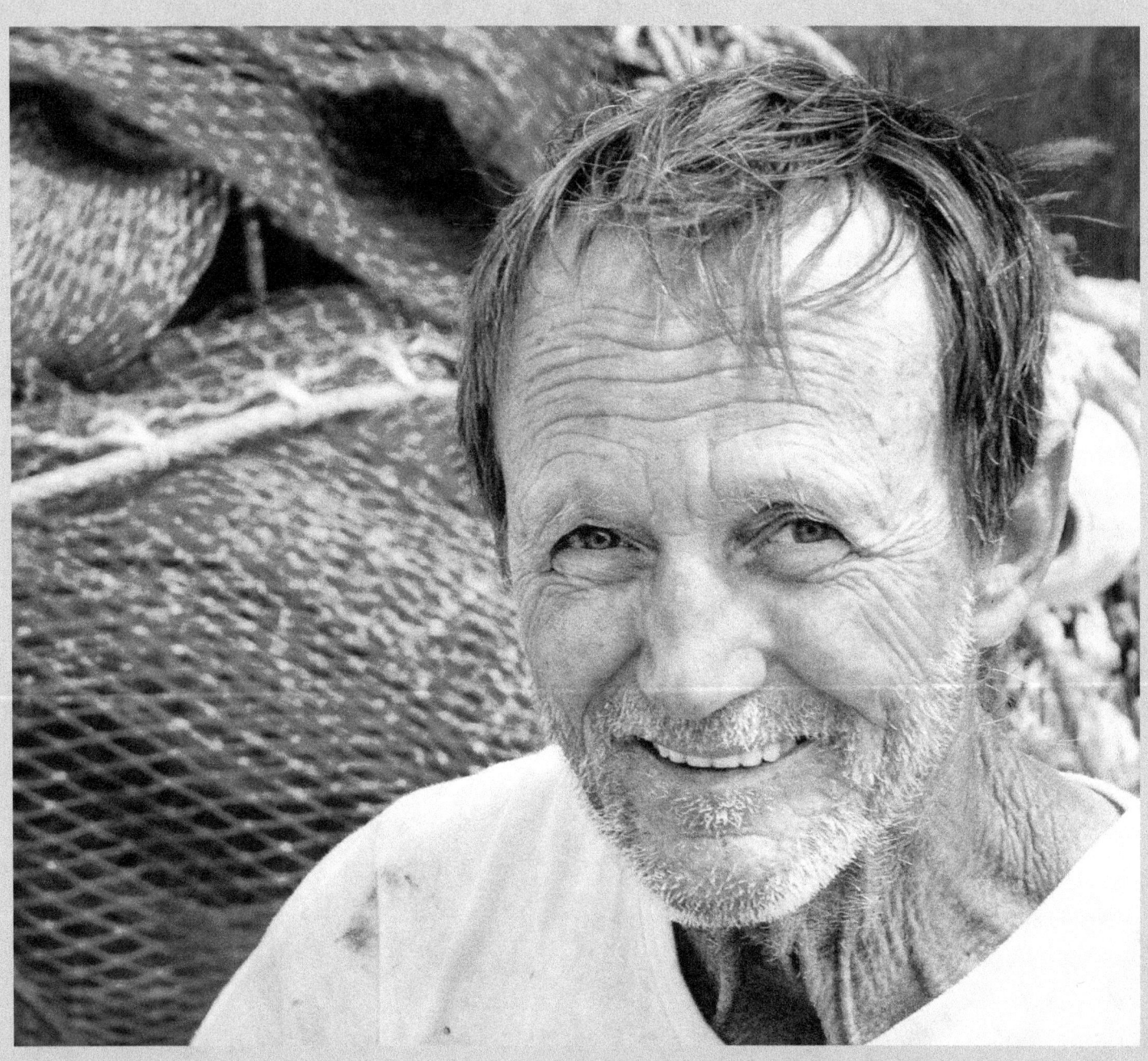

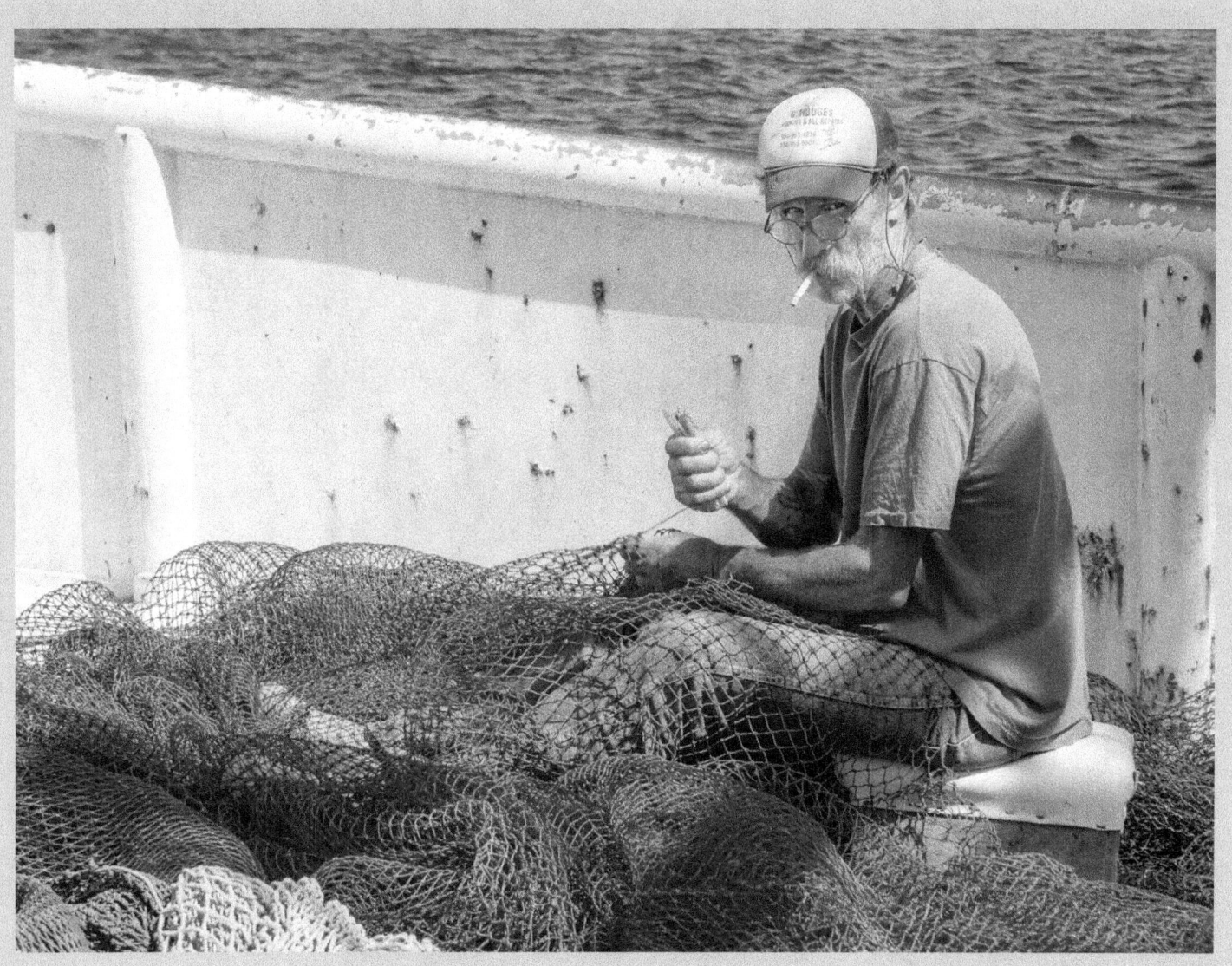

On my first visit to the shrimp boat dock. Cowboy, opposite page, and David repairing nets, 2007.

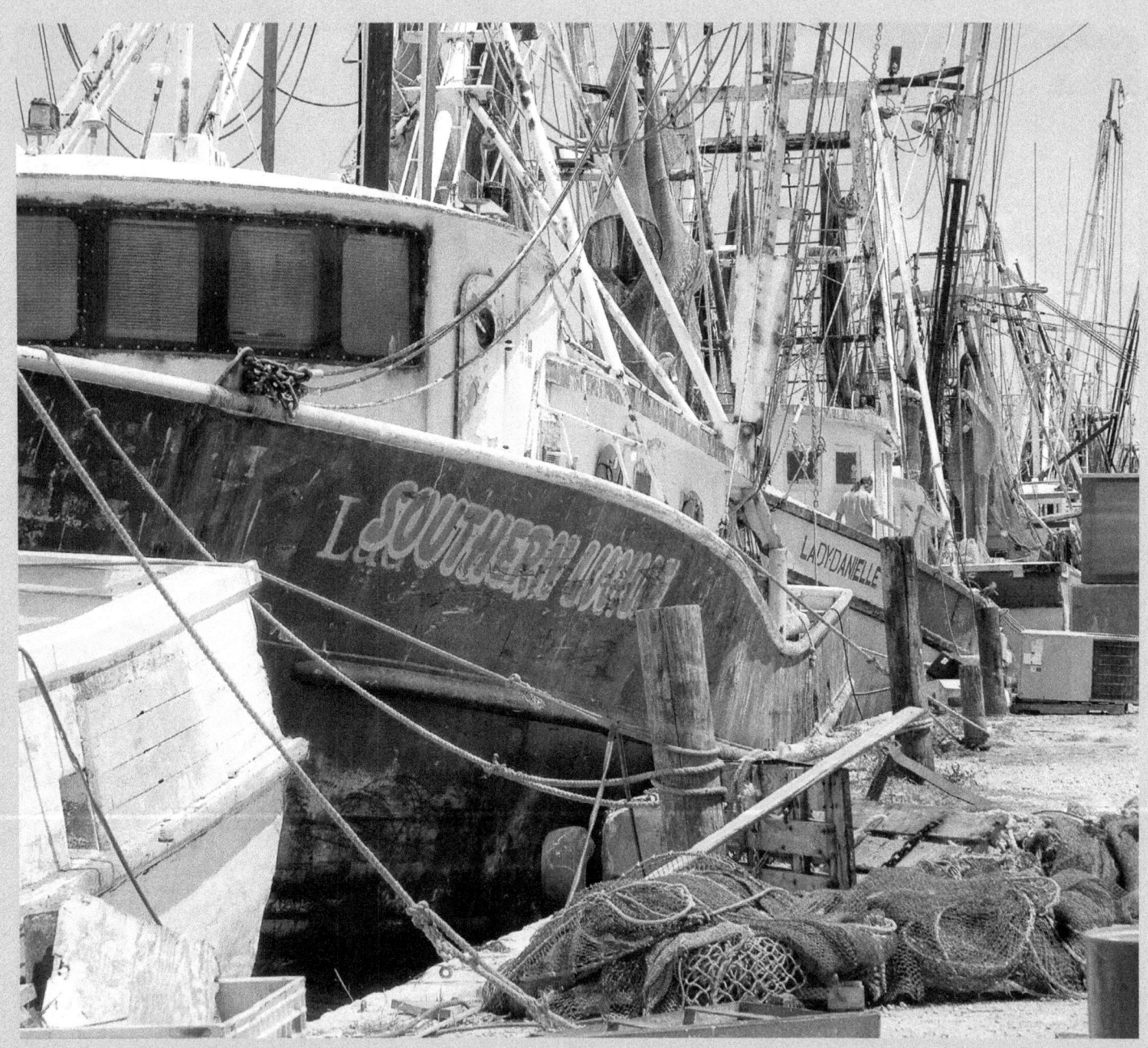

Above: *Lady-Danielle* behind the *Southern Lucille,* 2007.
Opposite: Mark, captain of *Lady-Danielle*, painting.

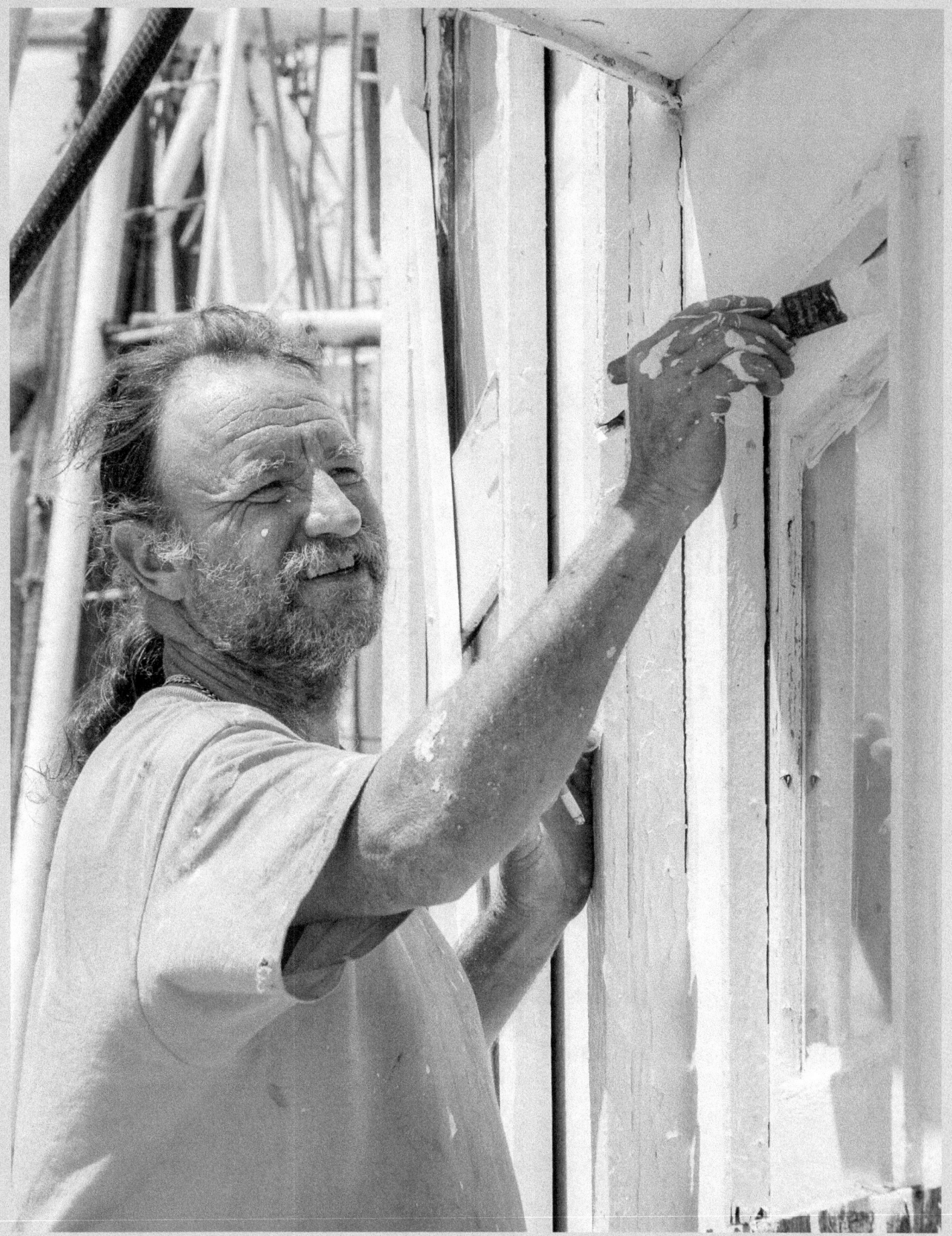

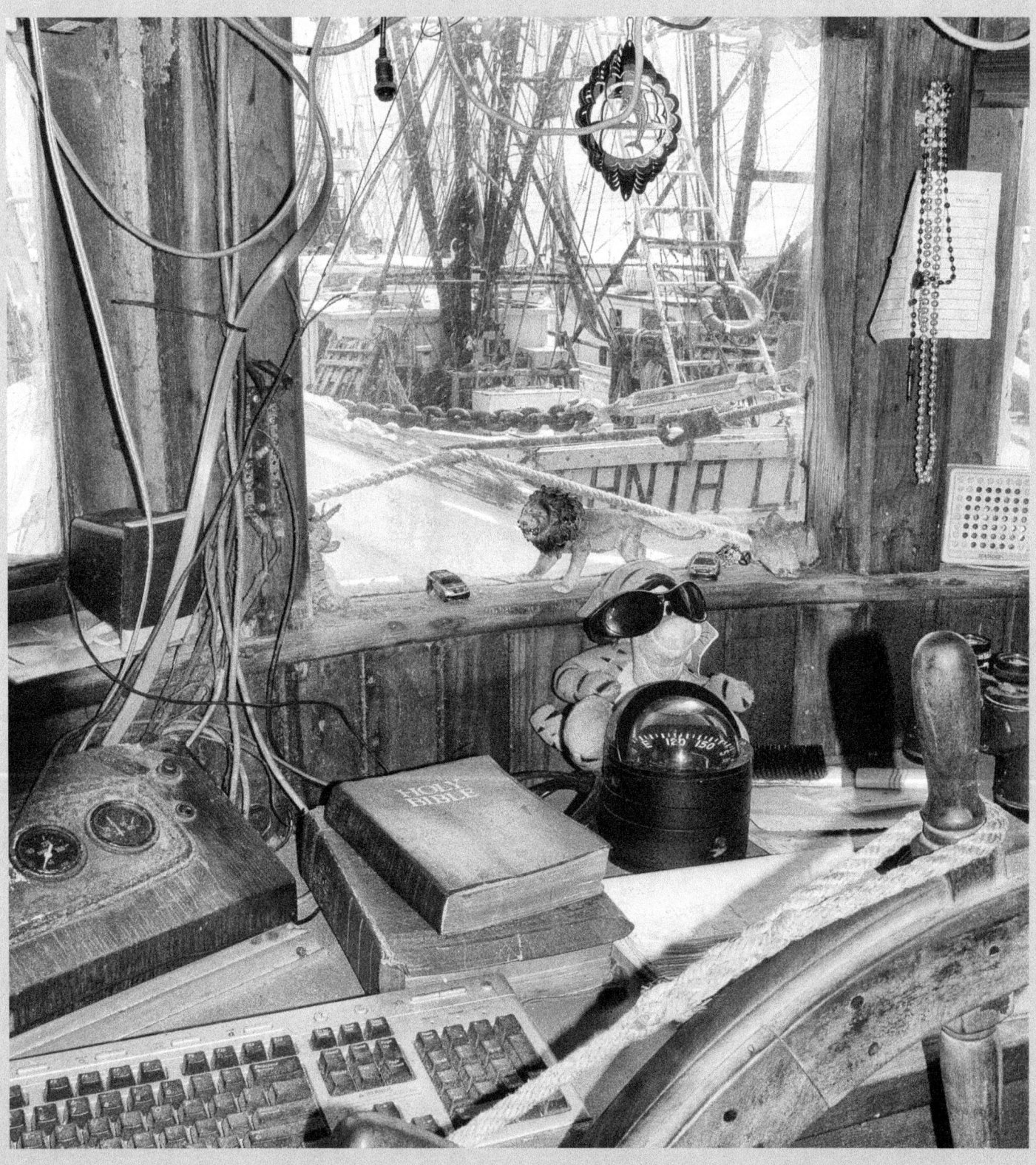

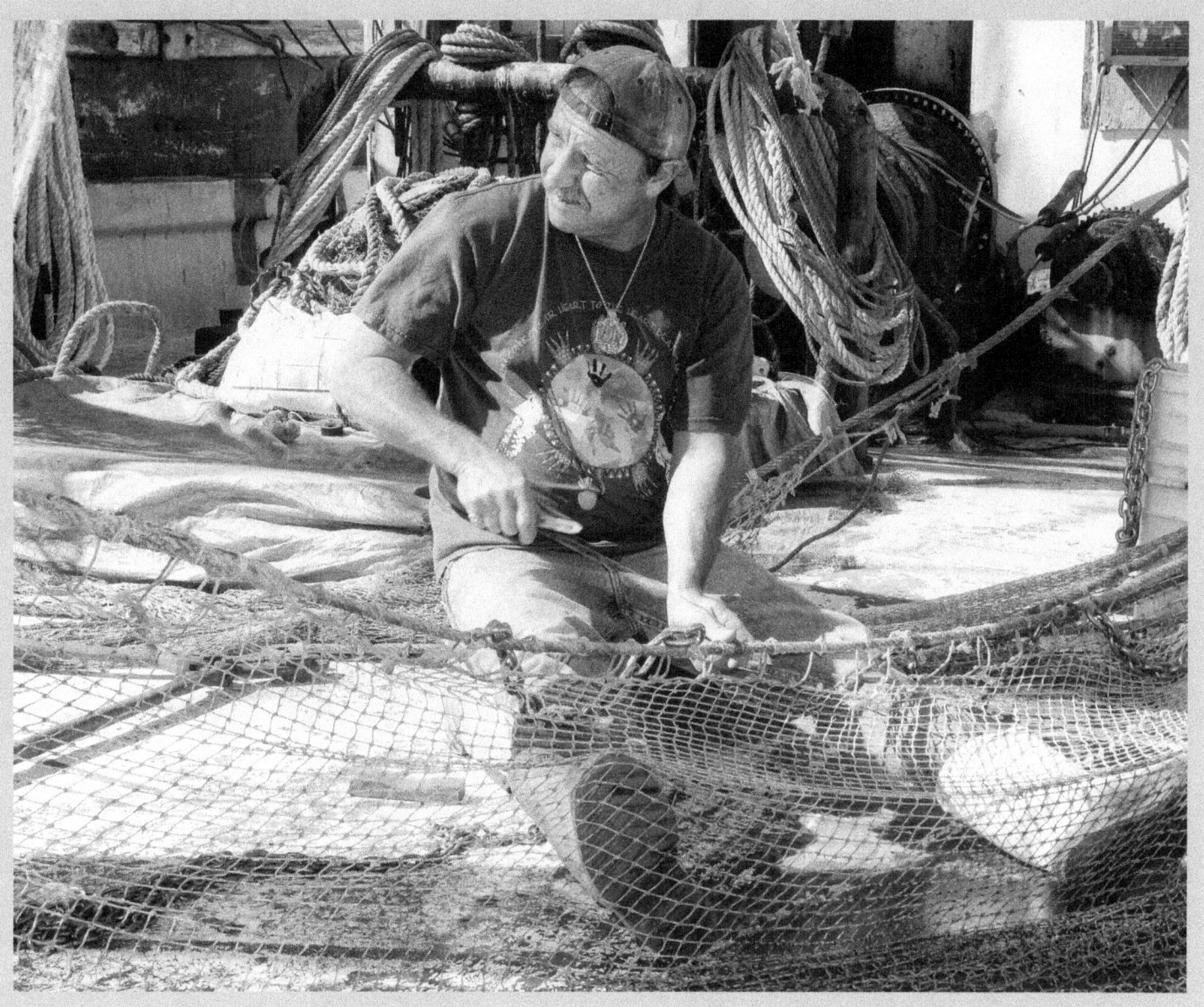

Opposite: The wheelhouse of the *Lady-Danielle*, 2008.
Above: Captain Mark mending nets.

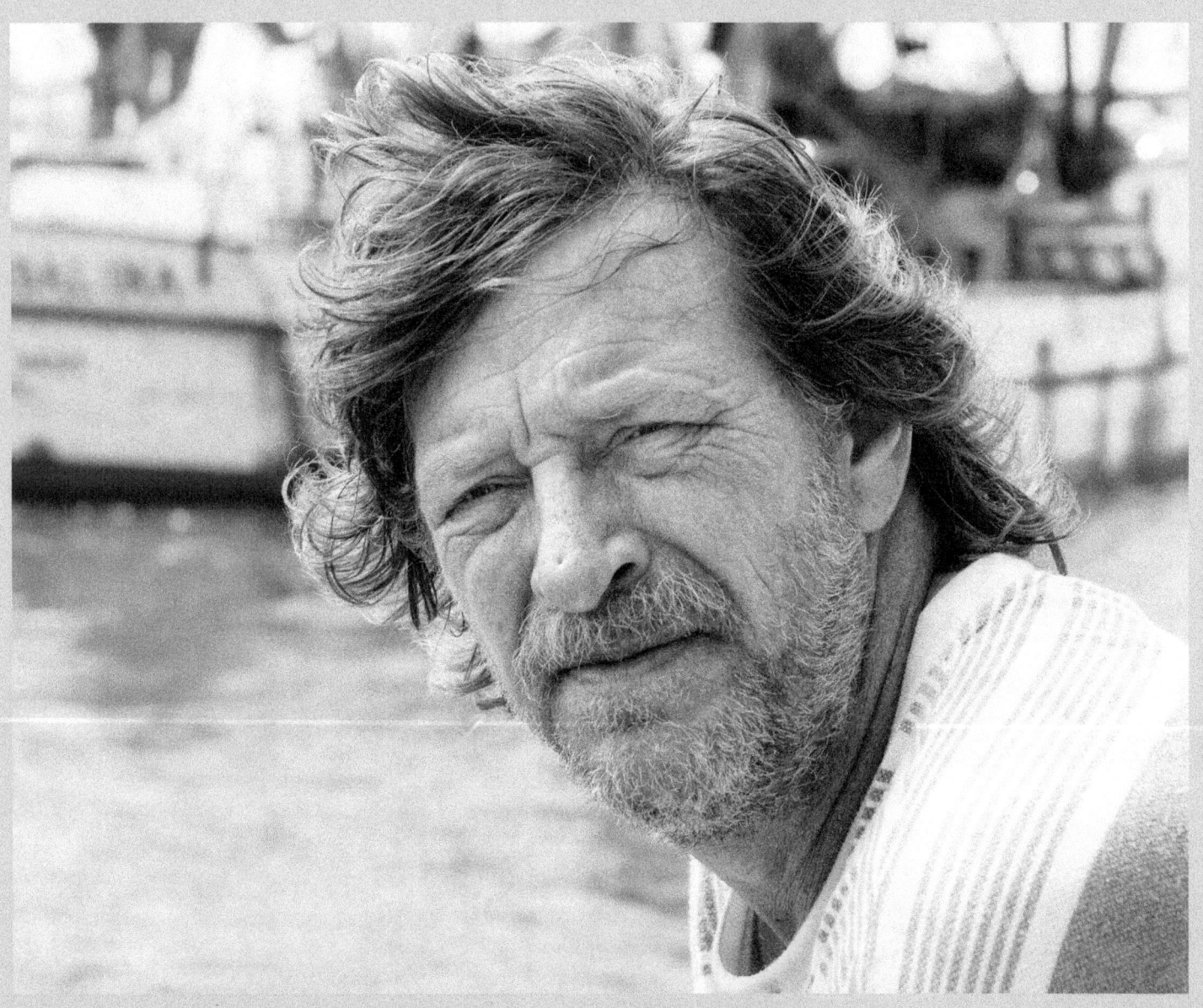

Above: Paul was crewman on the *Lady-Danielle*.
Opposite Top: Mark and his friend Annie.
Opposite Bottom: Mark taking a break from unloading
shrimp.

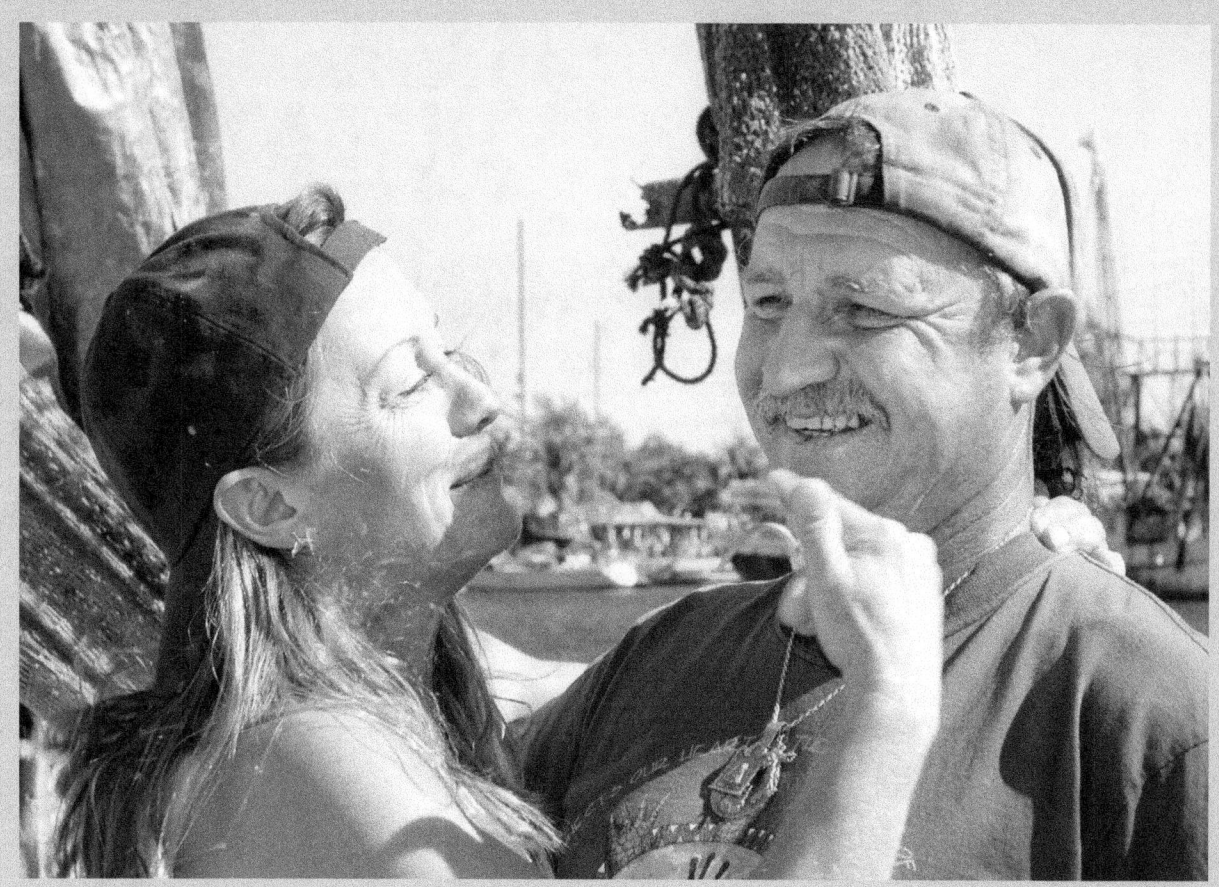

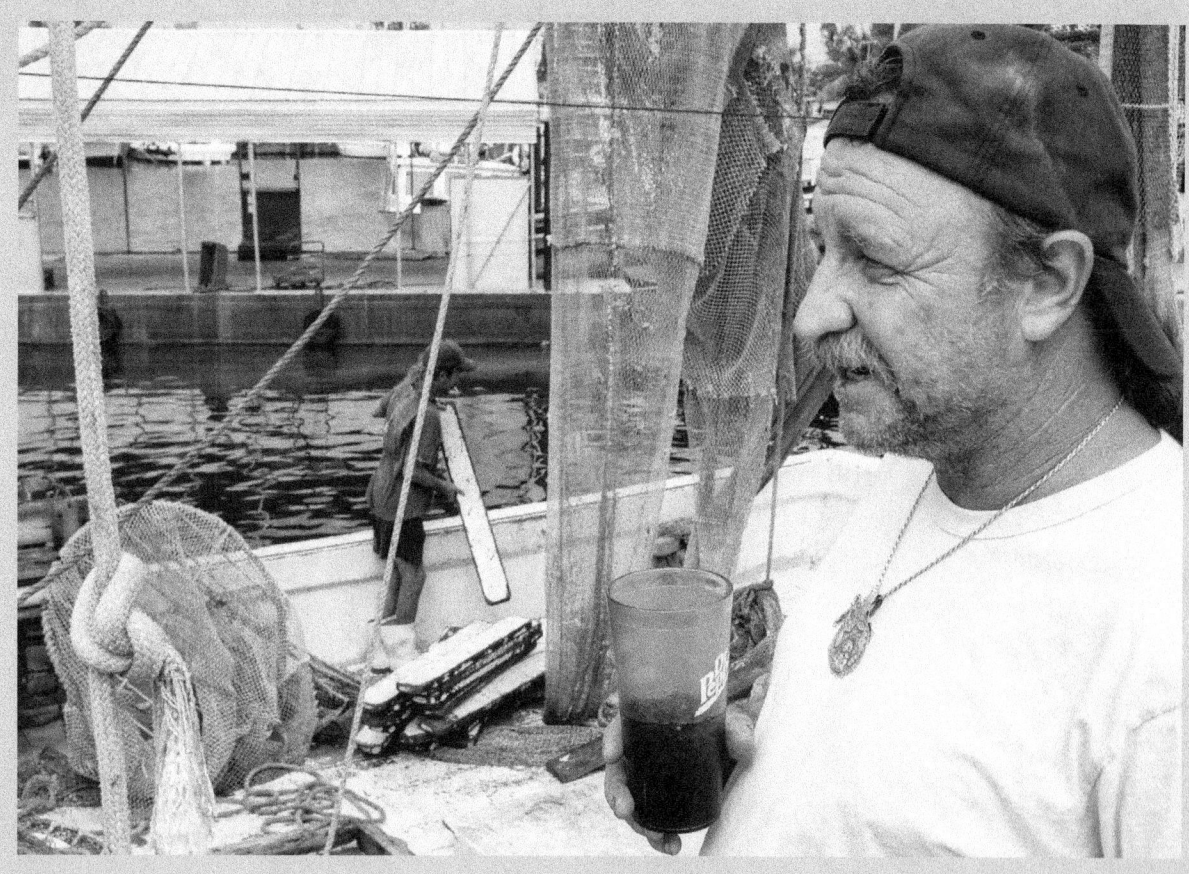

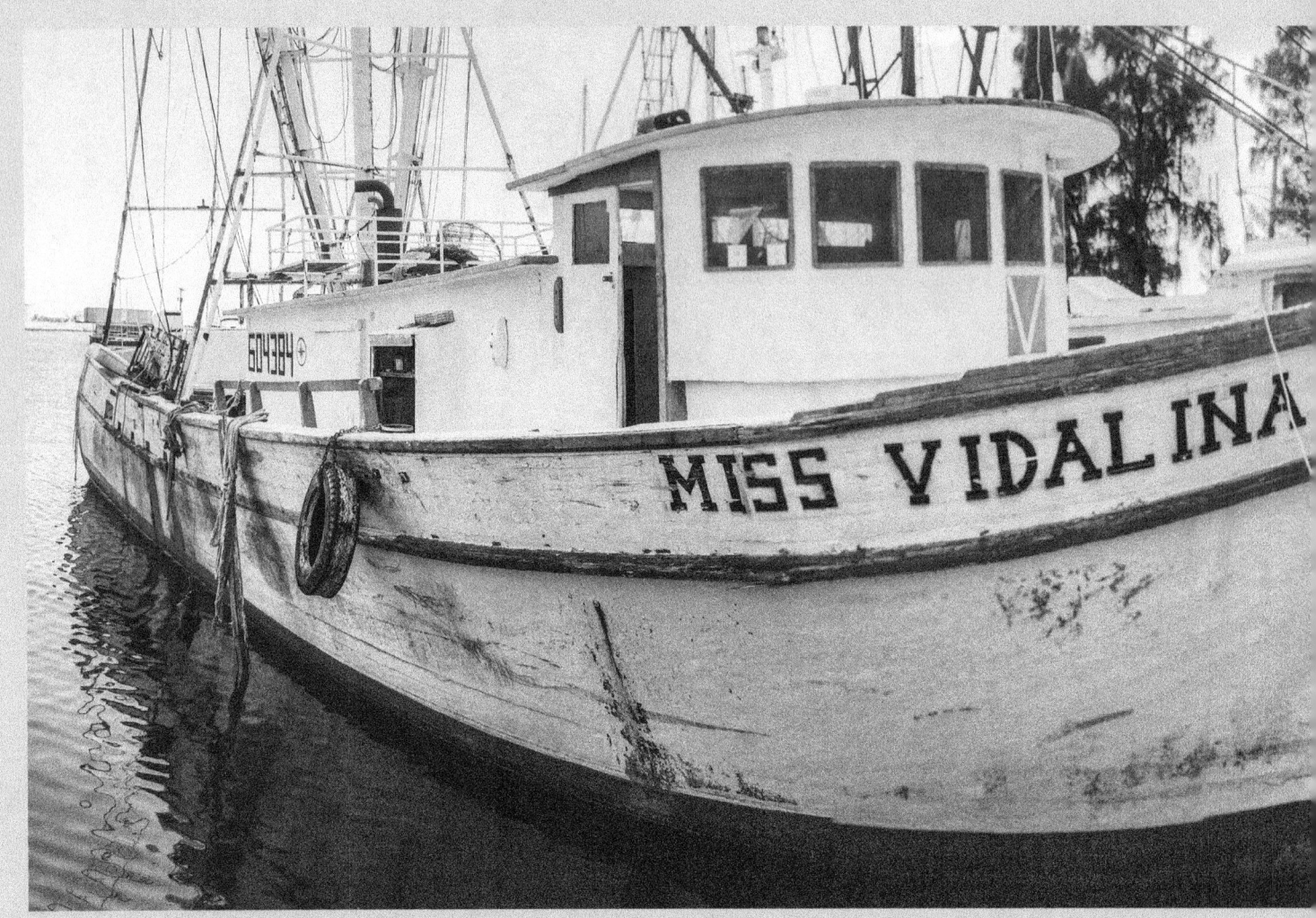

Miss Vidalina, Equalizer and *Lady-Danielle* being scaped, too old to be maintained and pass Coast Guard inspection, 2011.

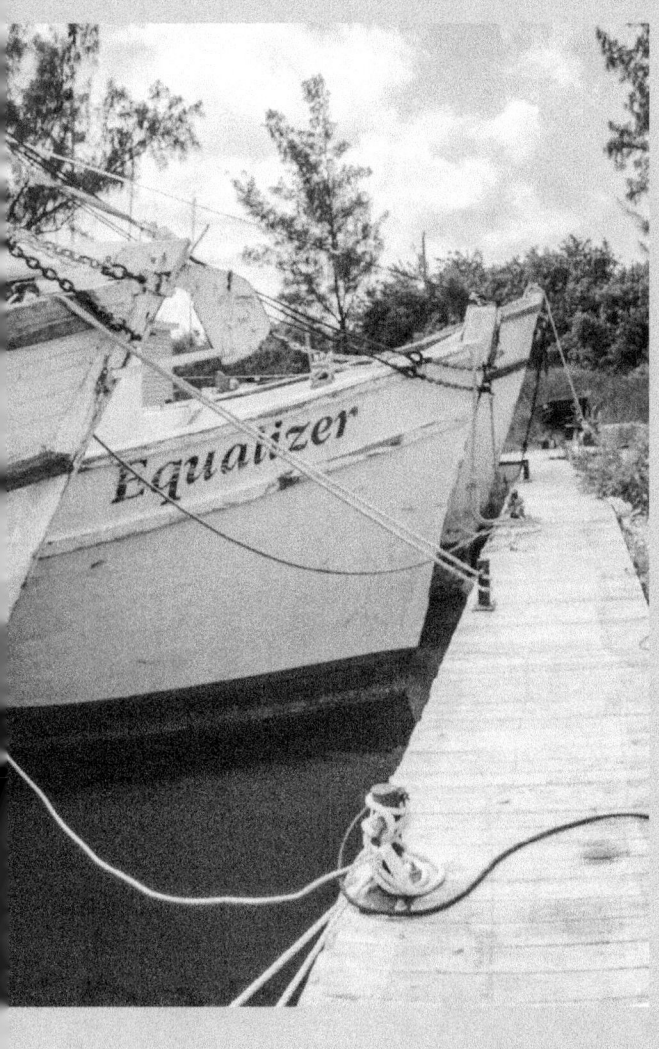

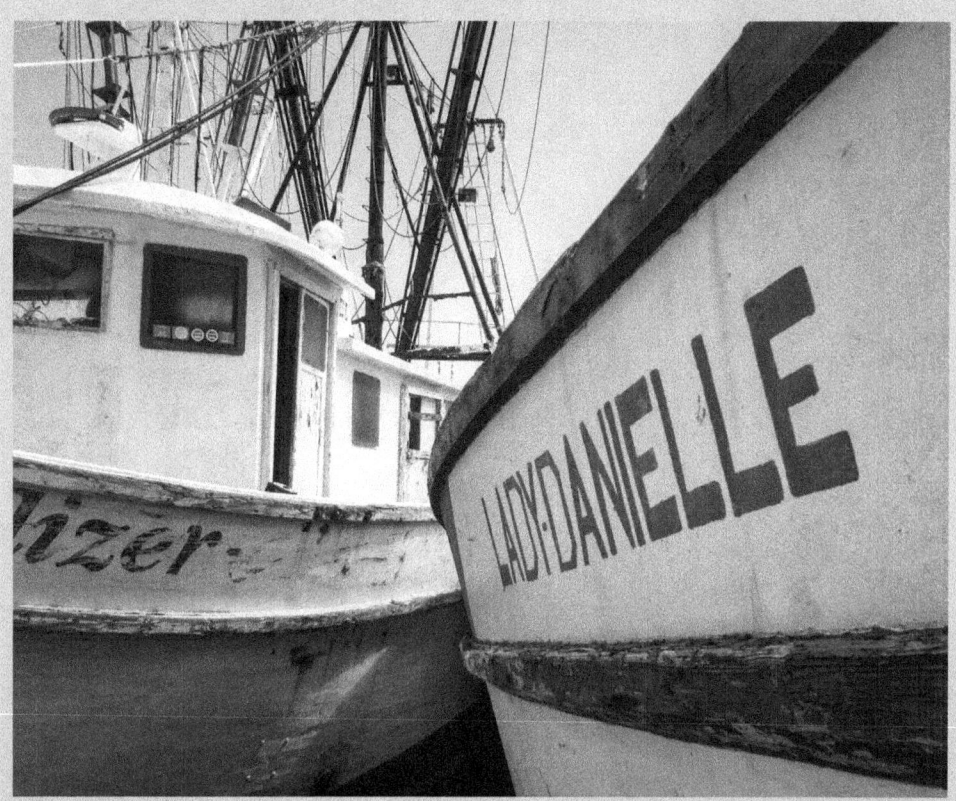

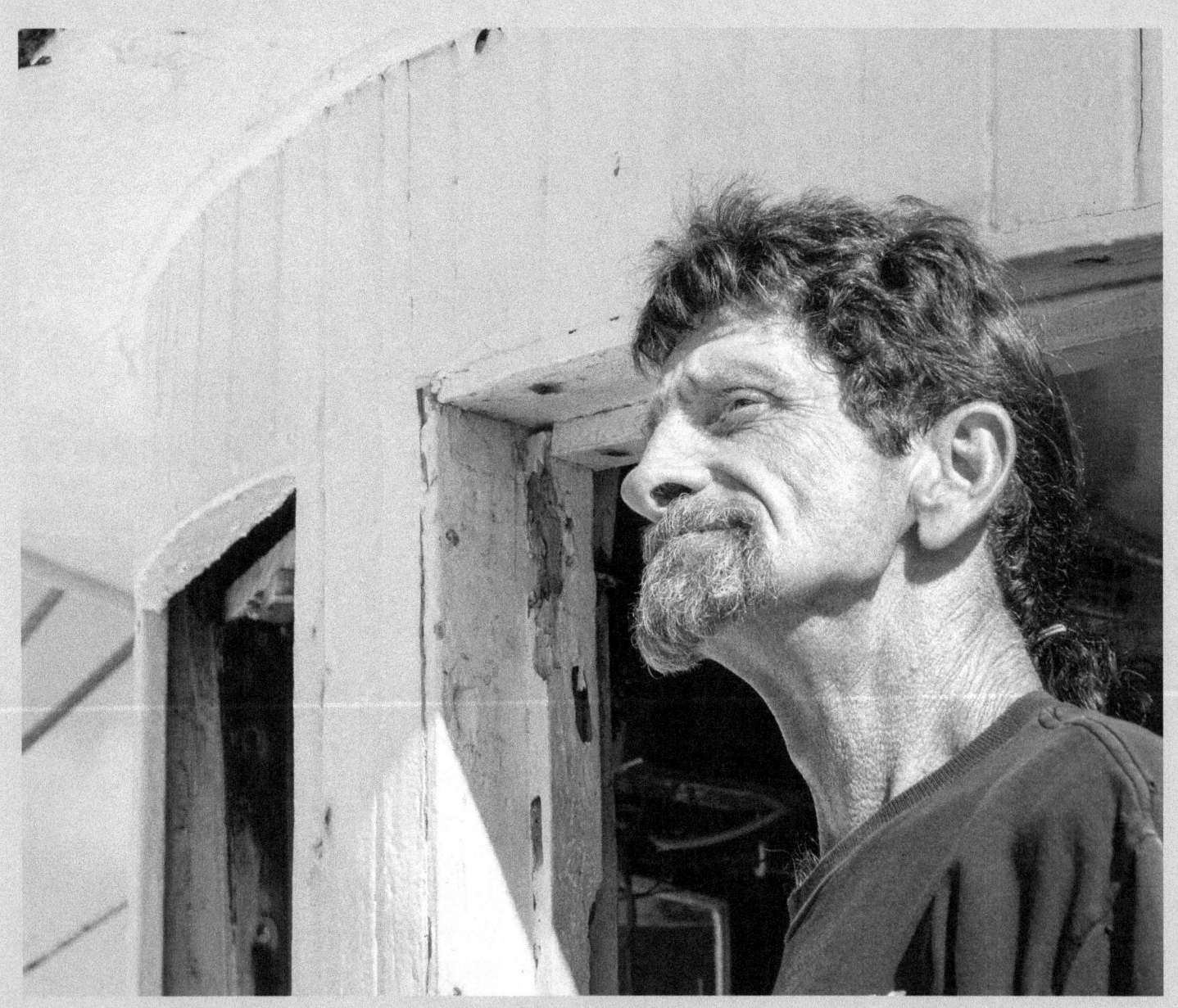

Tim, the new owner of the *Michael James*, 2007.

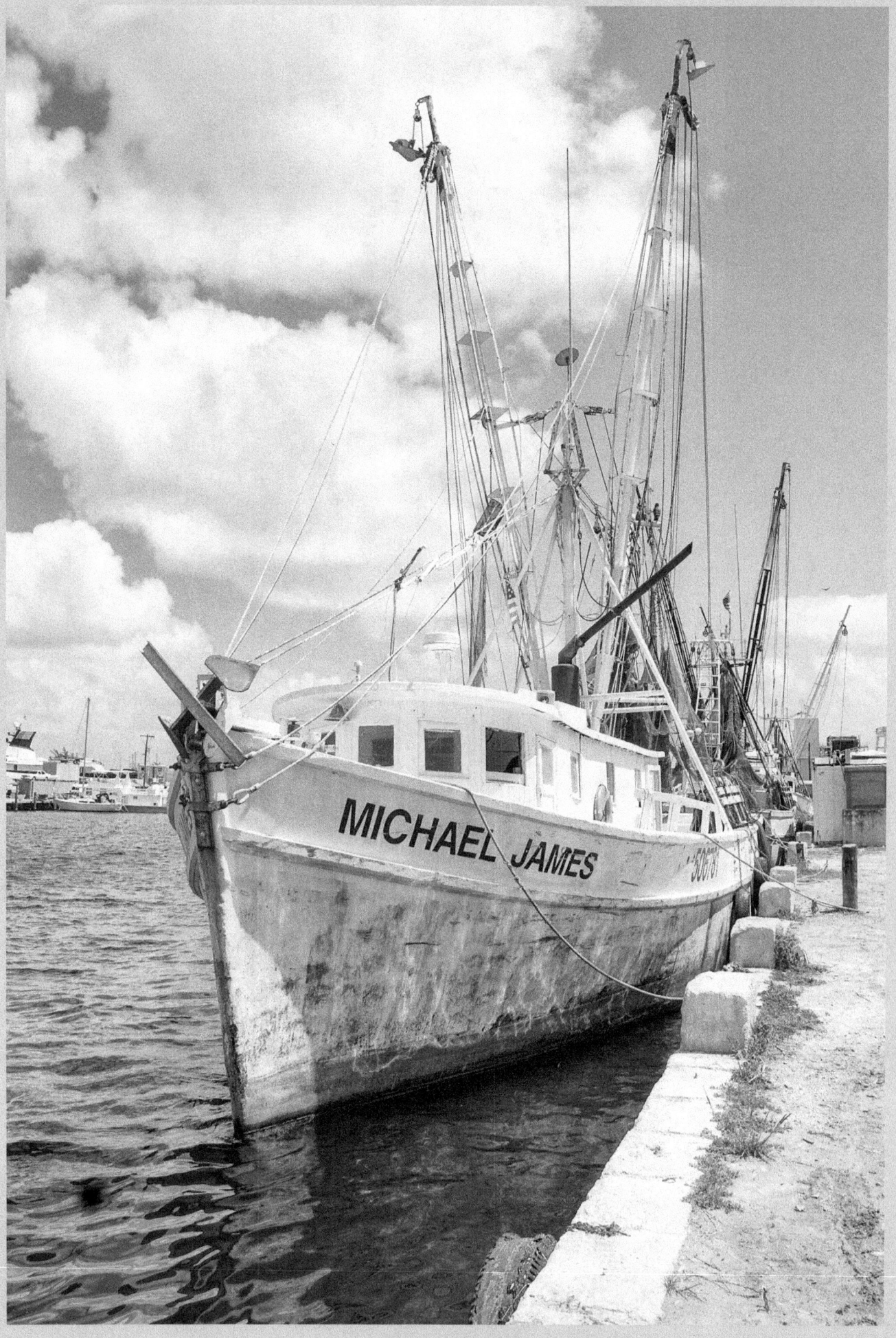

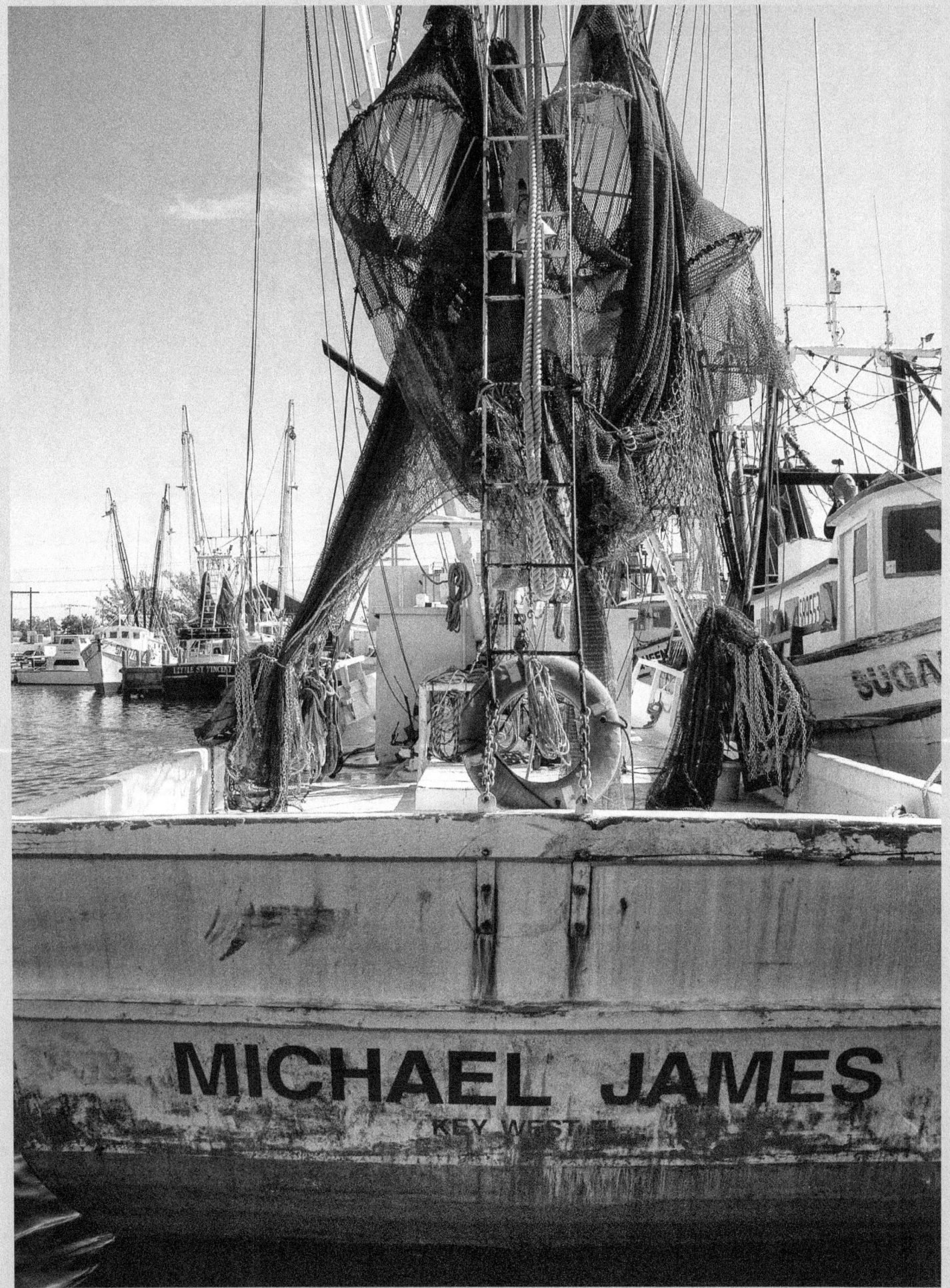

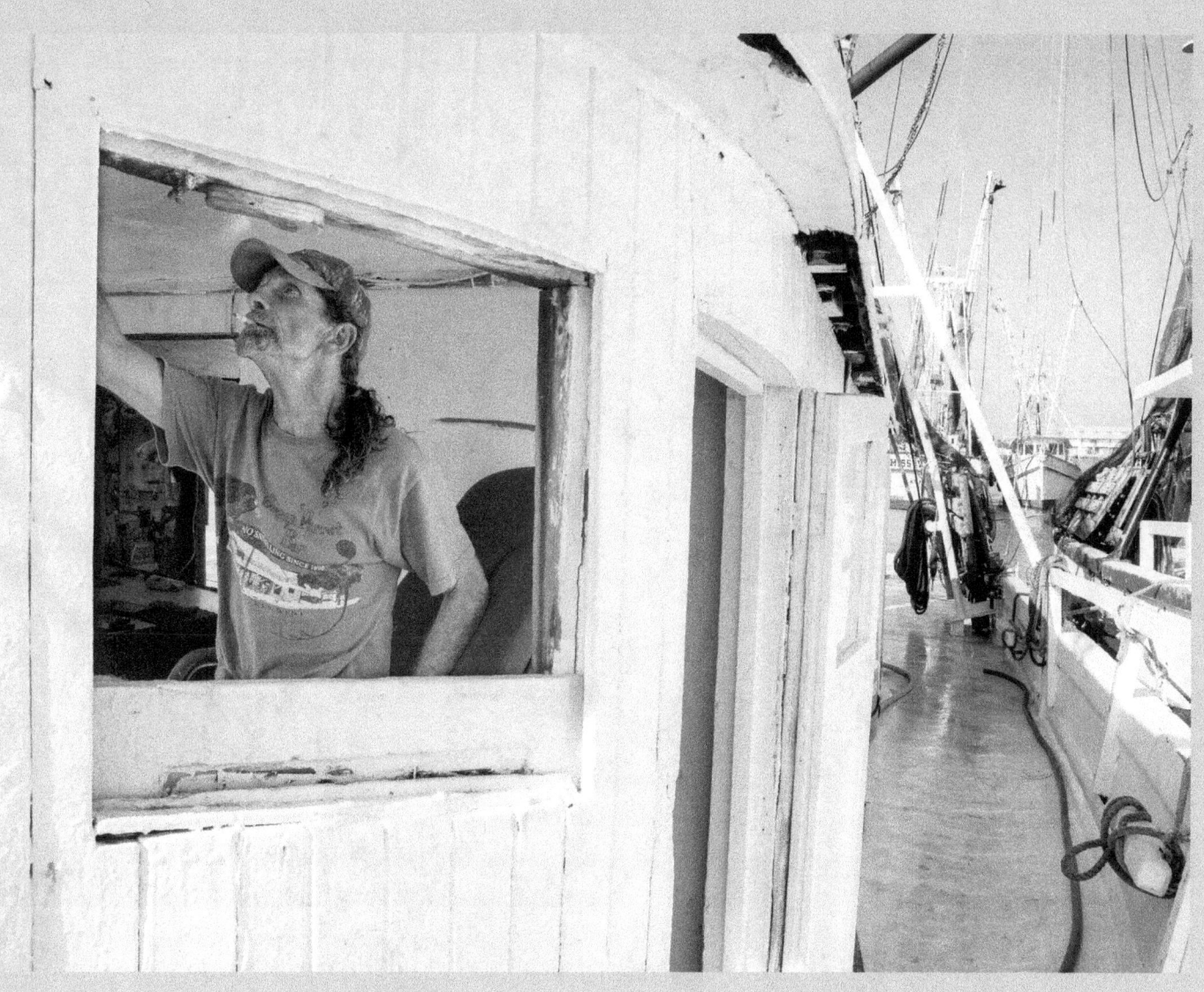

Captain Tim with the *Michael James,* which was stuck
at the dock with mechanical problems, 2008.

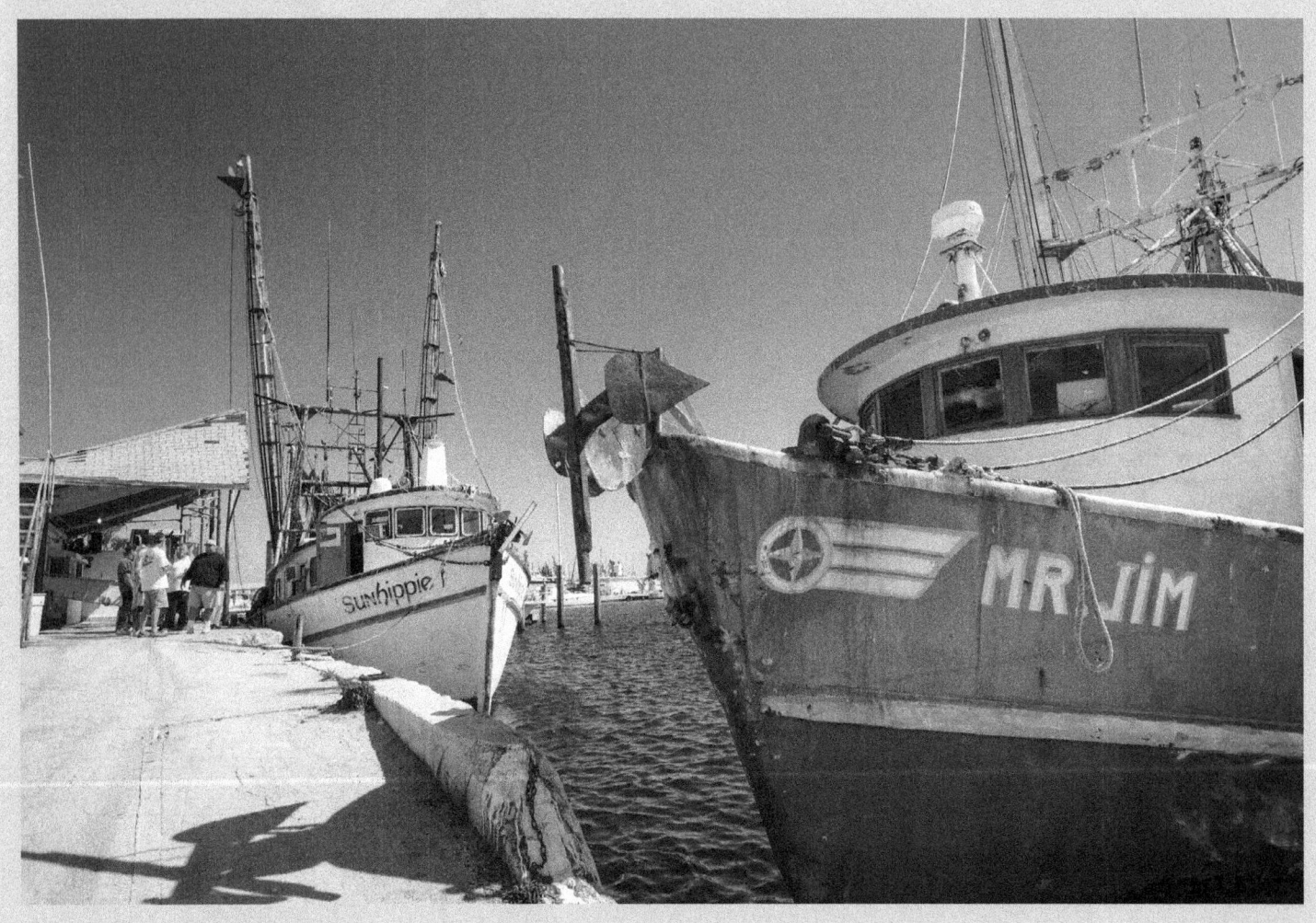

Above: *Mr. Jim* and *Sunhippie* on the Shrimp Road dock, 2007.

Opposite: Red is from Brunswick, Georgia. He often captained the *Sunhippie*, 2013.

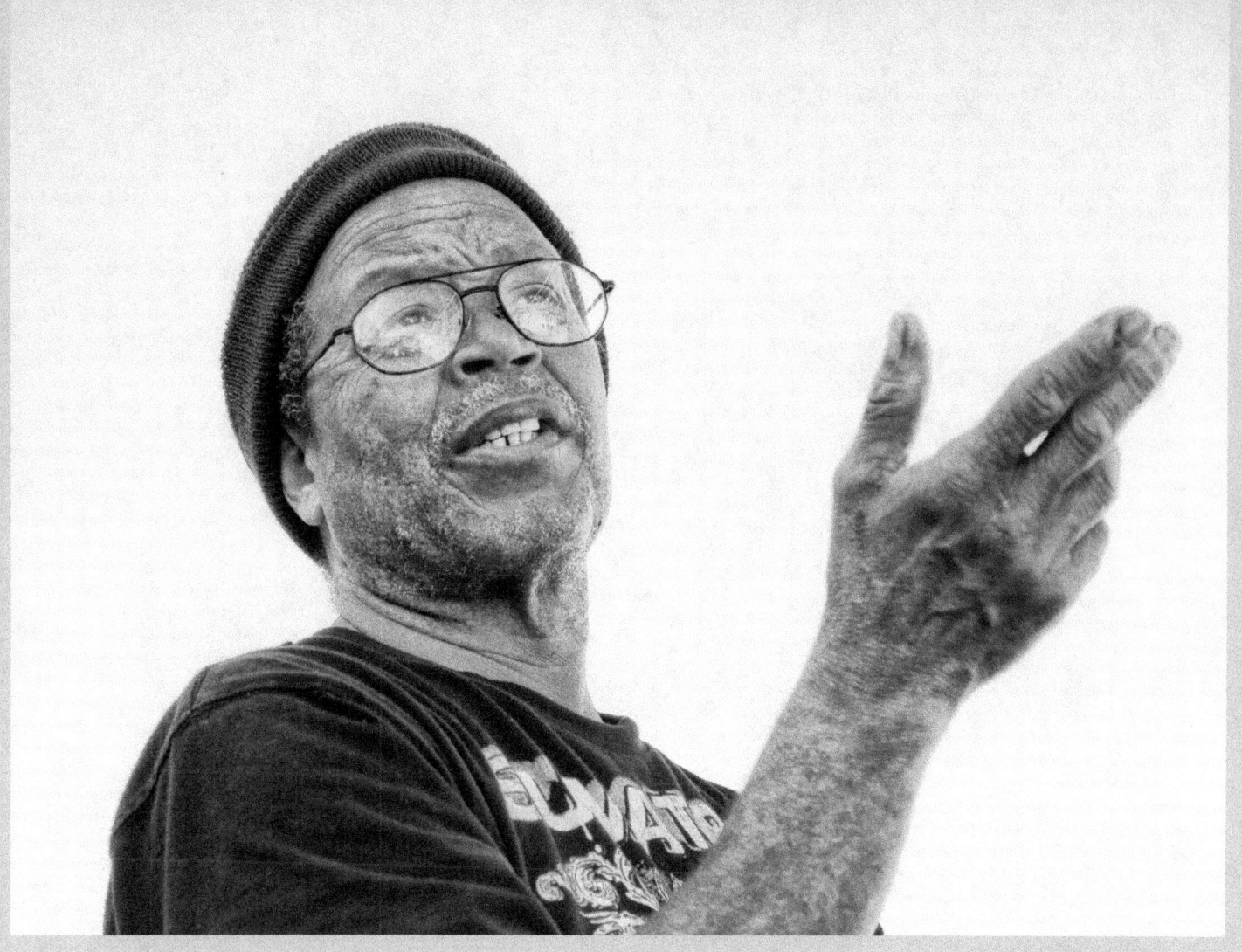

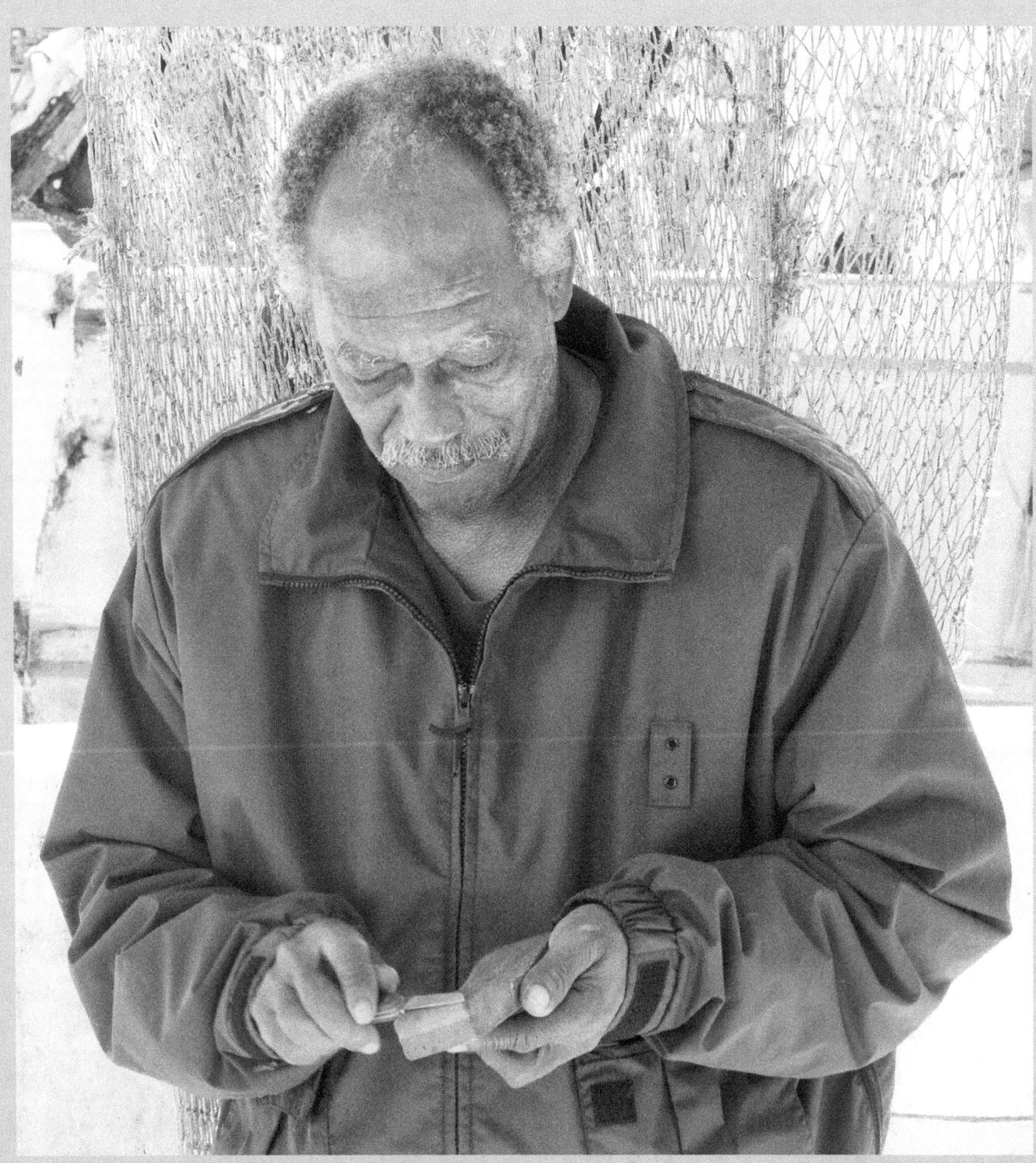

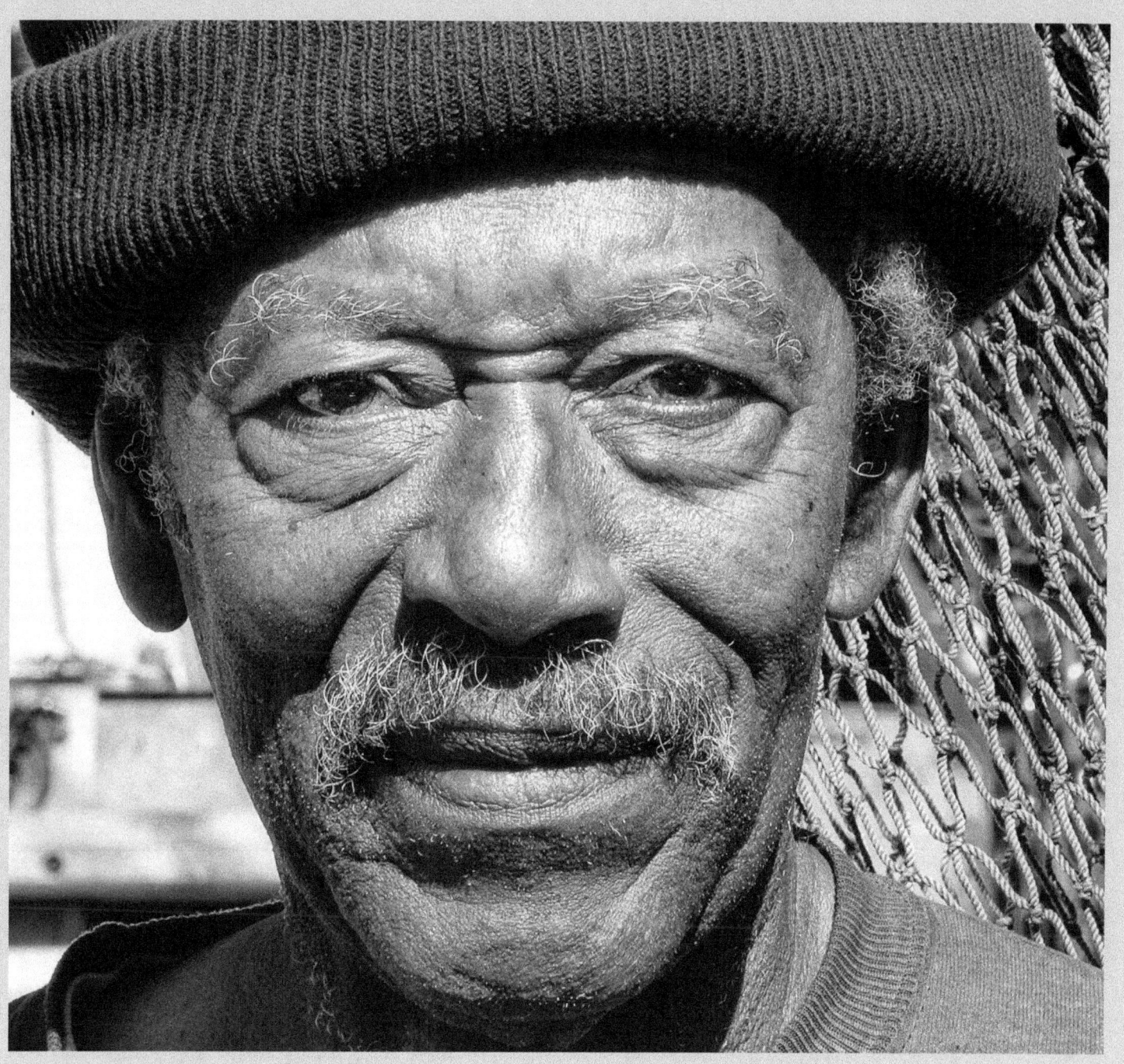

Opposite: Randolph, who often crewed with his
younger brother Red on the *Sunhippie*, sharpening a
knife while repairing nets, 2008.
Above: Randolph, 2013.

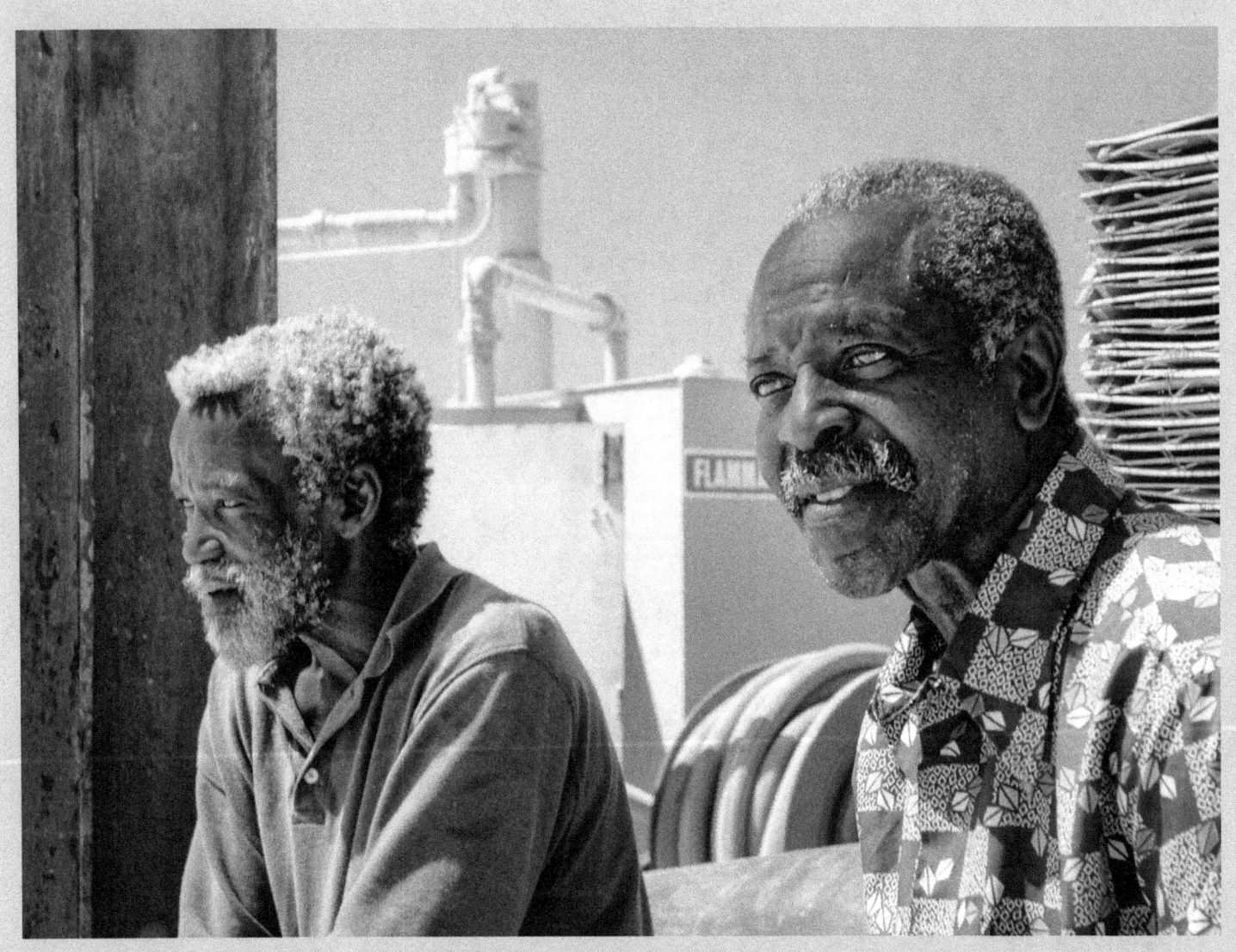

Above: Charlie and Albert, 2007
Opposite: Albert on his shrimp boat *D&S*.

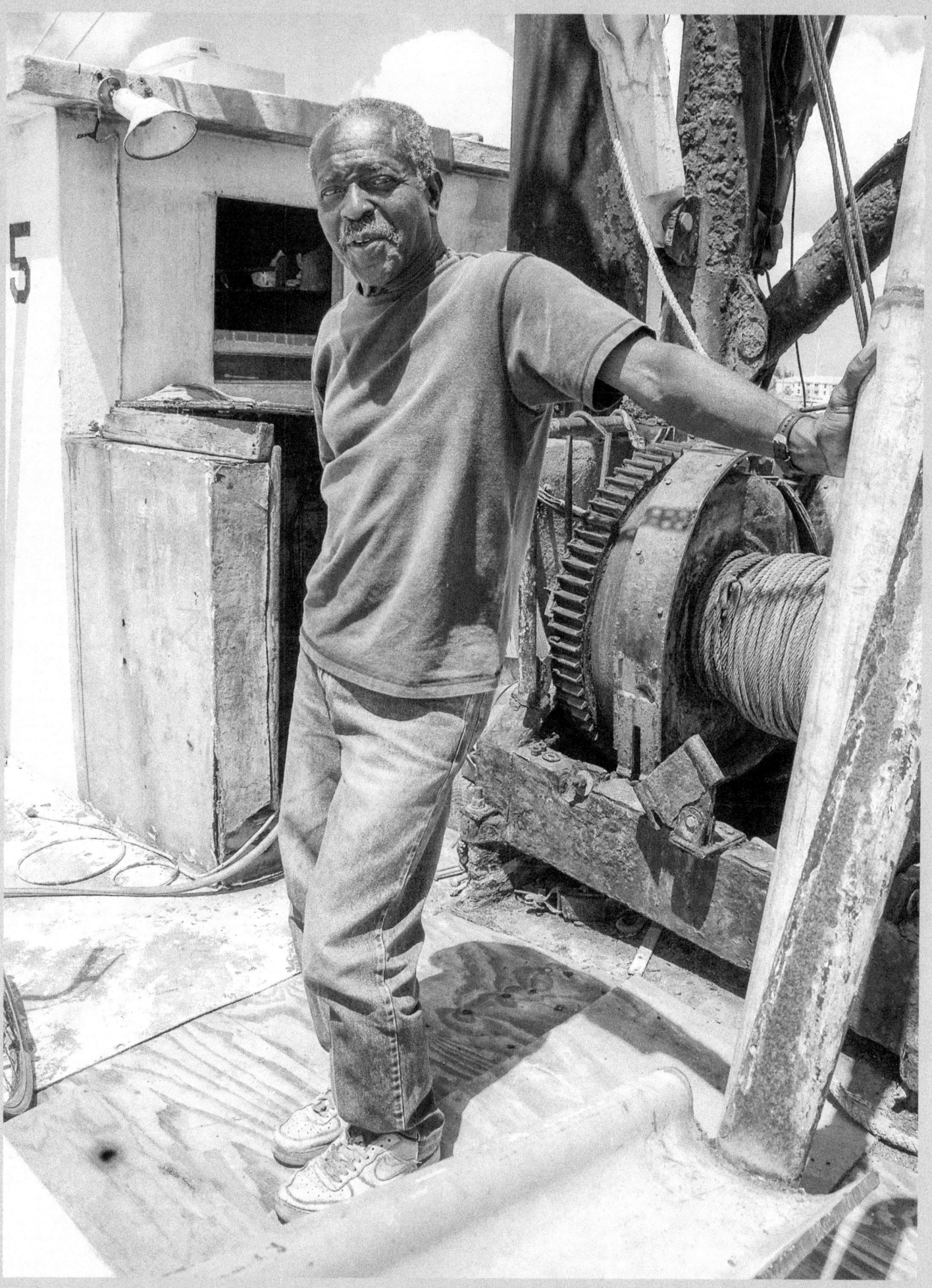

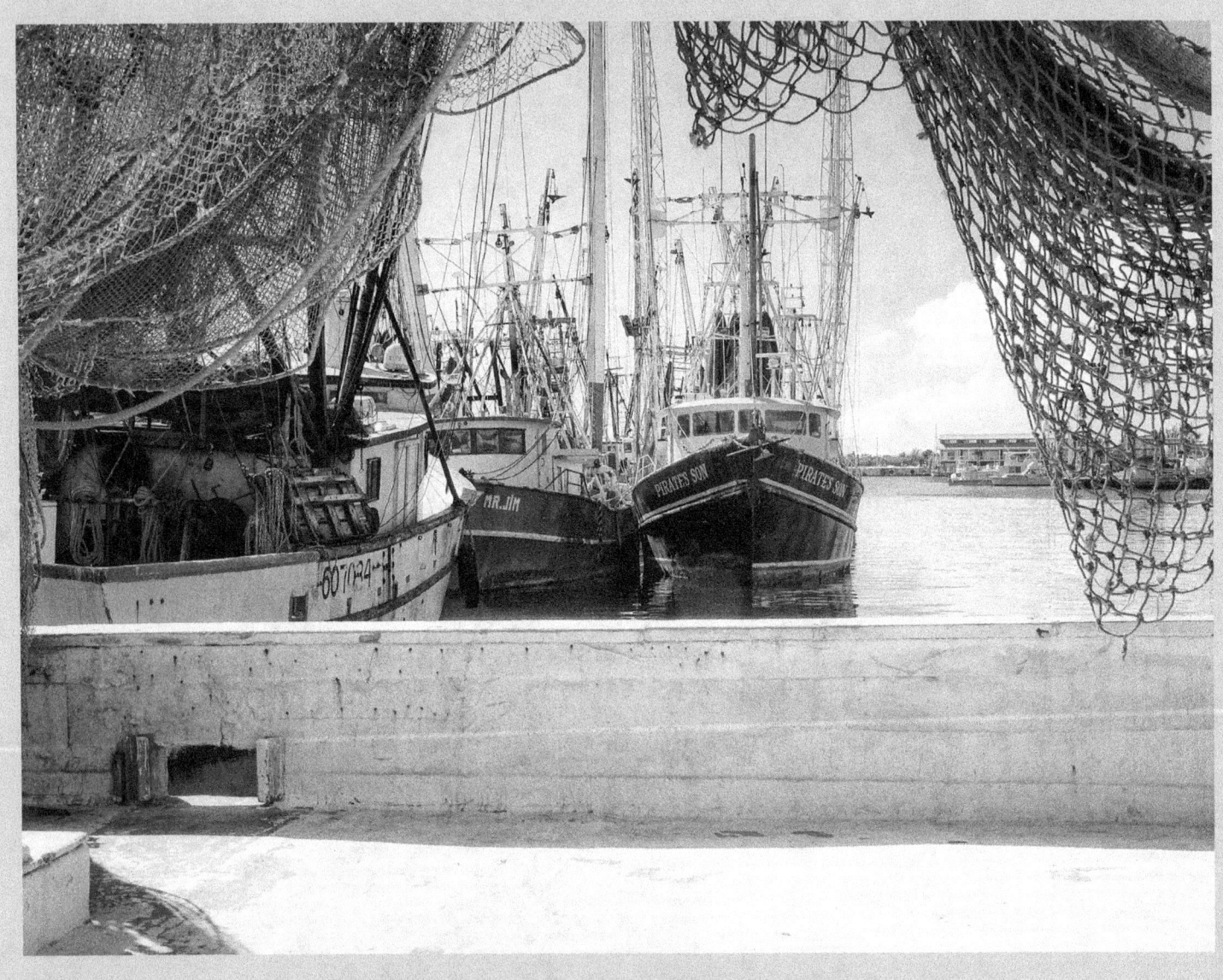

Above: Shrimp boats at Fishbusterz dock, 2008.
Opposite: Ever-present foul weather gear.

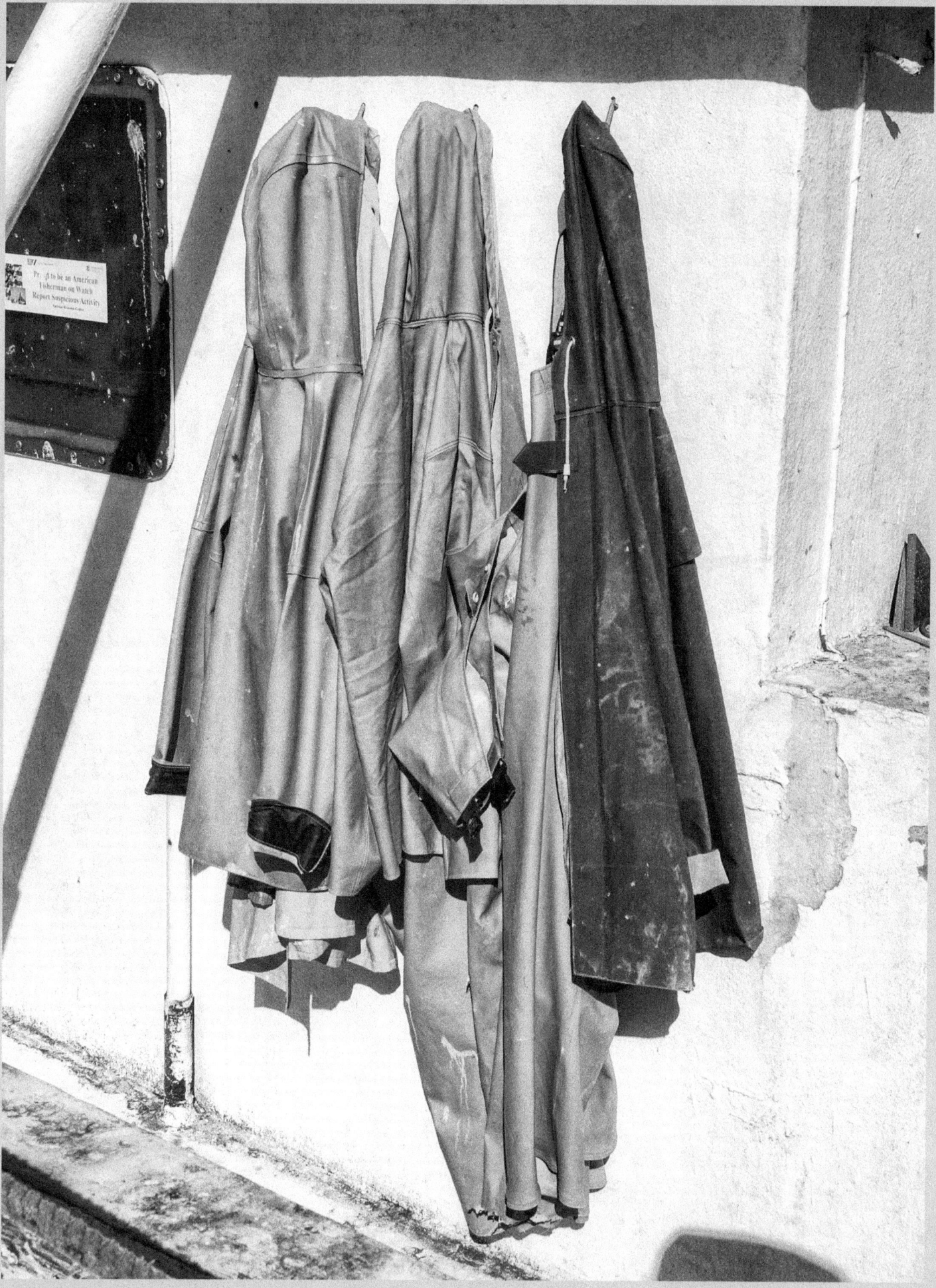

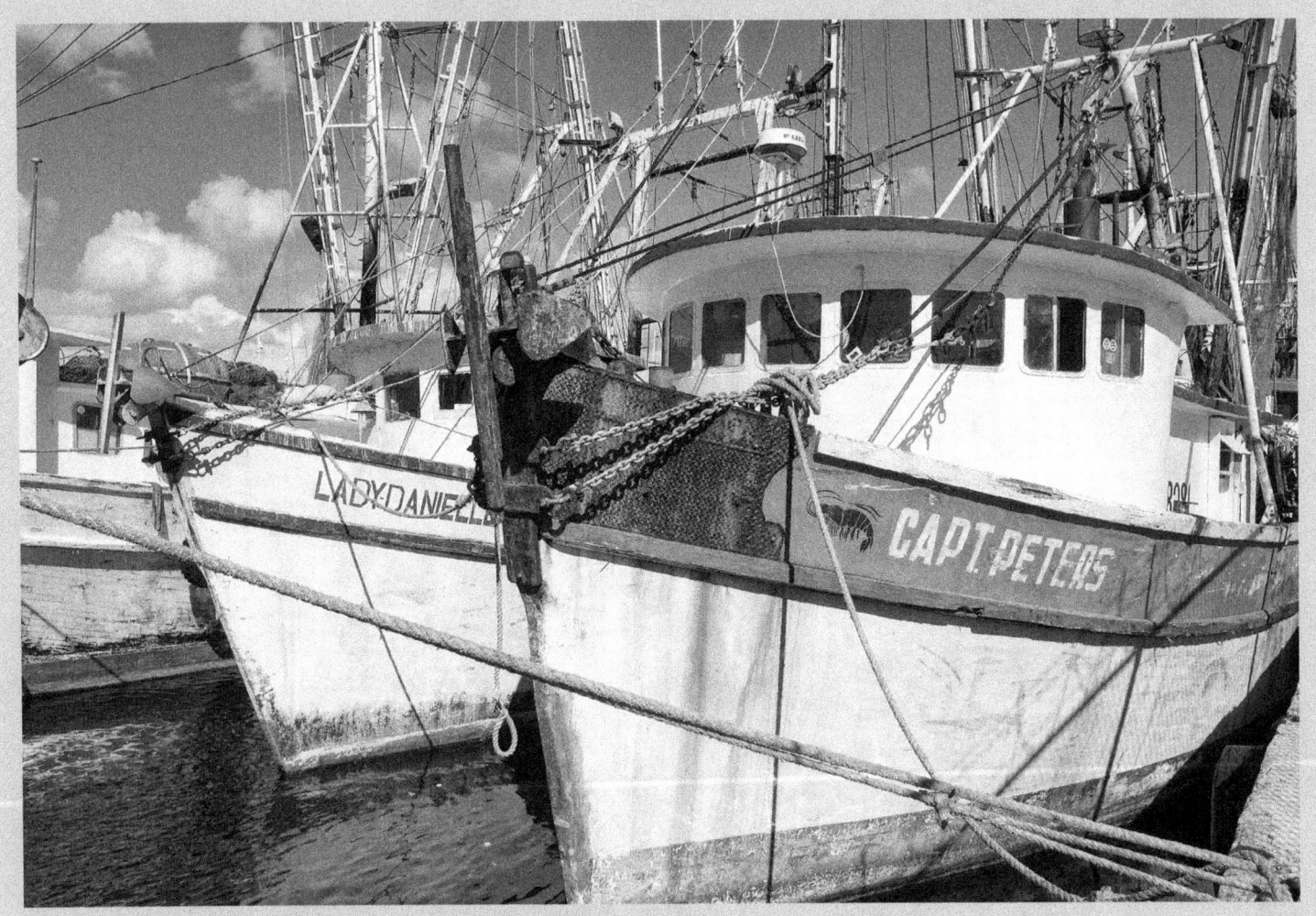

Above: *Capt. Peters*, 2008
Opposite: Charlie, my favorite subject and crewmember
on the *Capt. Peters*.

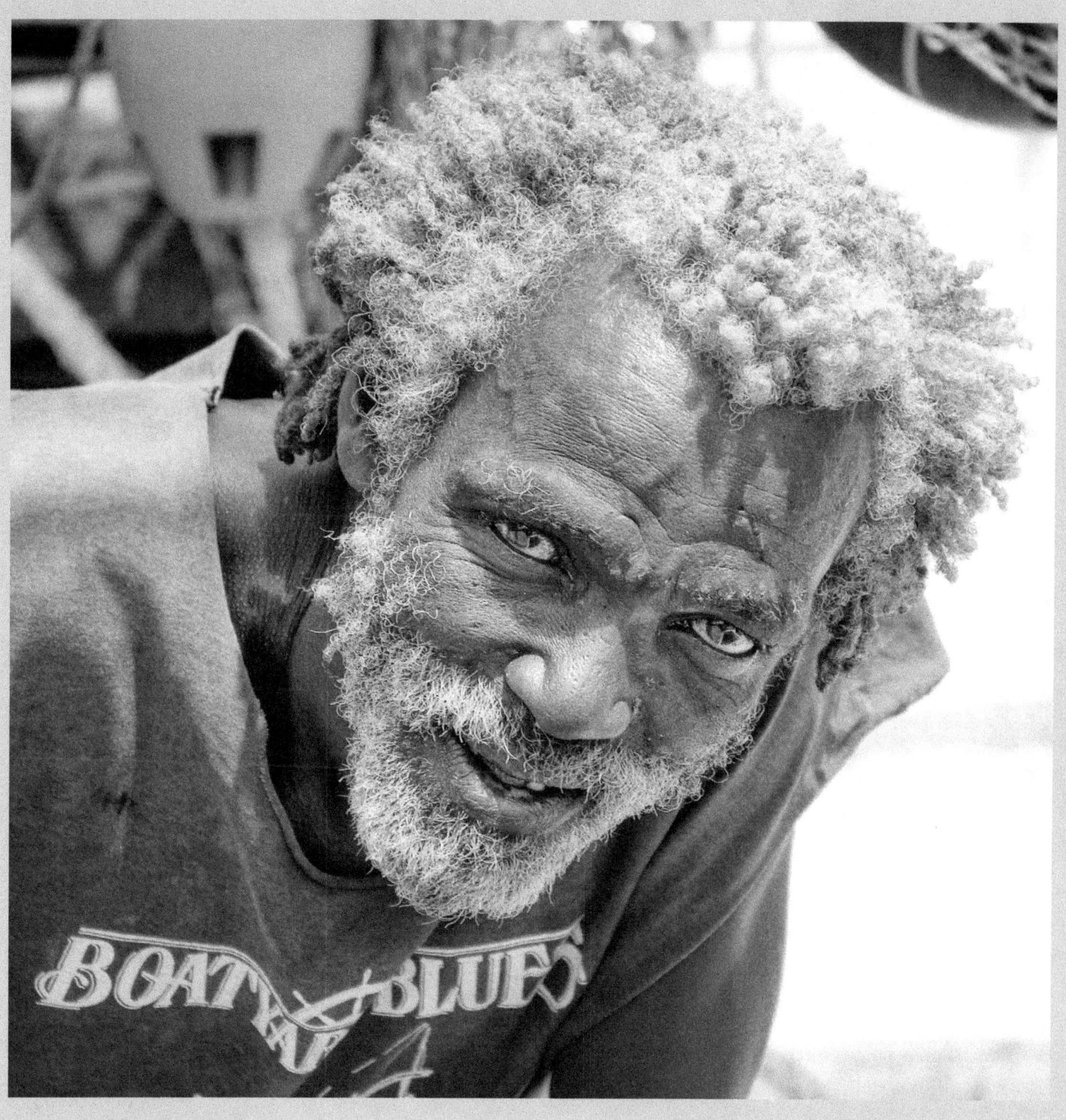

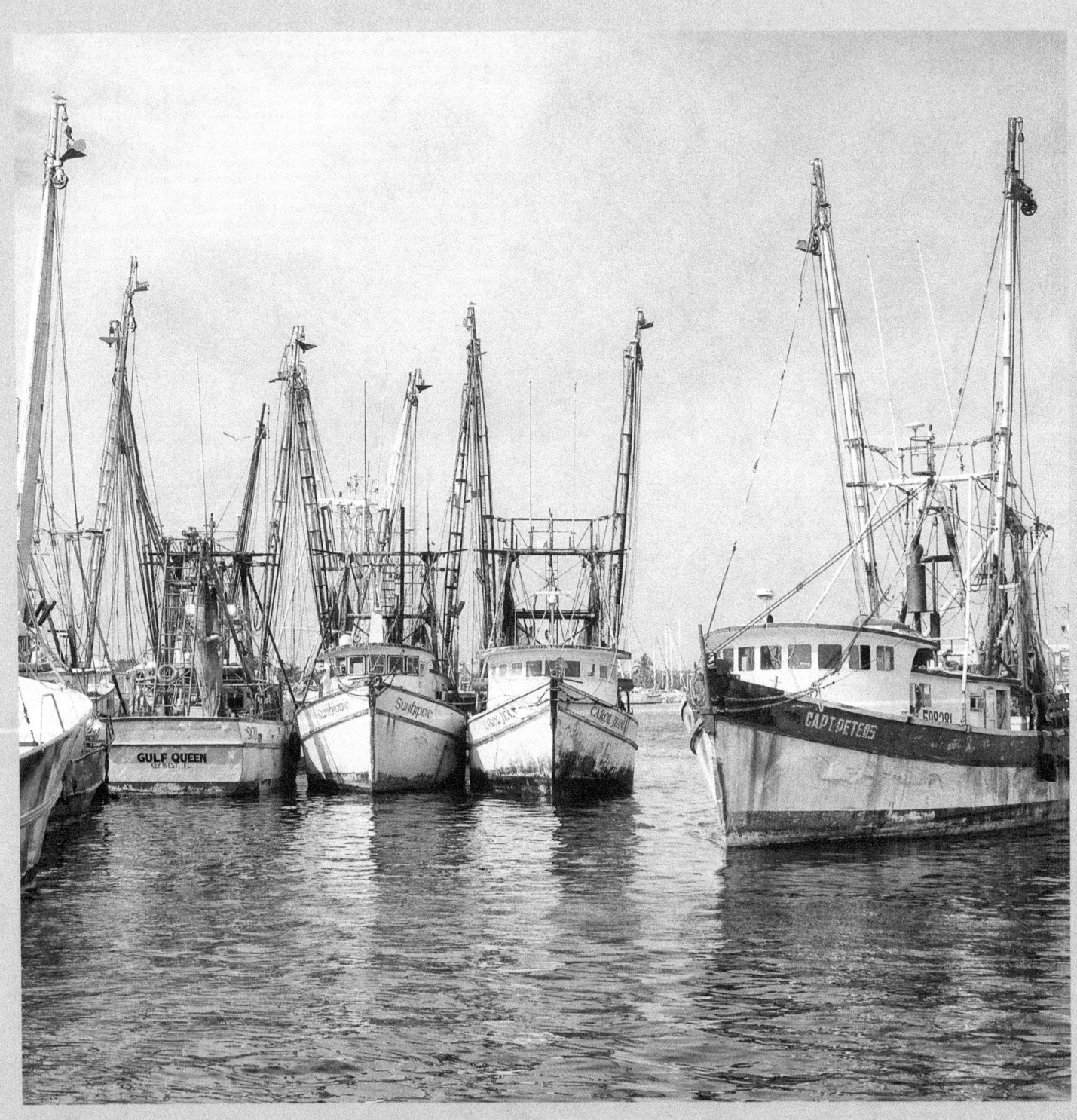

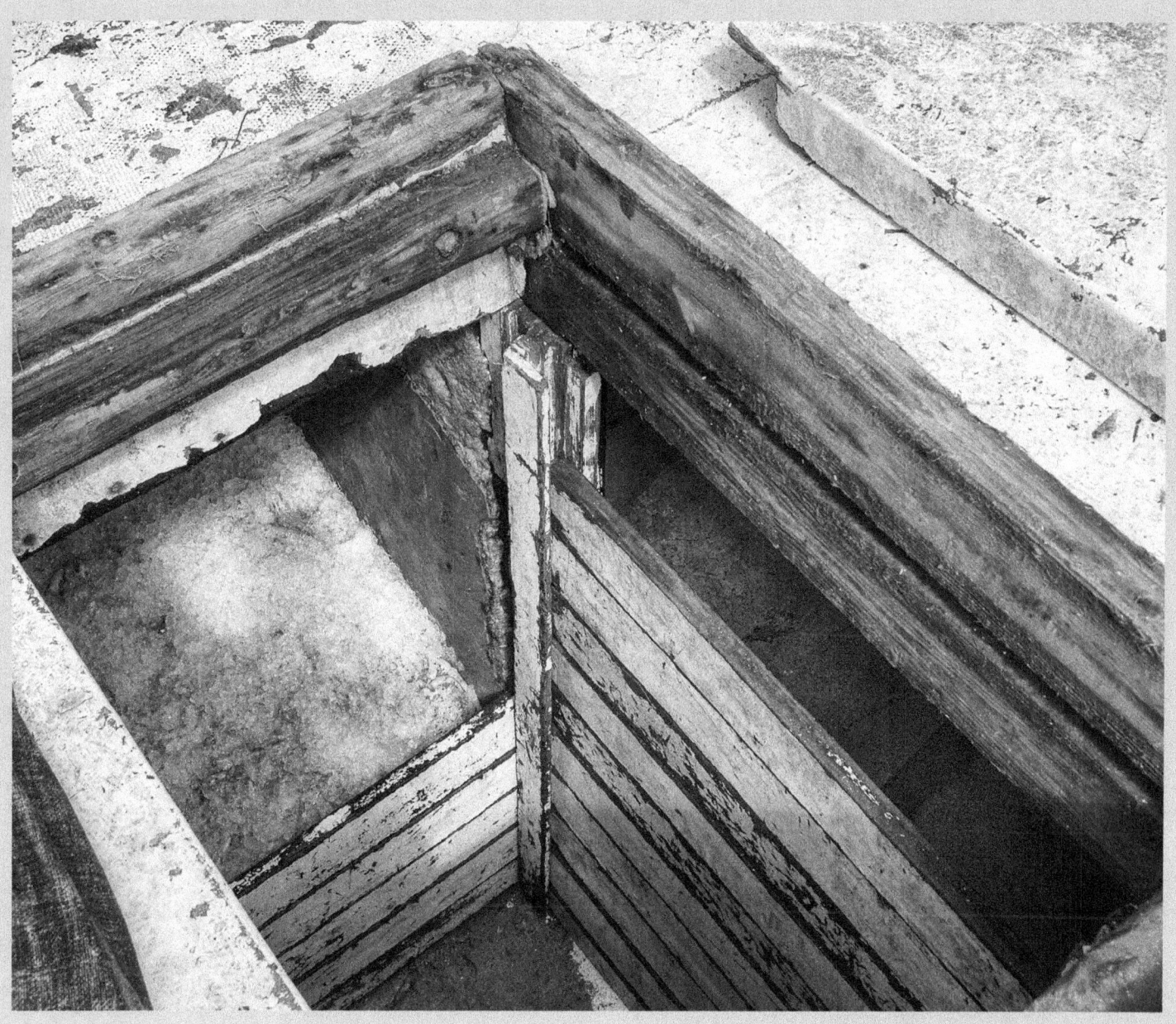

Opposite: *Capt. Peters* returning from shrimping.
Above: Shrimp on ice in the hold. Boats like the *Capt. Peters* keep the shrimp fresh by storing them in ice.

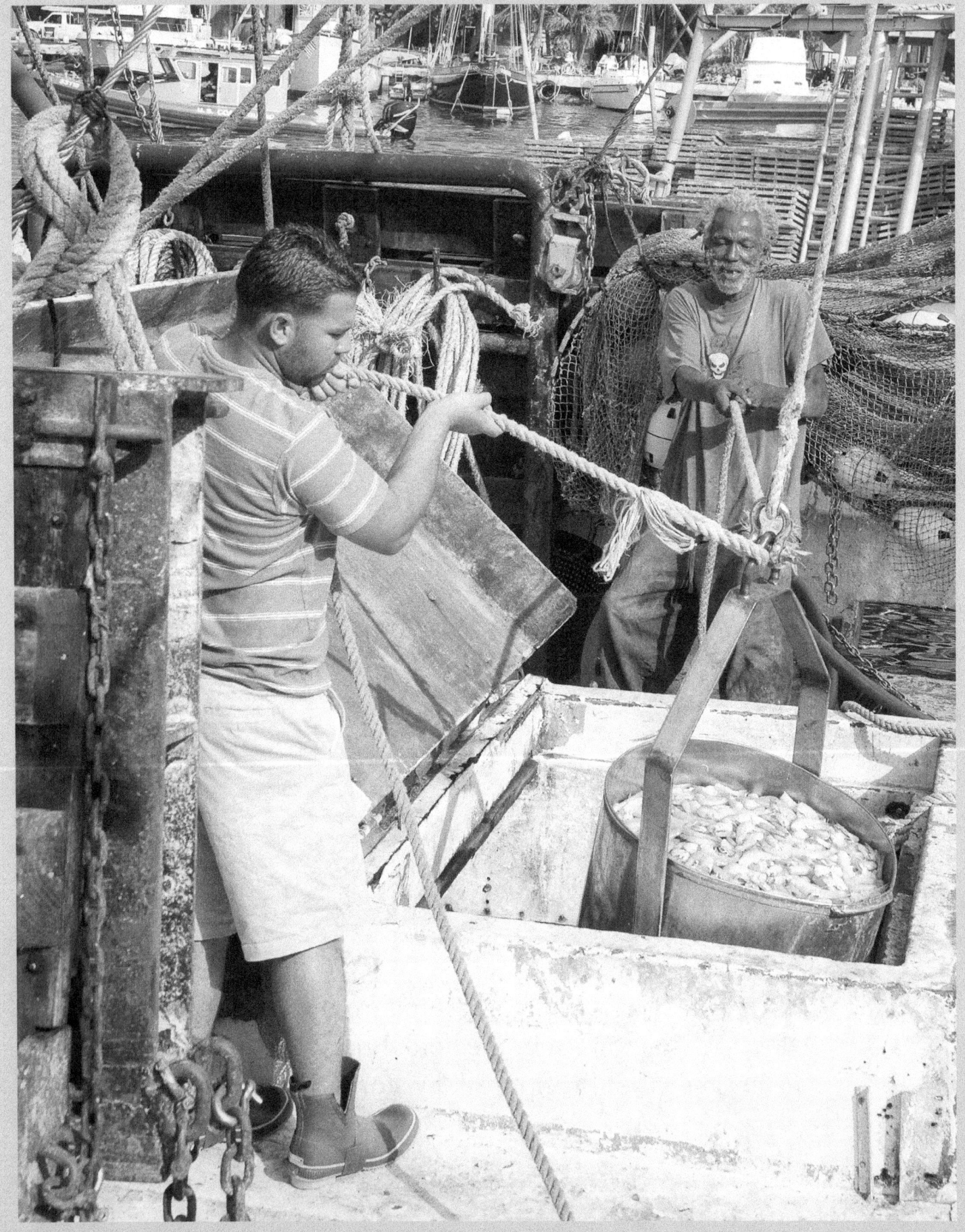

Unloading shrimp from the *Capt. Peters*.

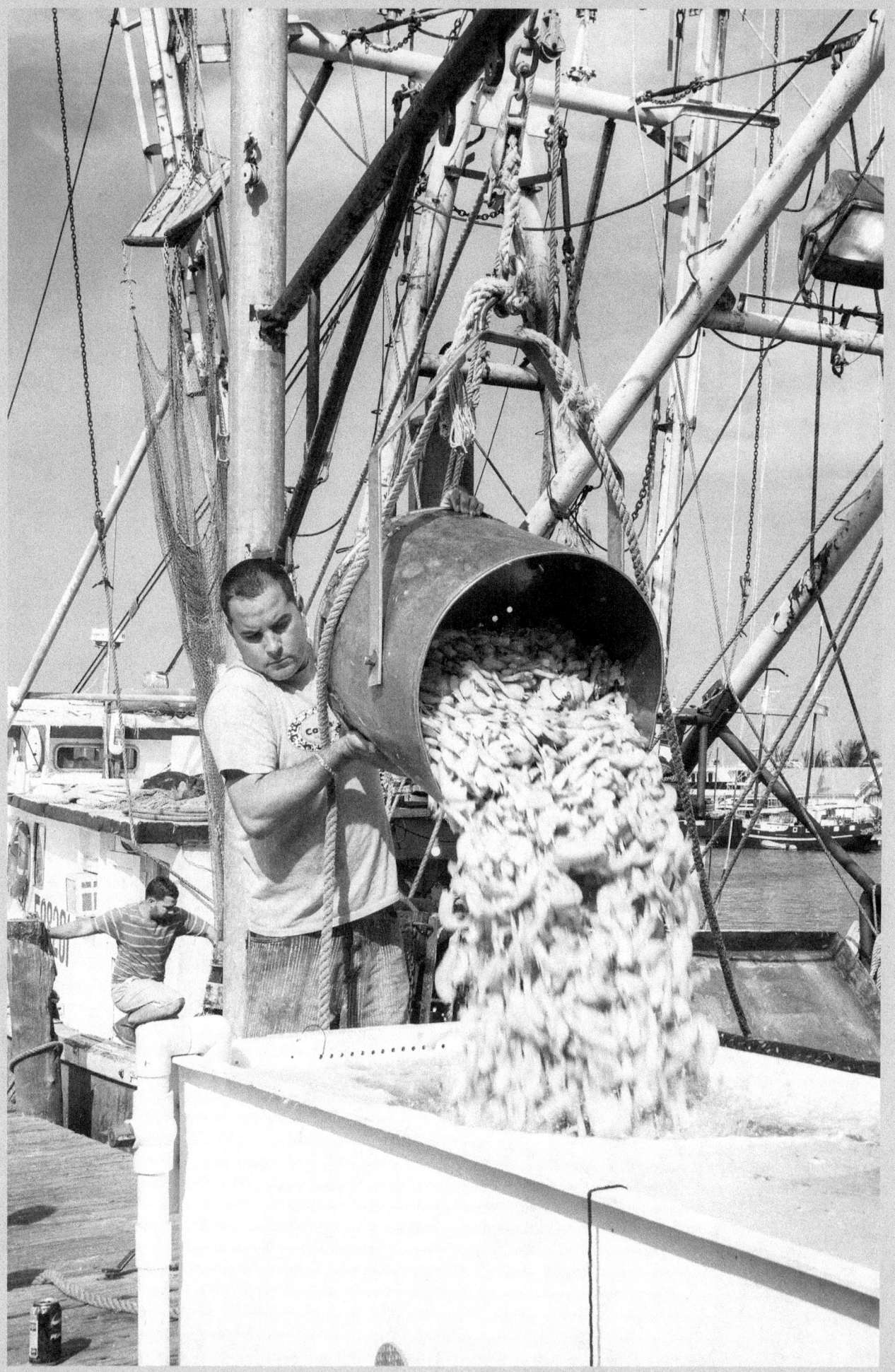

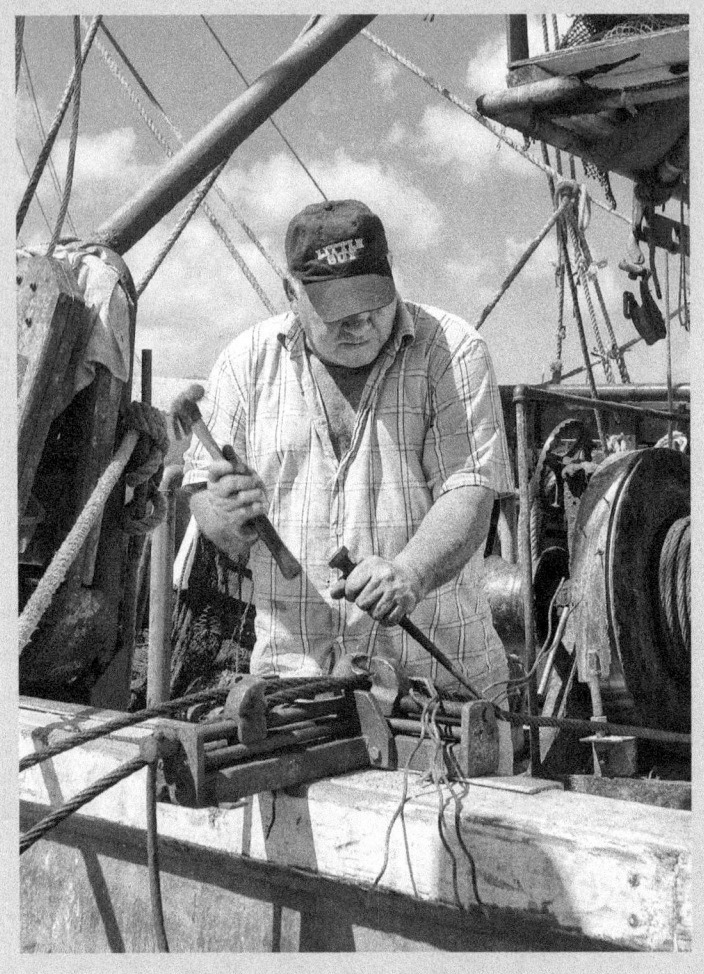
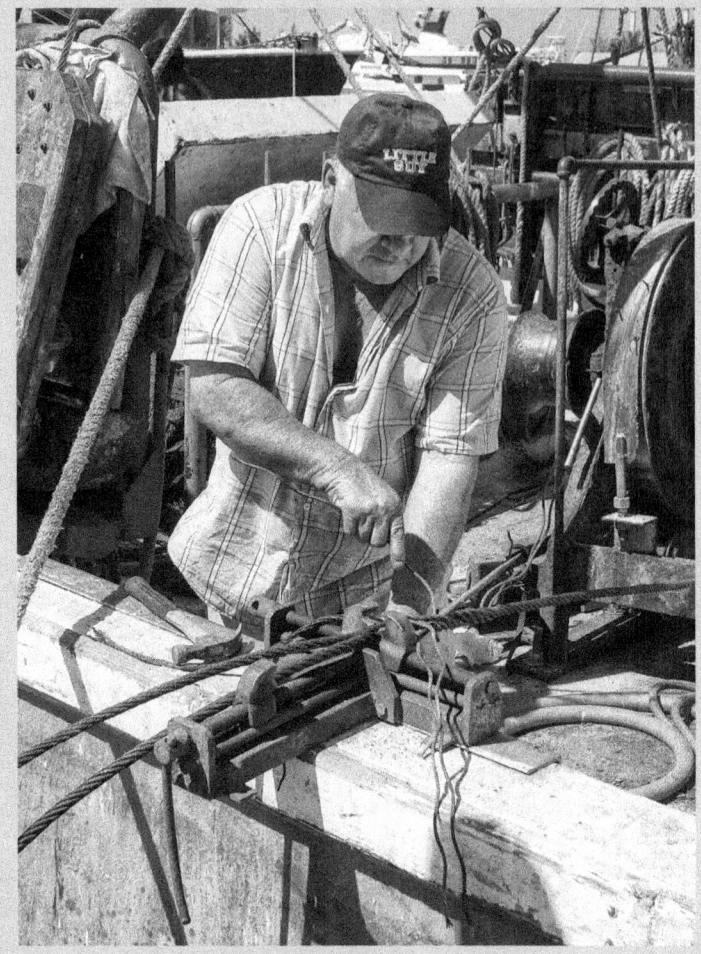
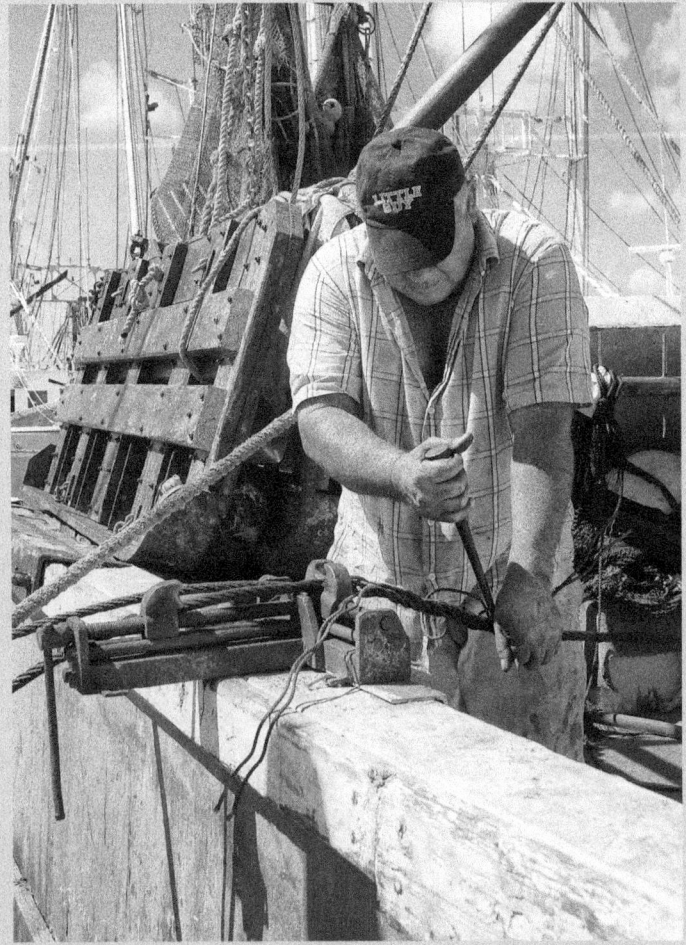
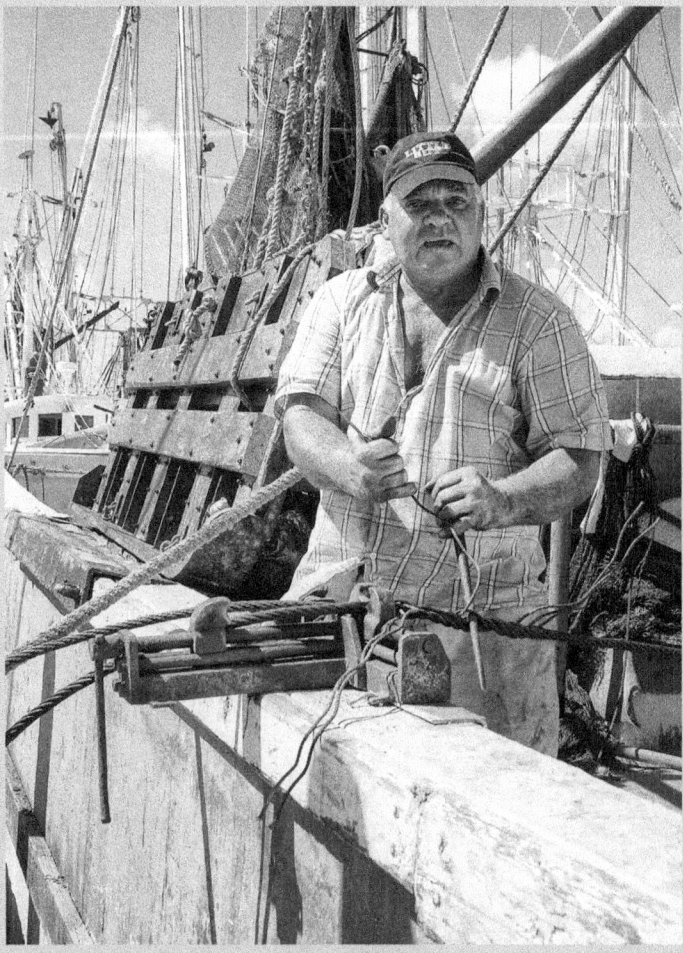

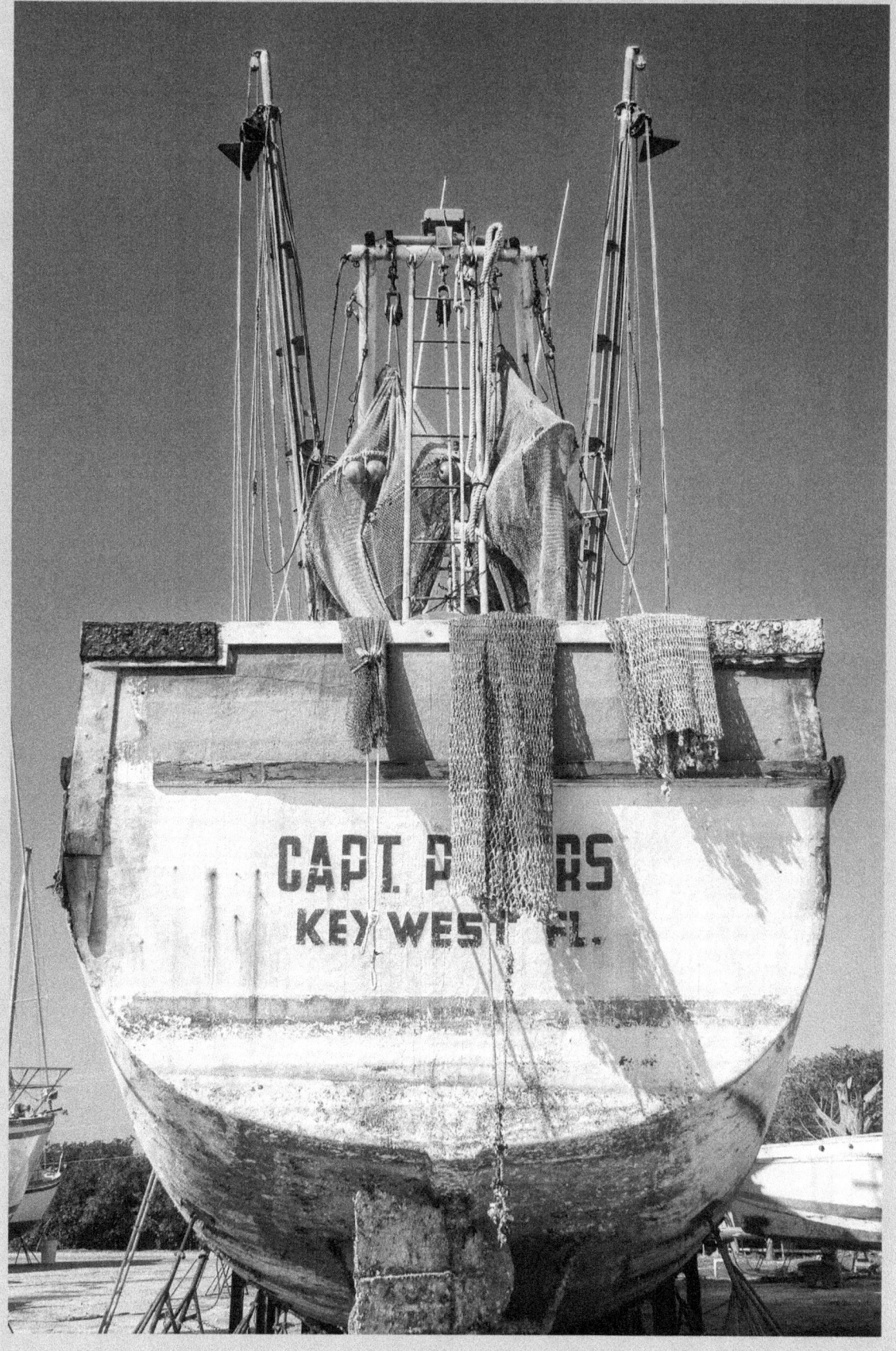

Opposite: Juan, owner of the *Capt. Peters,* splicing
steel cable, 2008.
Above: The *Capt. Peters* hauled out for the last time, 2011.

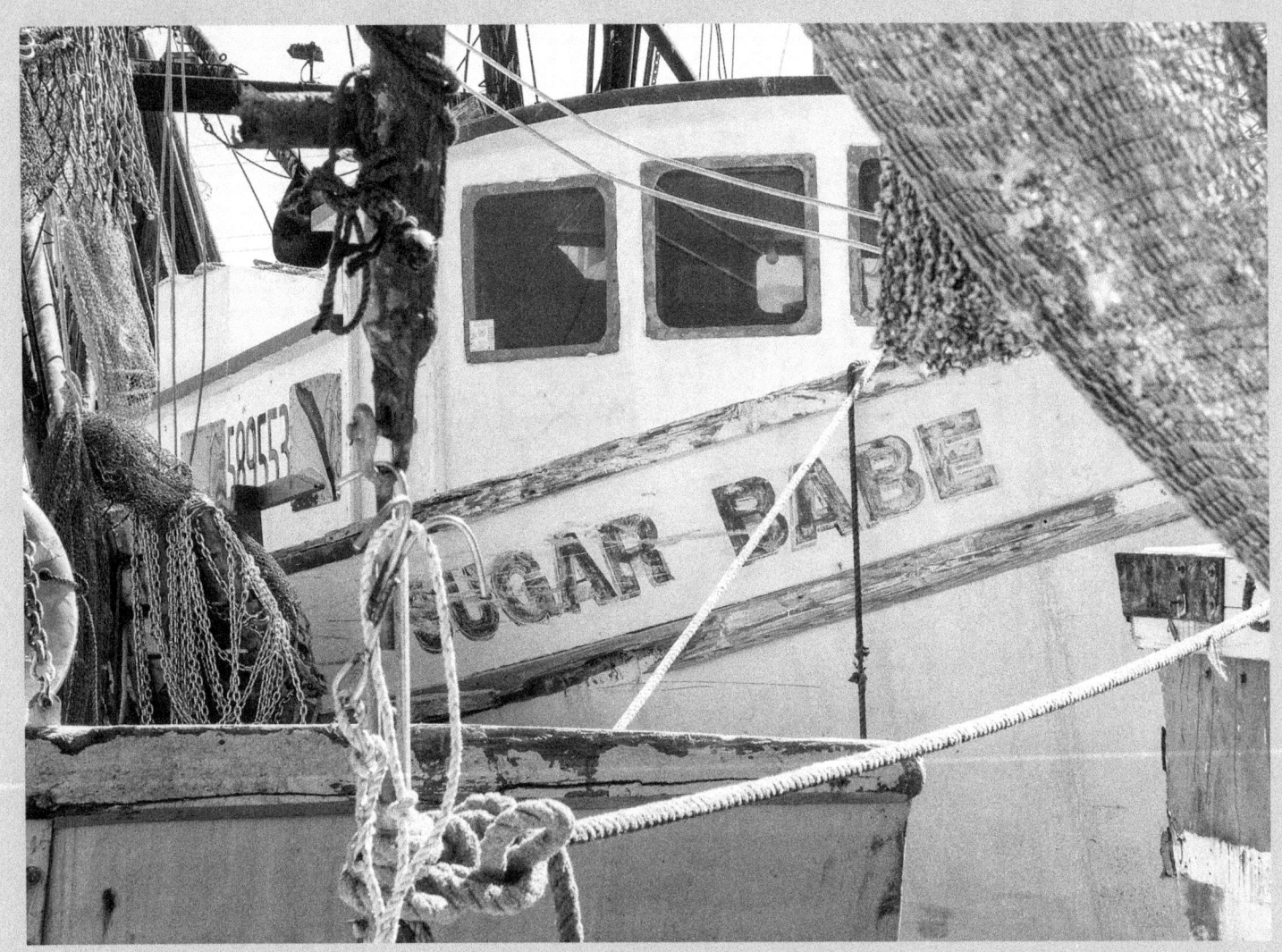

Above: *Sugar Babe*, 2008.
Opposite: Brenda and Dewey working on the
Sugar Babe.

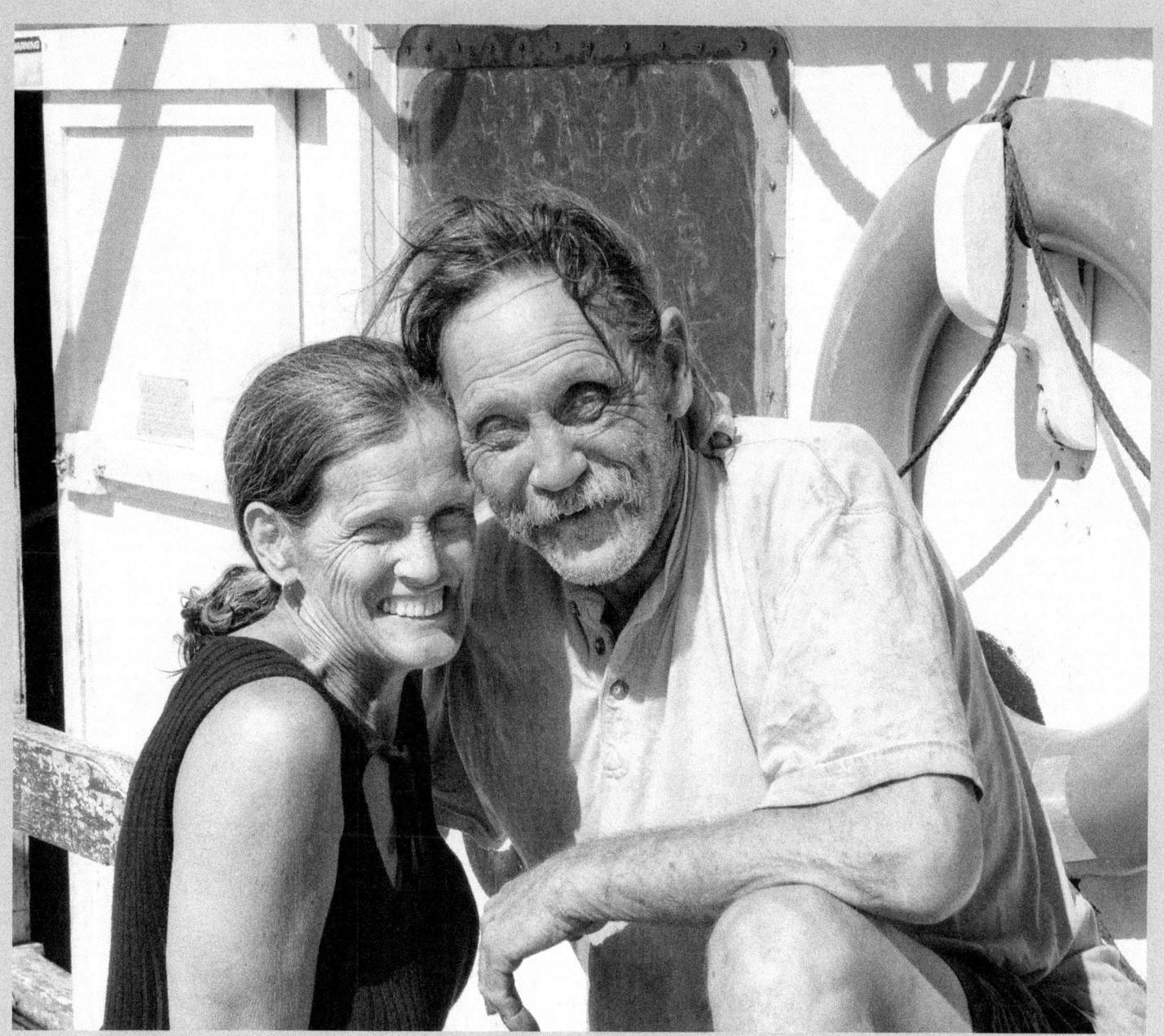

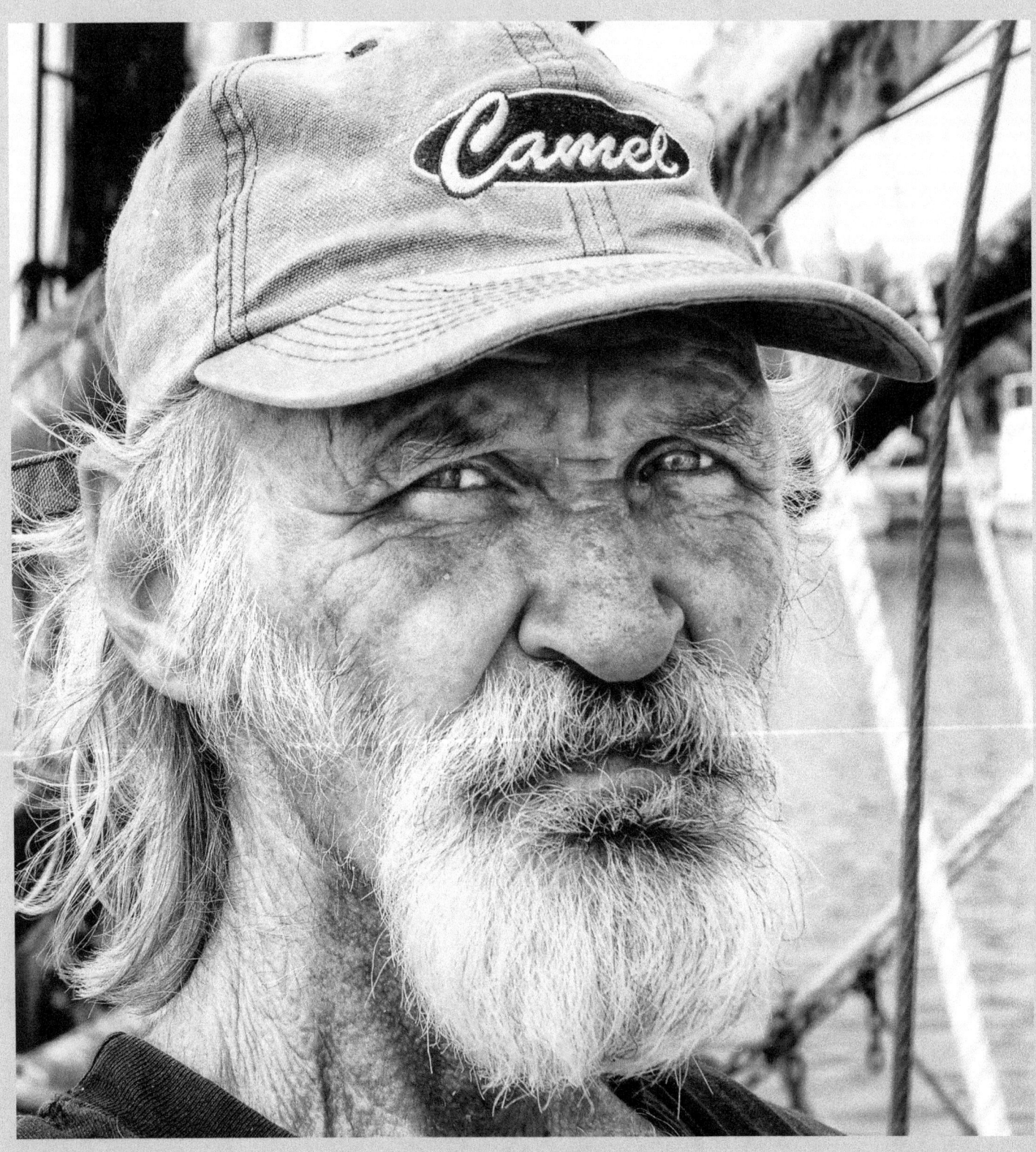

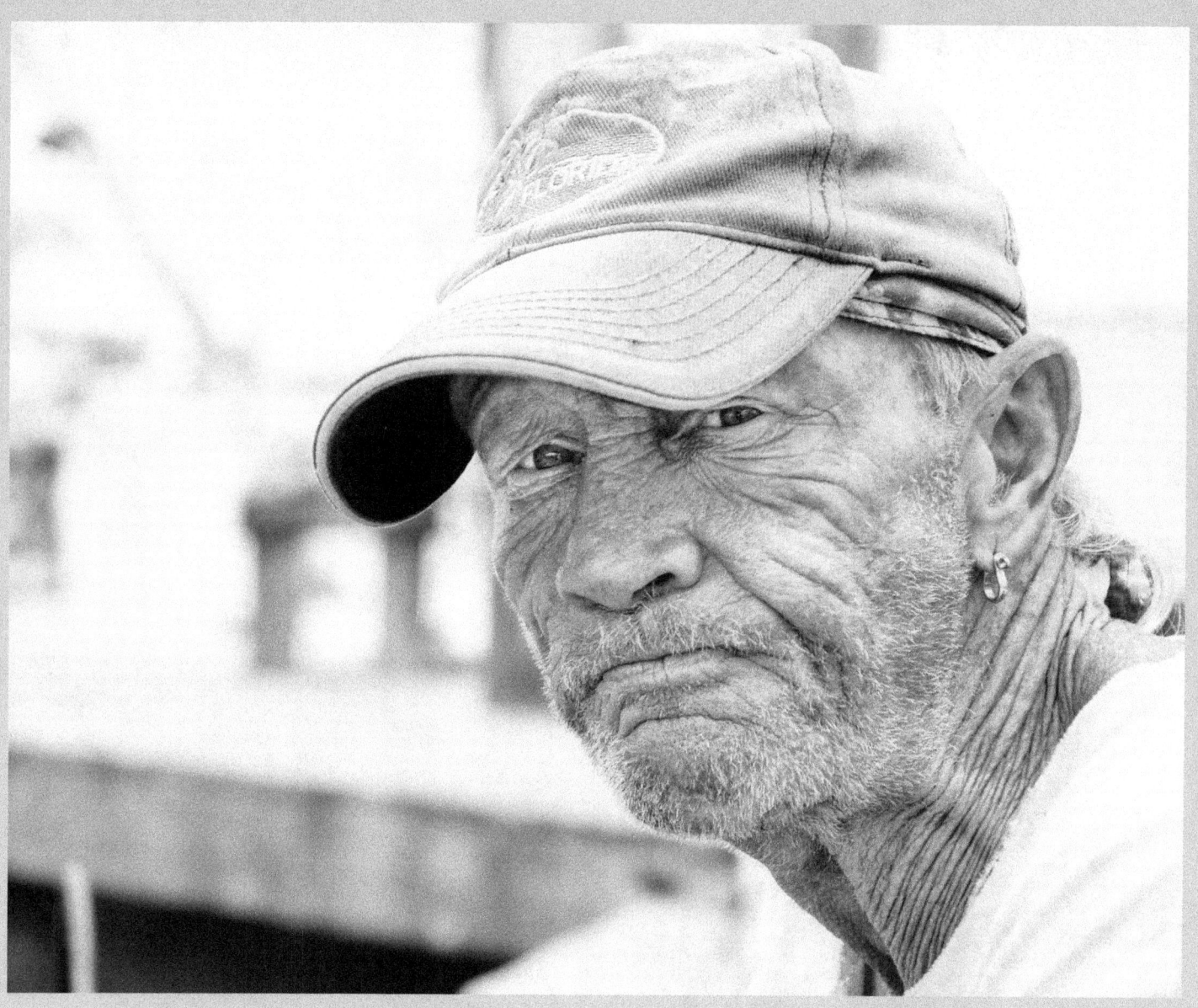

Opposite: John, deck crewmember on various boats.
Above: Frank at the Fishbusterz fuel dock.

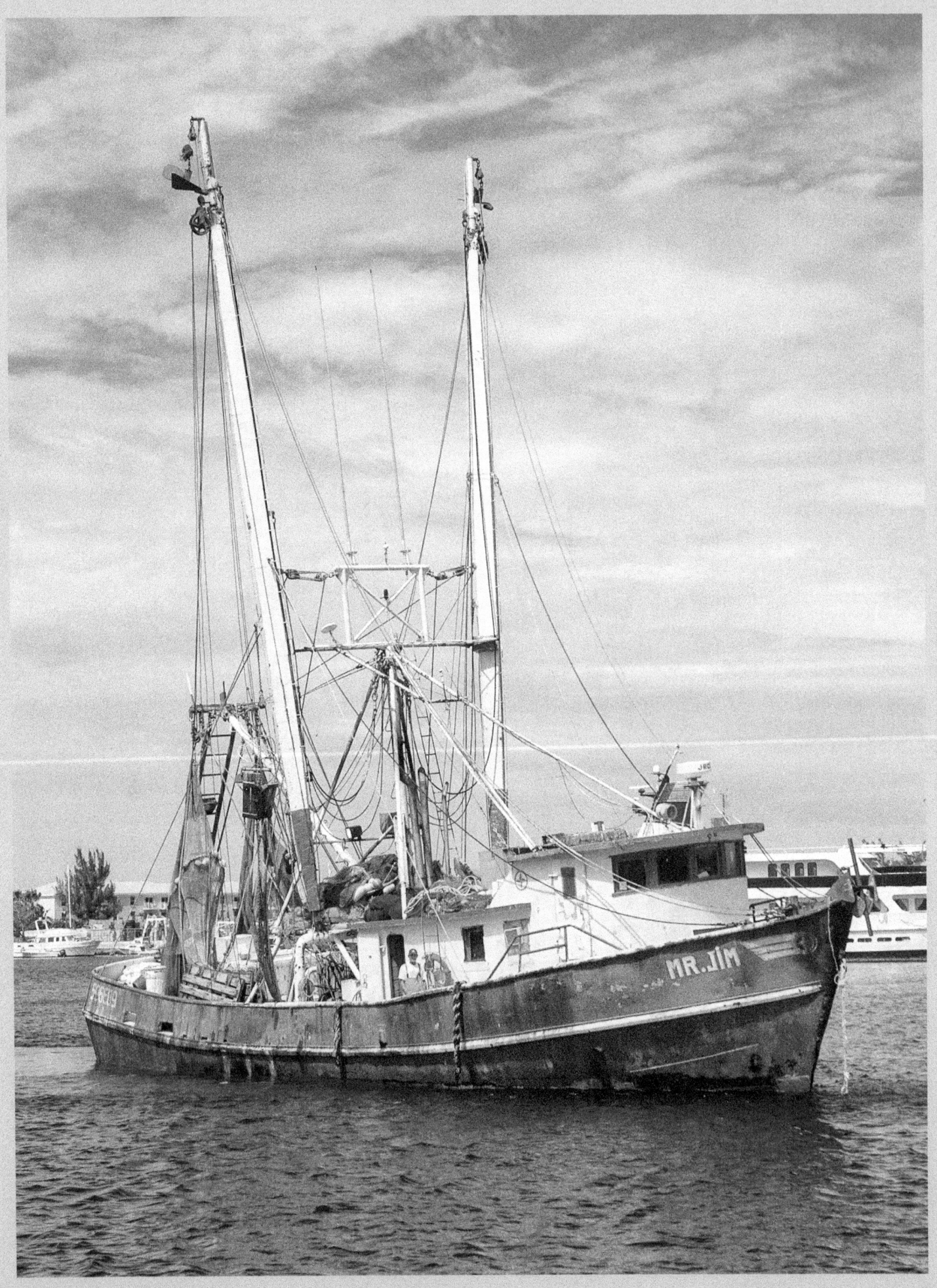

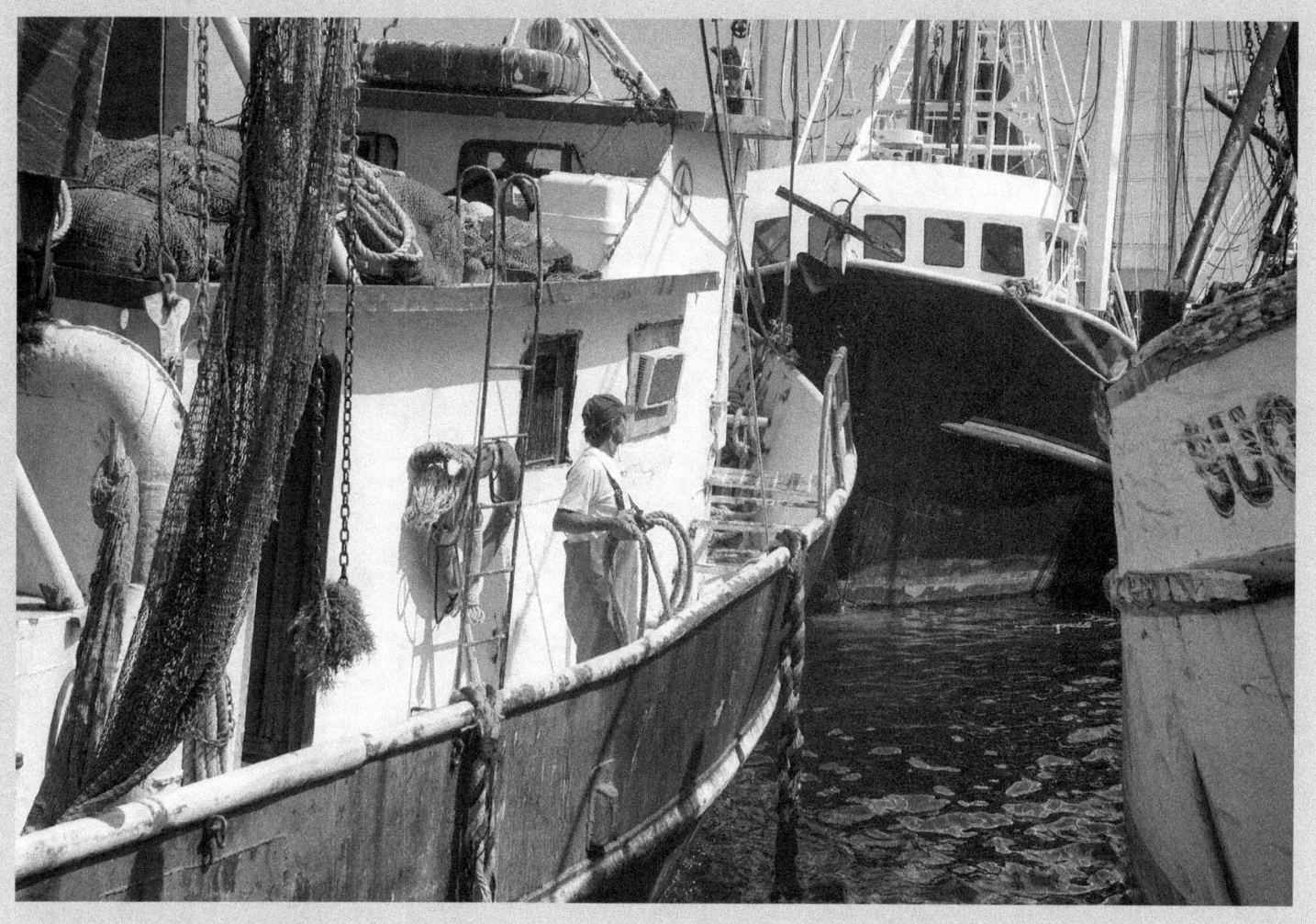

Opposite: The *Mr. Jim* arrives at the Fishbusterz dock, 2008.
Above: Cowboy with the line waiting to tie up.

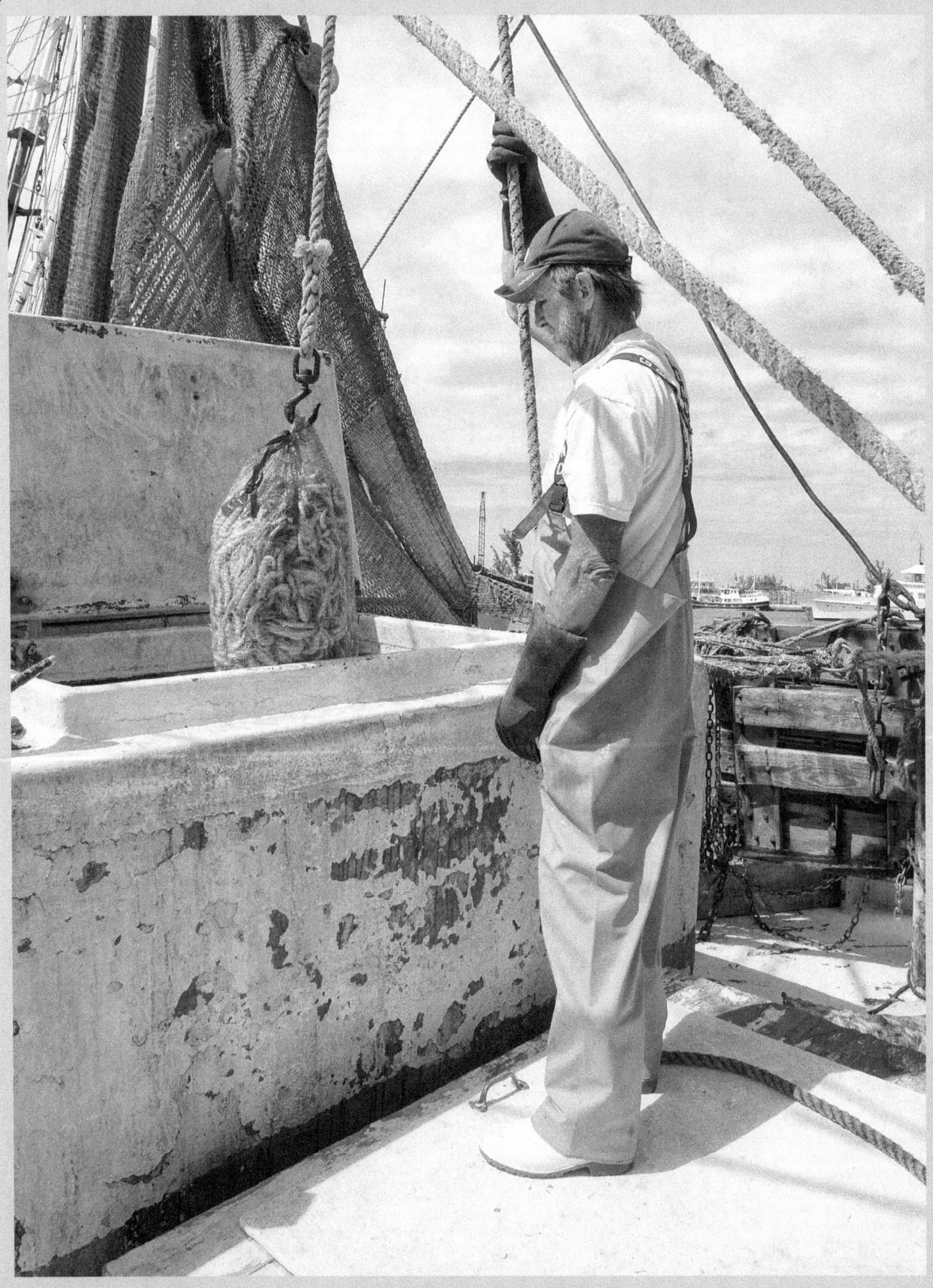

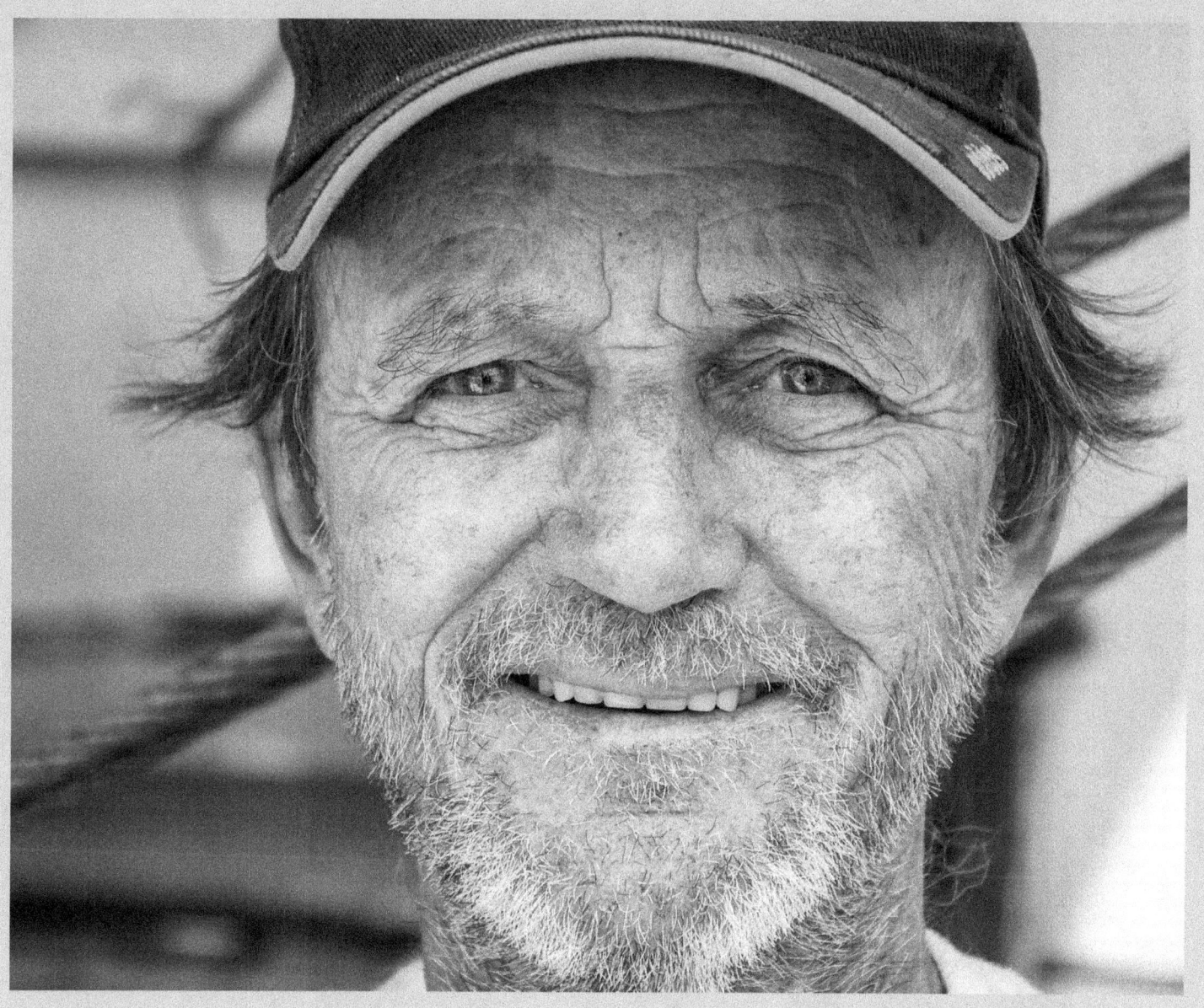

Opposite: Cowboy and freezer box on the *Mr. Jim*.
Above: Cowboy, unshaven after a long cruise.

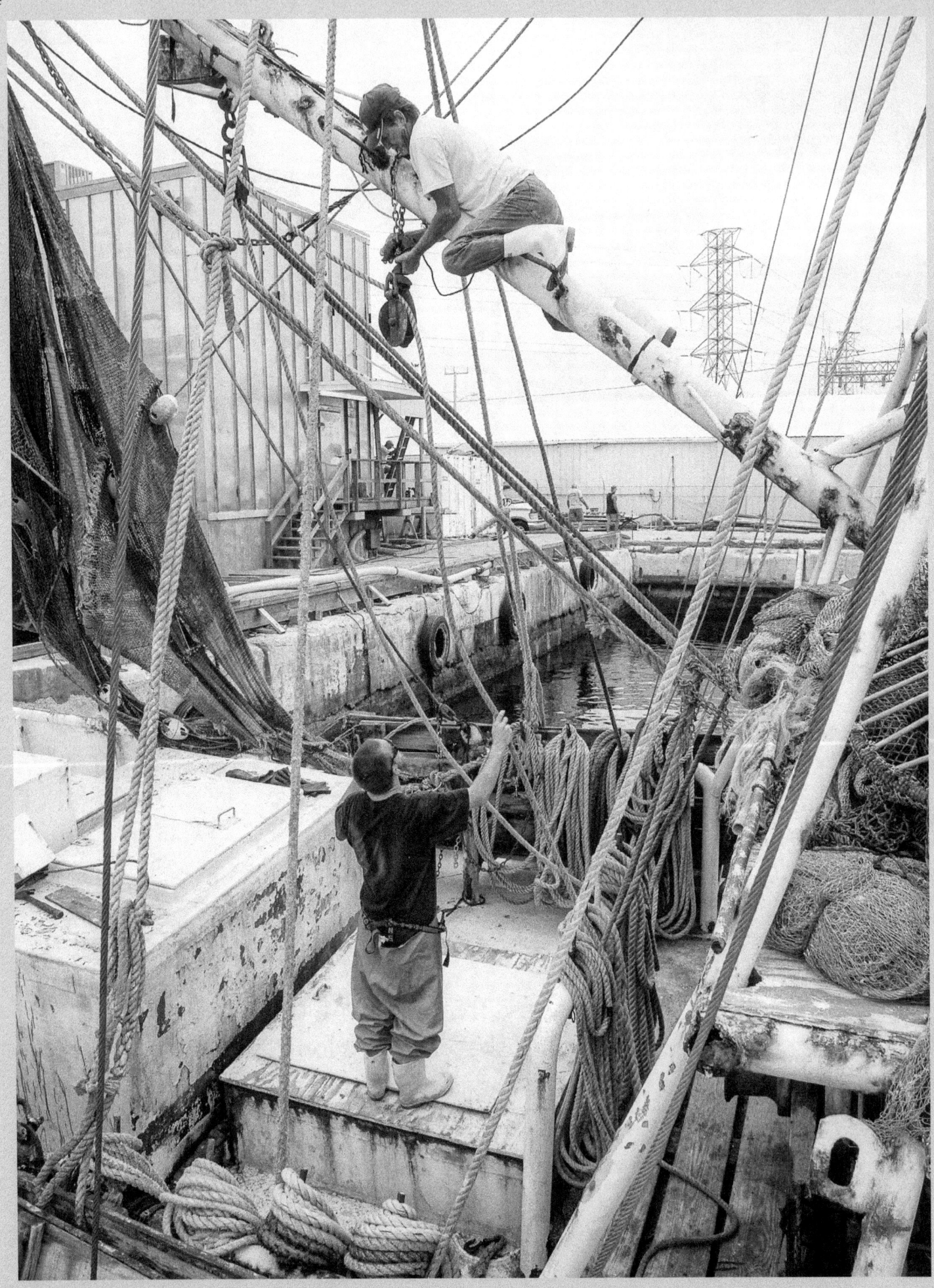

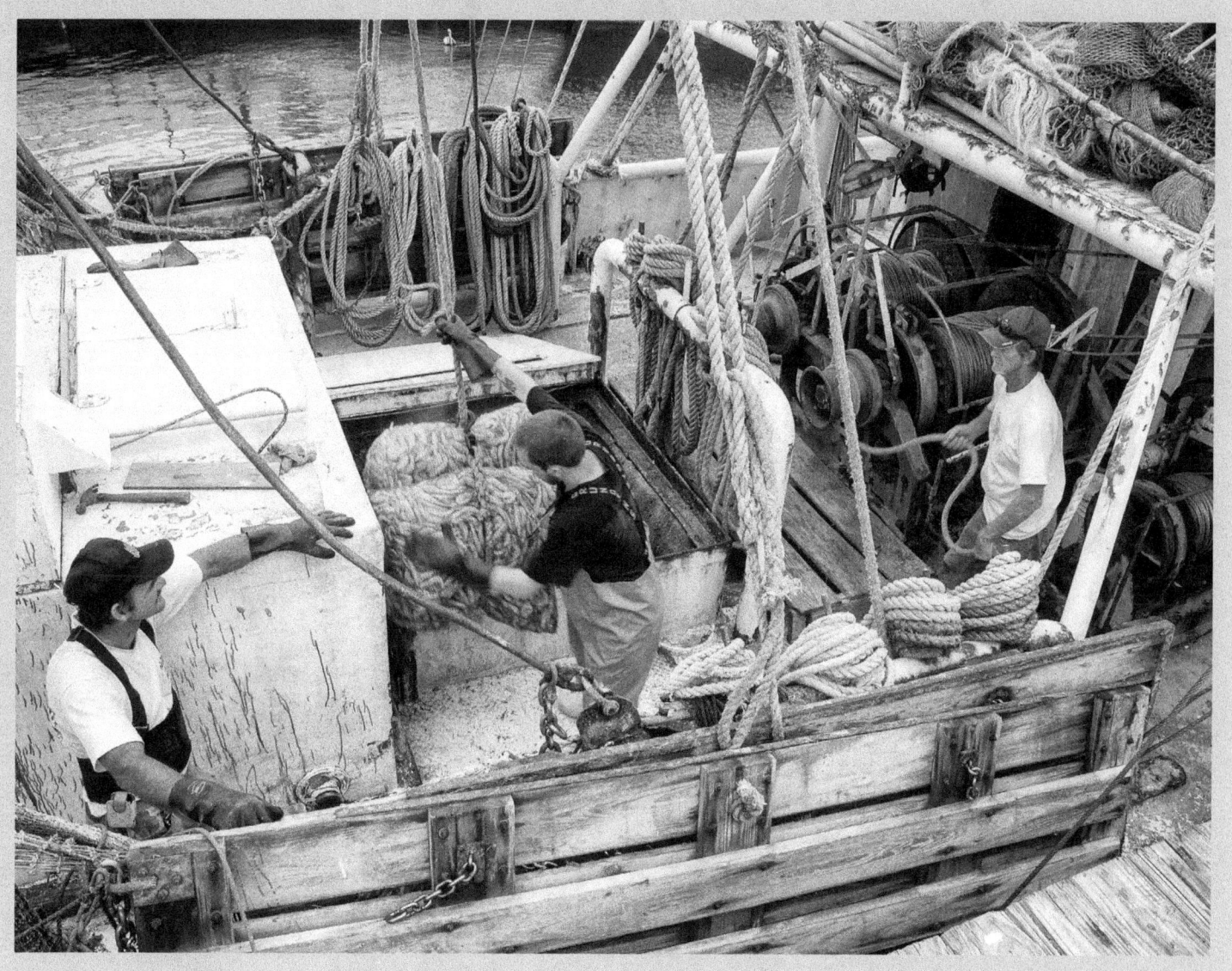

Preparing to unload—and unloading—bags of frozen shrimp.

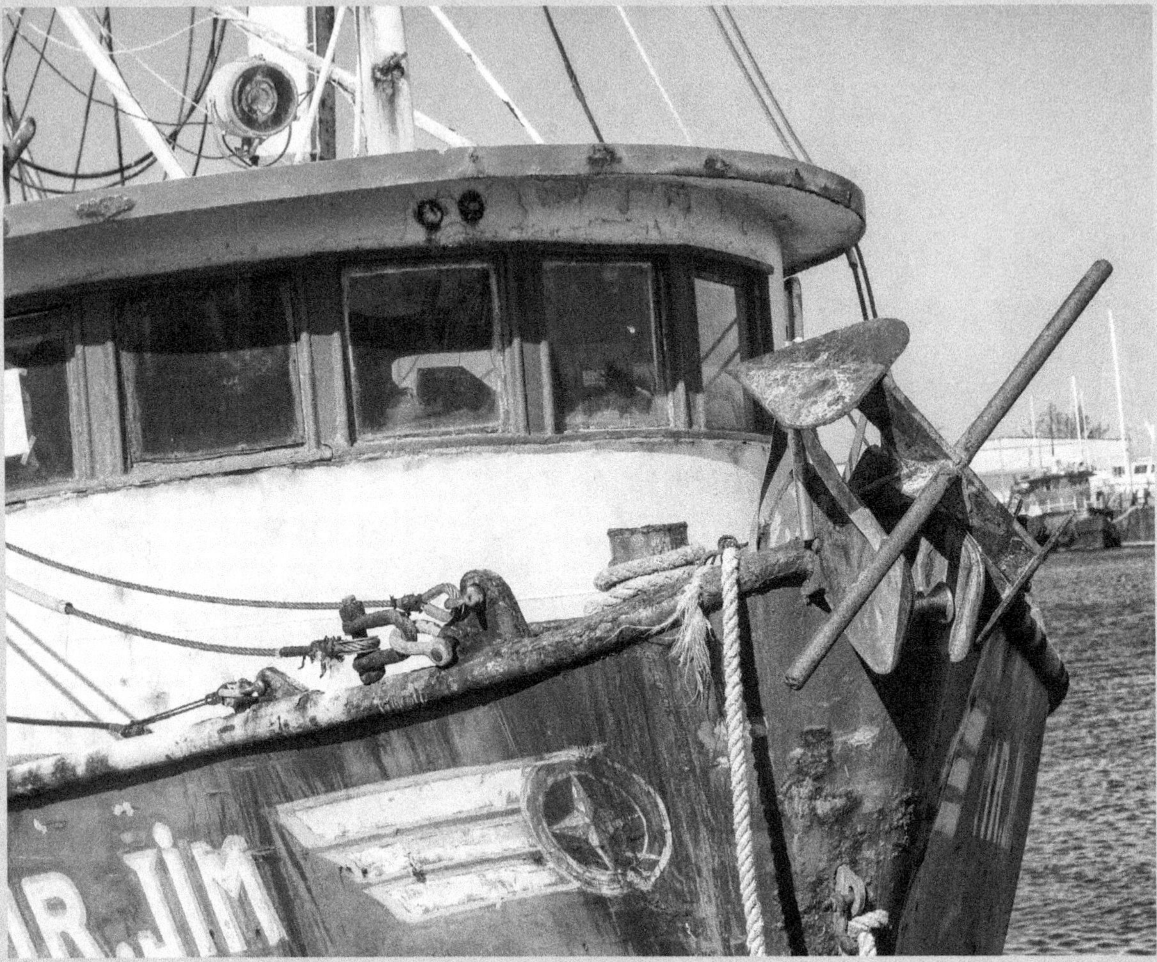
R.JIM

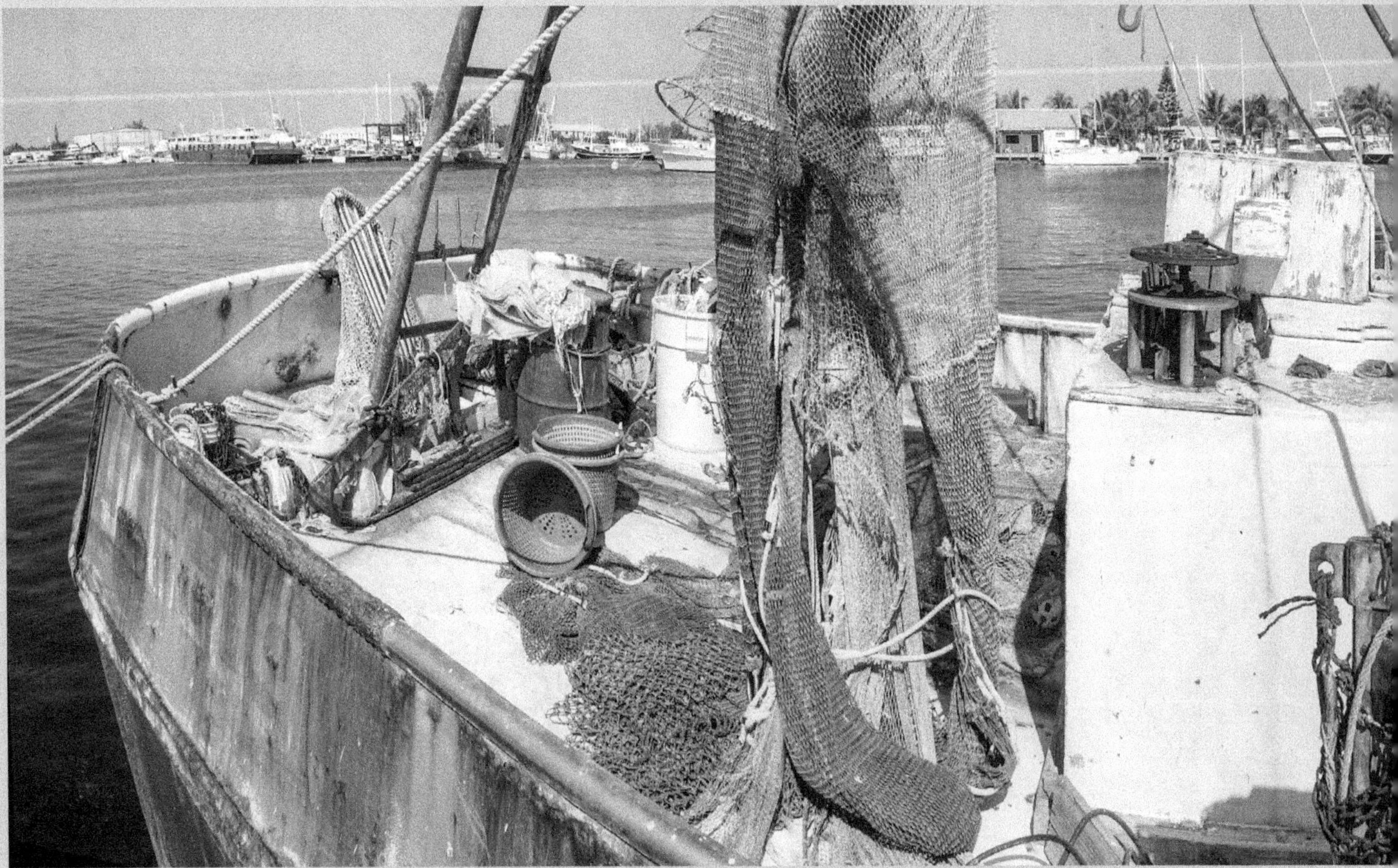

Mr. Jim, abandoned after the owner died, 2011.

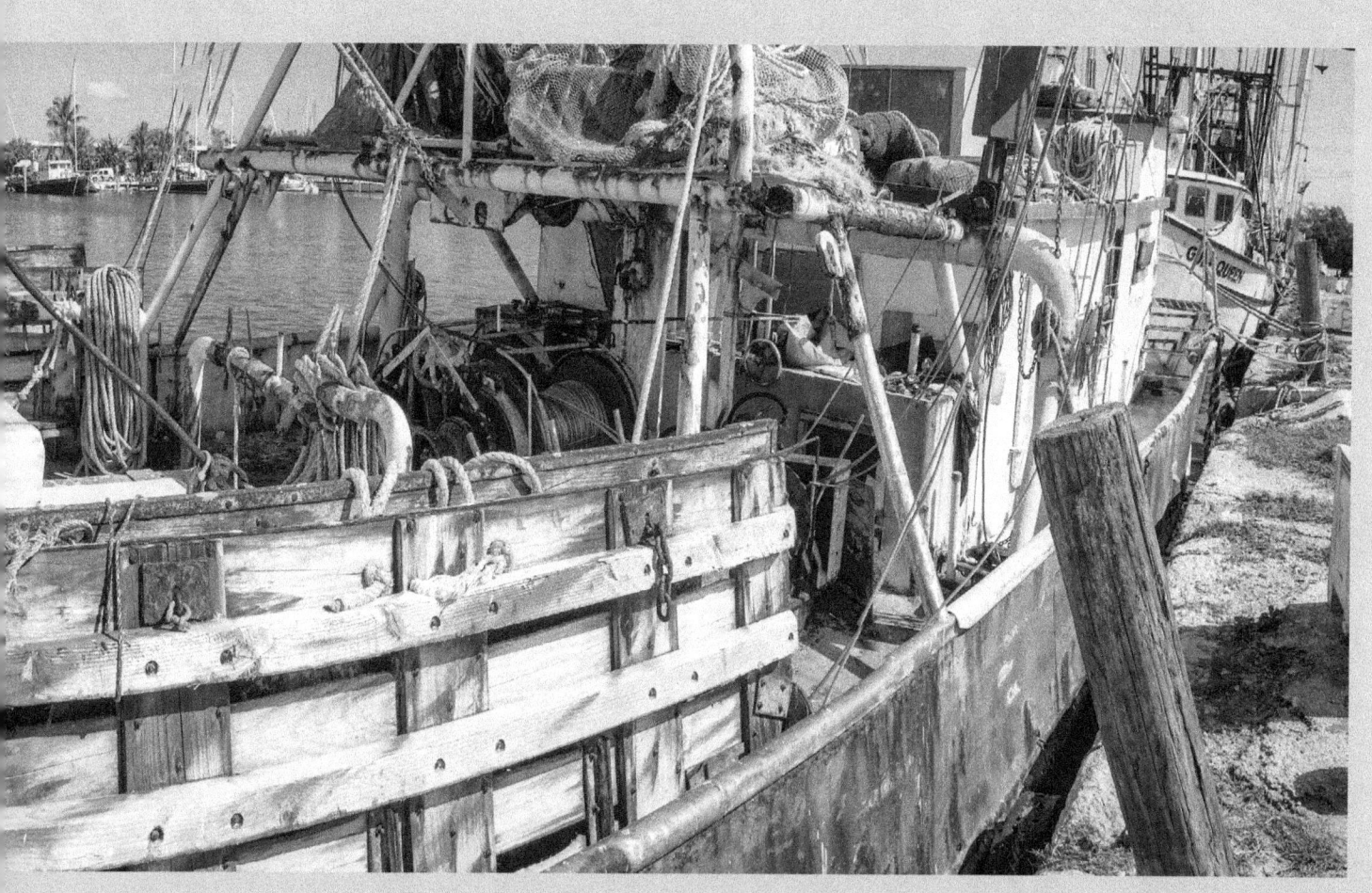

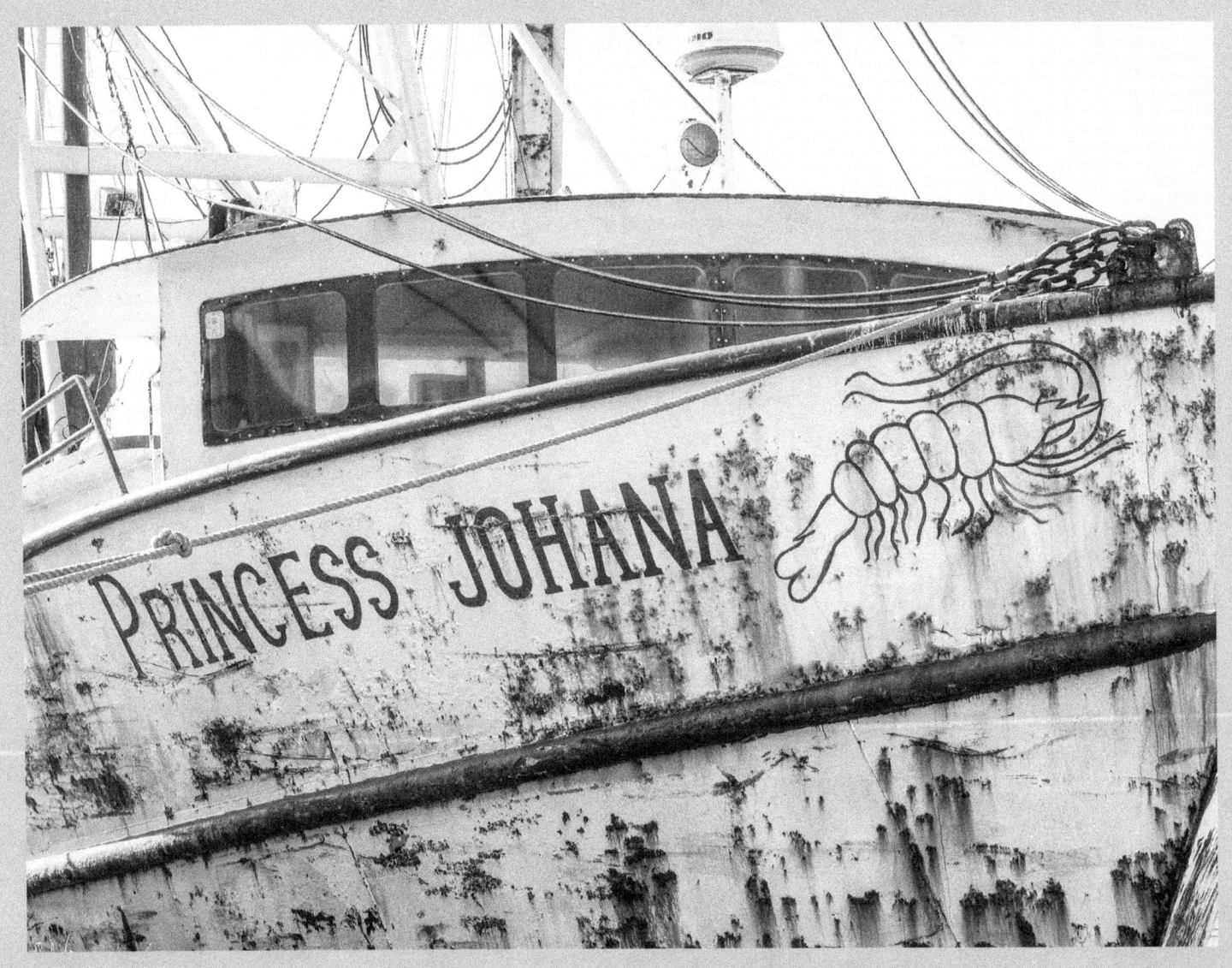

Above: *Princess Johana*, 2011.
Opposite: Juan, former owner of *Capt. Peters*, now in charge of crew on the *Princess Johana*.

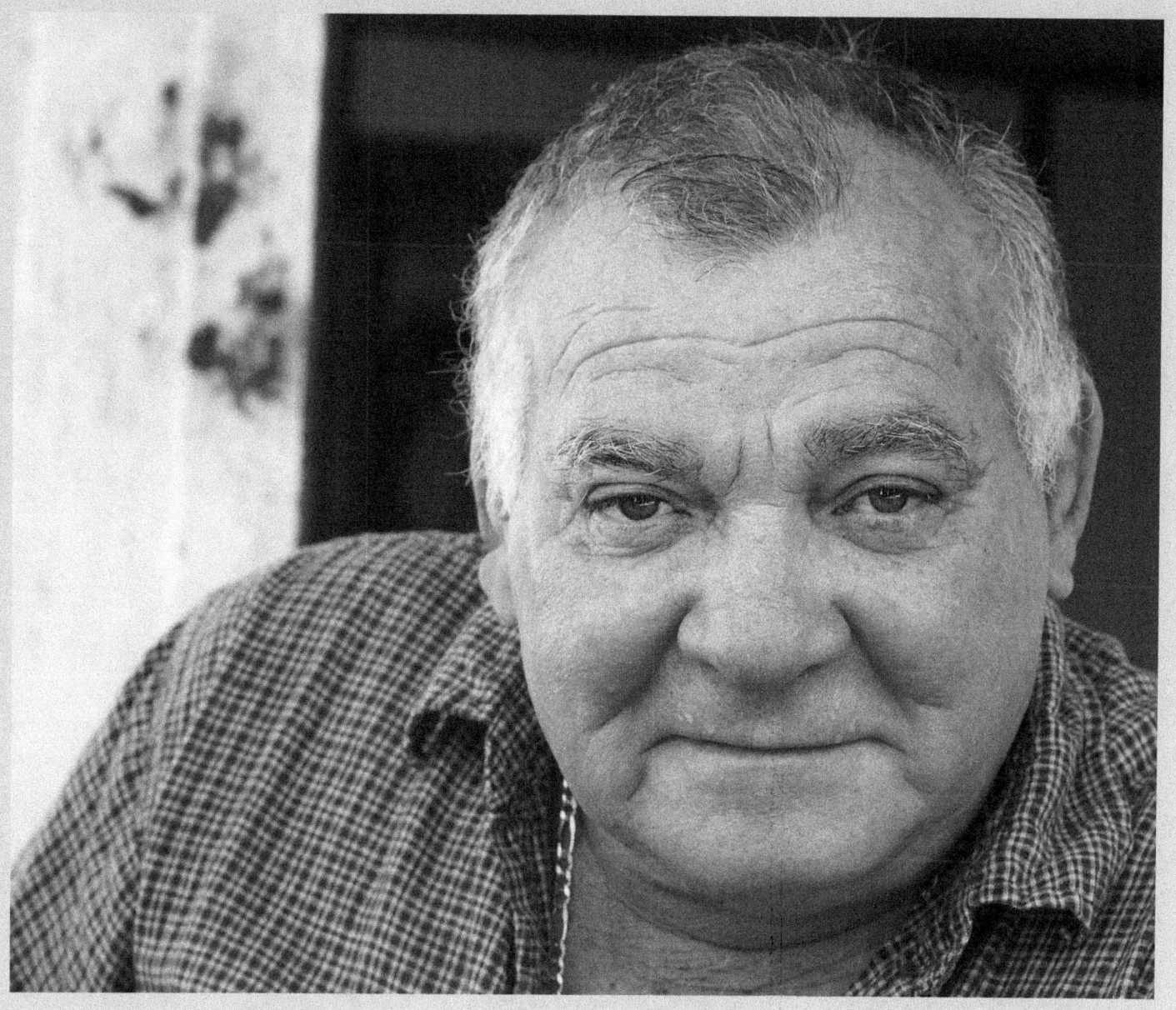

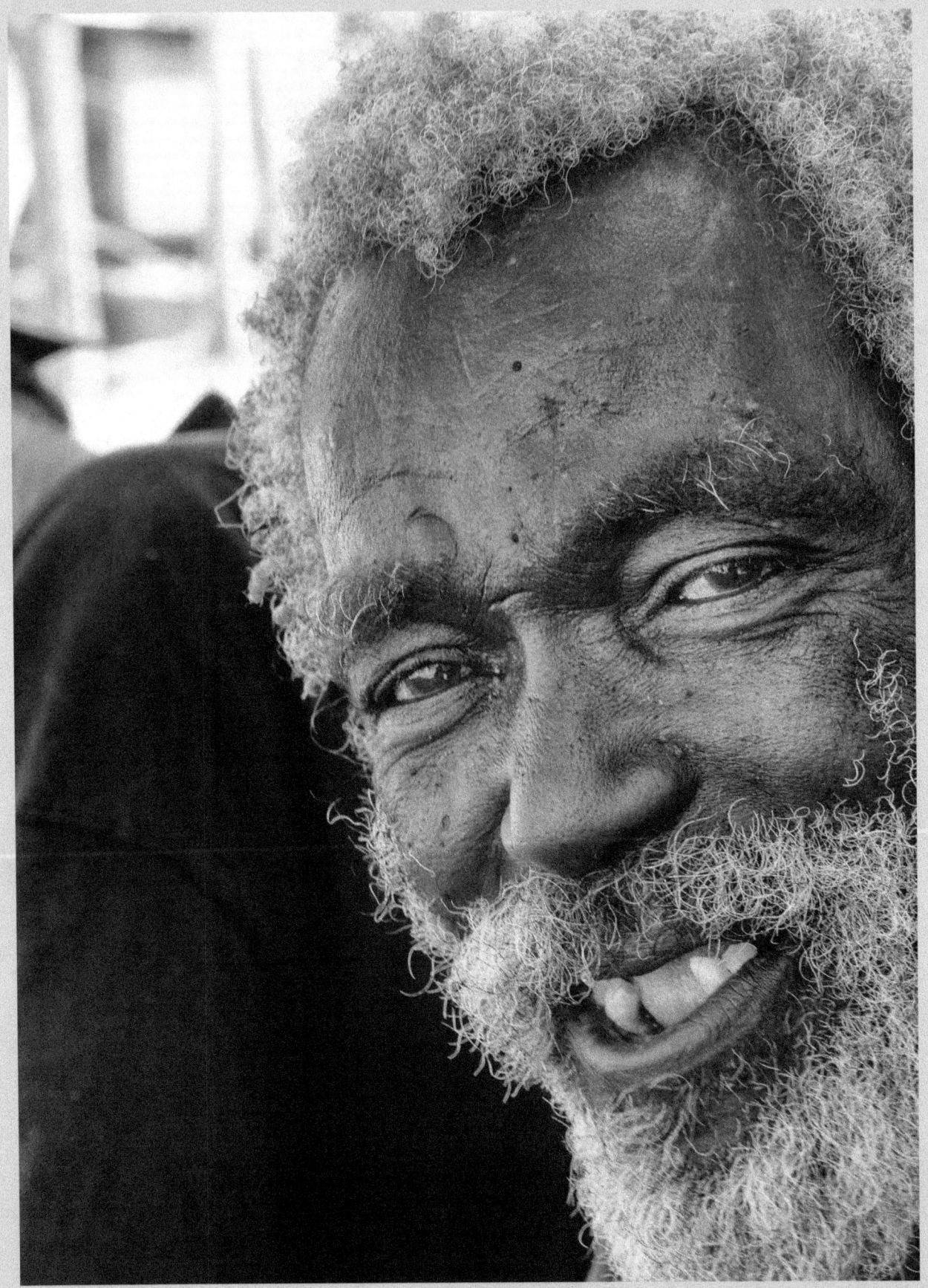

Above: Charlie came over from the *Capt. Peters* to work
for Juan on the *Princess Johana*.
Opposite: Cowboy repairing nets on the *Princess Johana*.

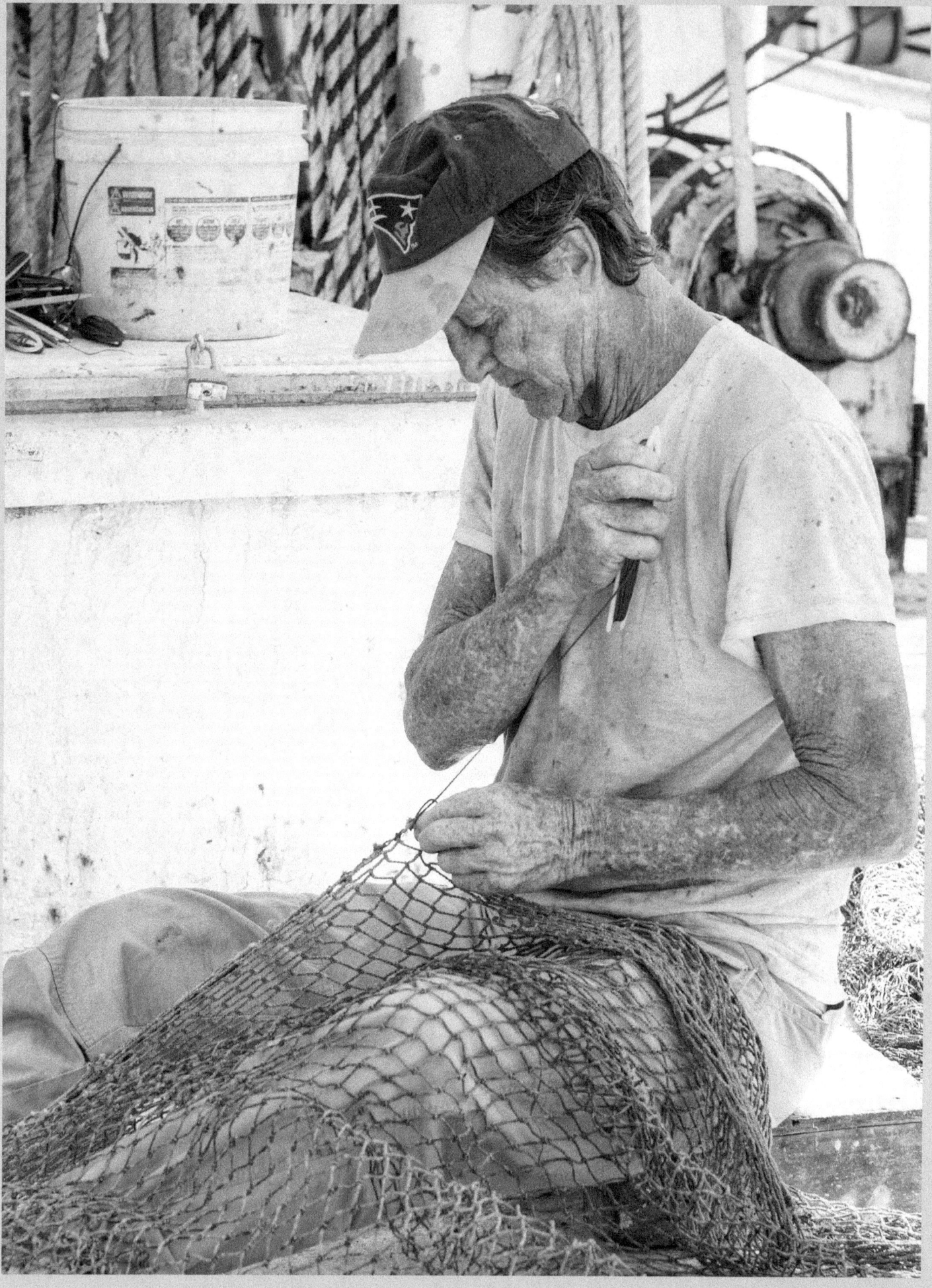

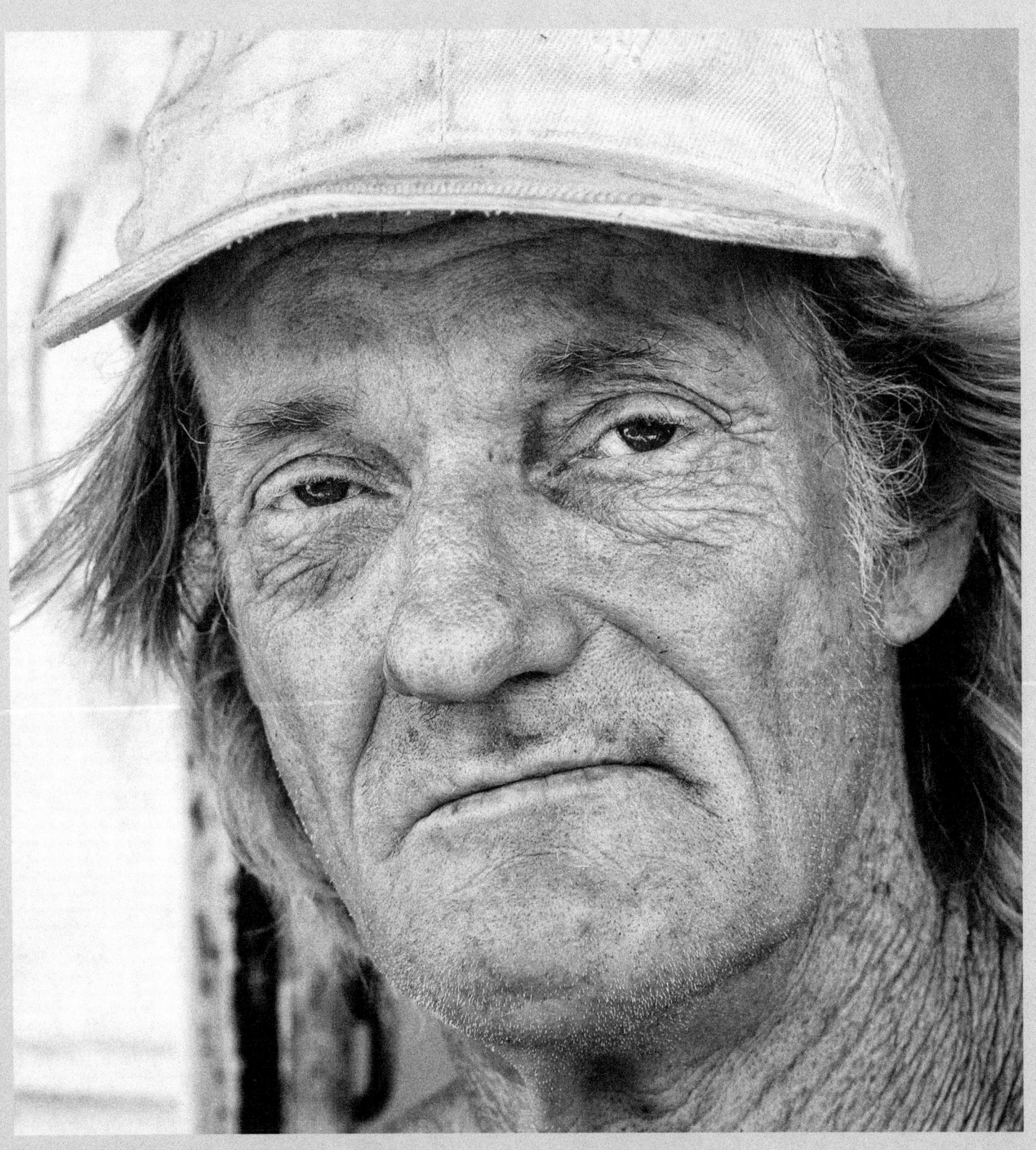

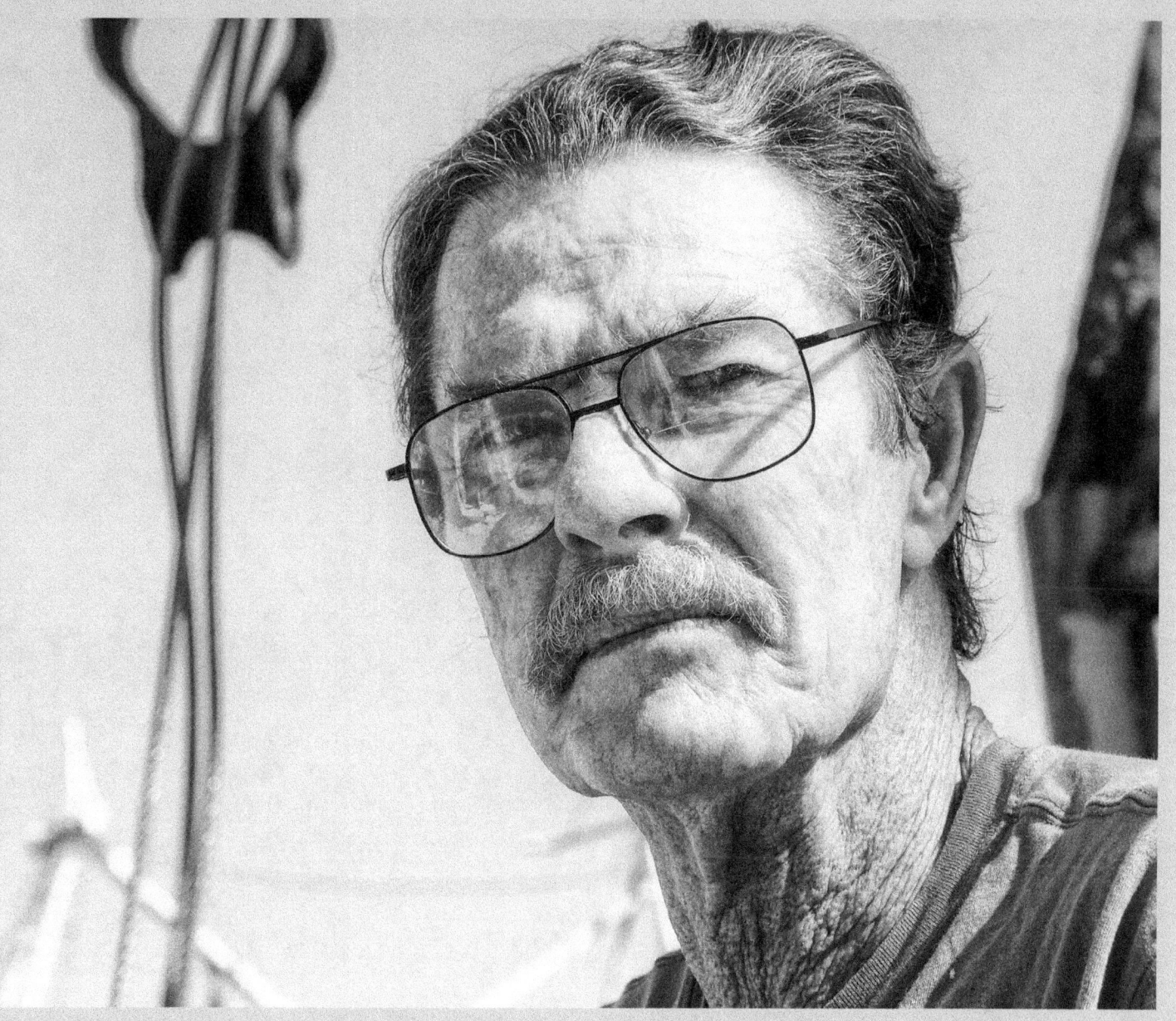

Opposite: Key West Red, crewmember, *Priness Johana*.
Above: Frank, cook, *Princess Johana*.

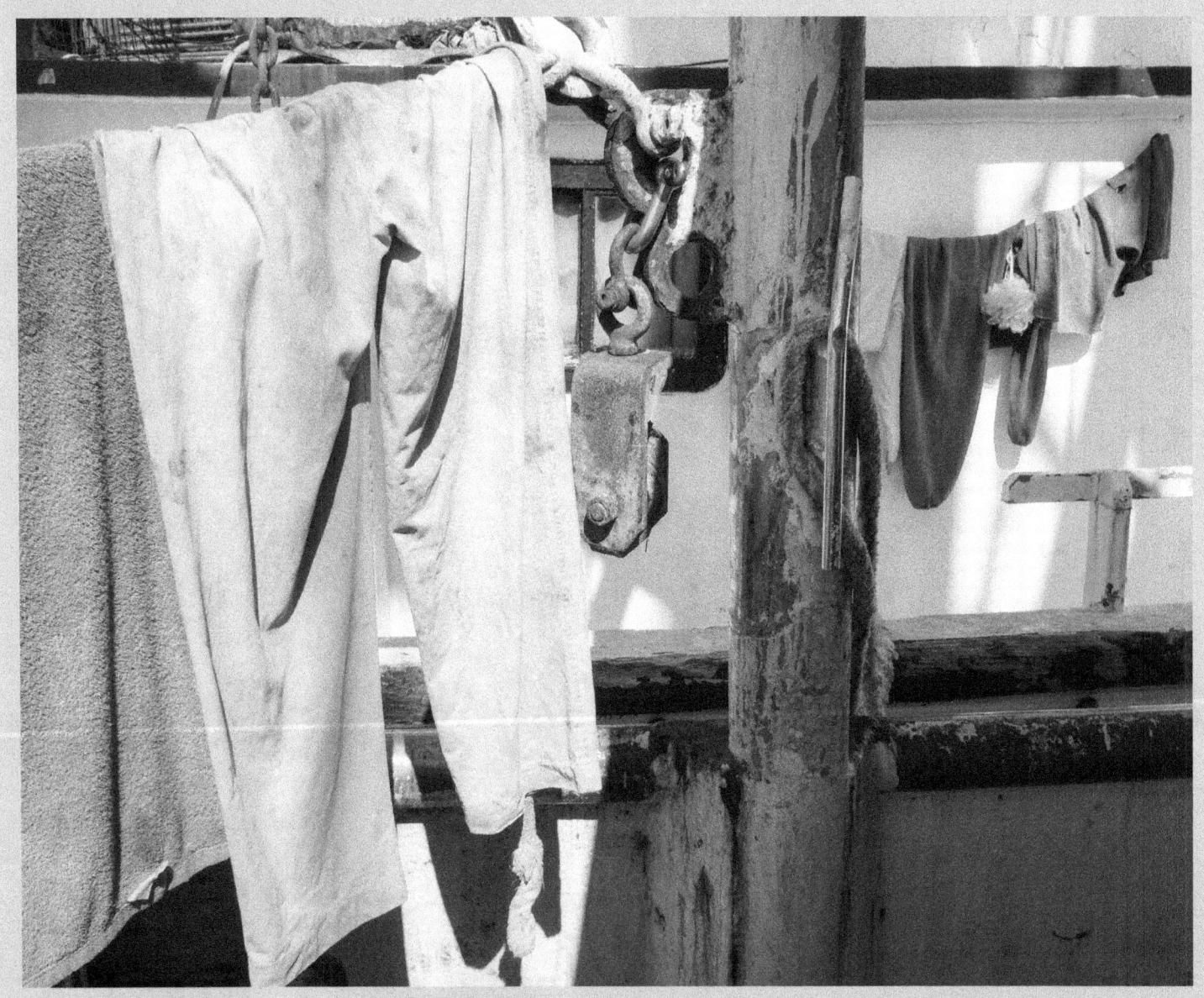

Above: Wash Day.
Opposite: Charlie with Mr. Dog, another crewmember
from the *Capt. Peters*.

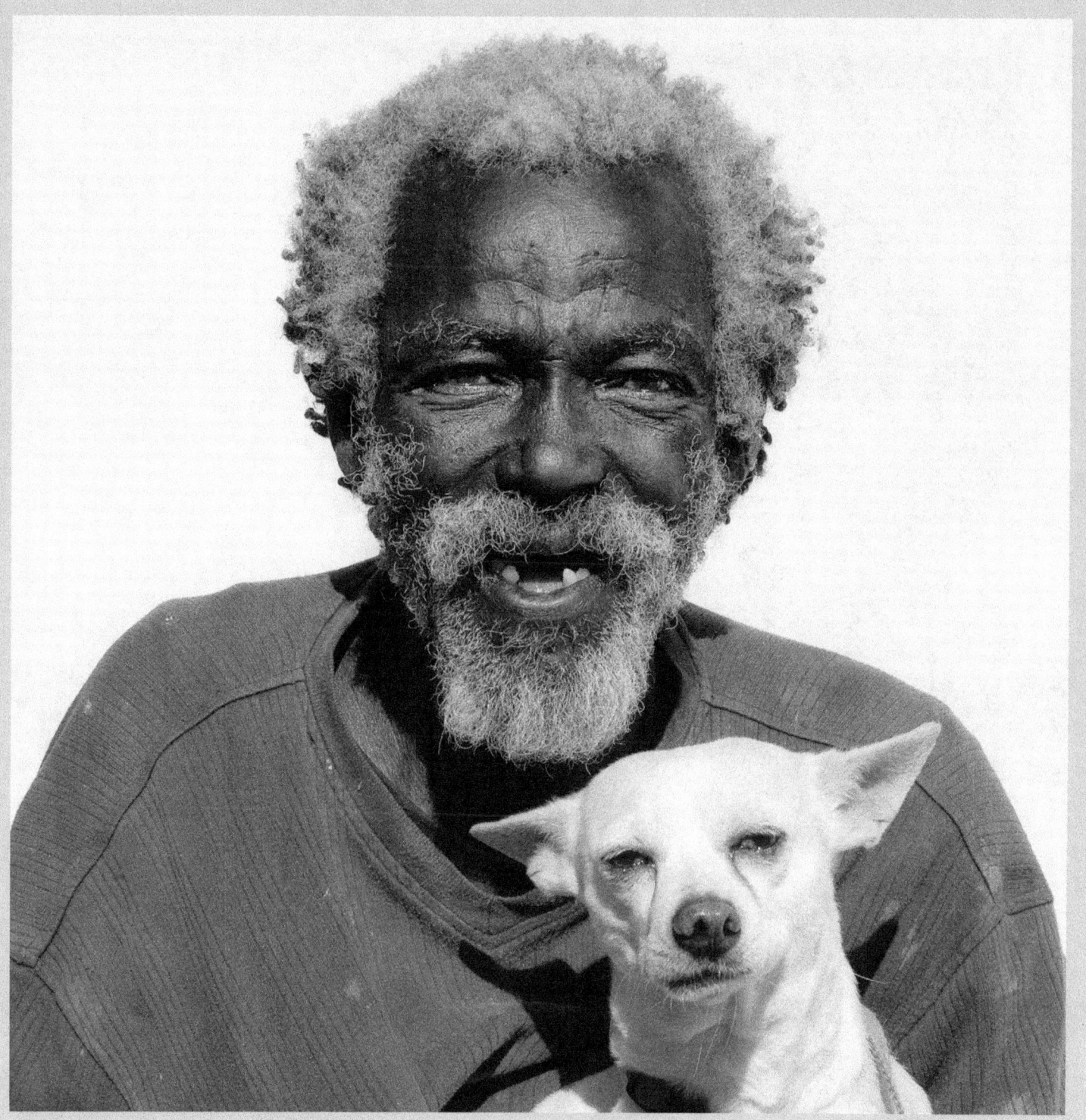

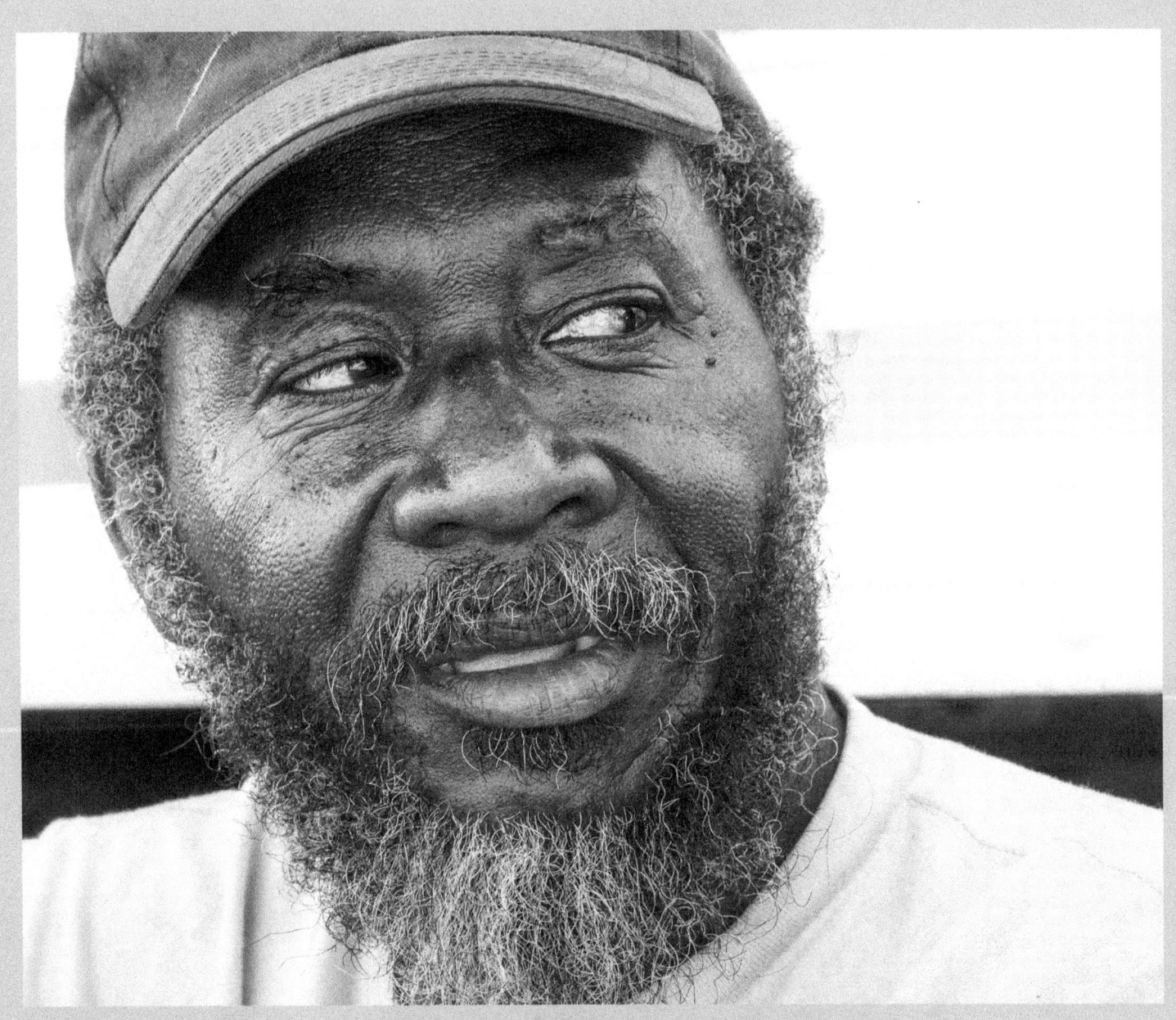

Pee Wee, crewmember on the *Gulf Queen*, 2011.

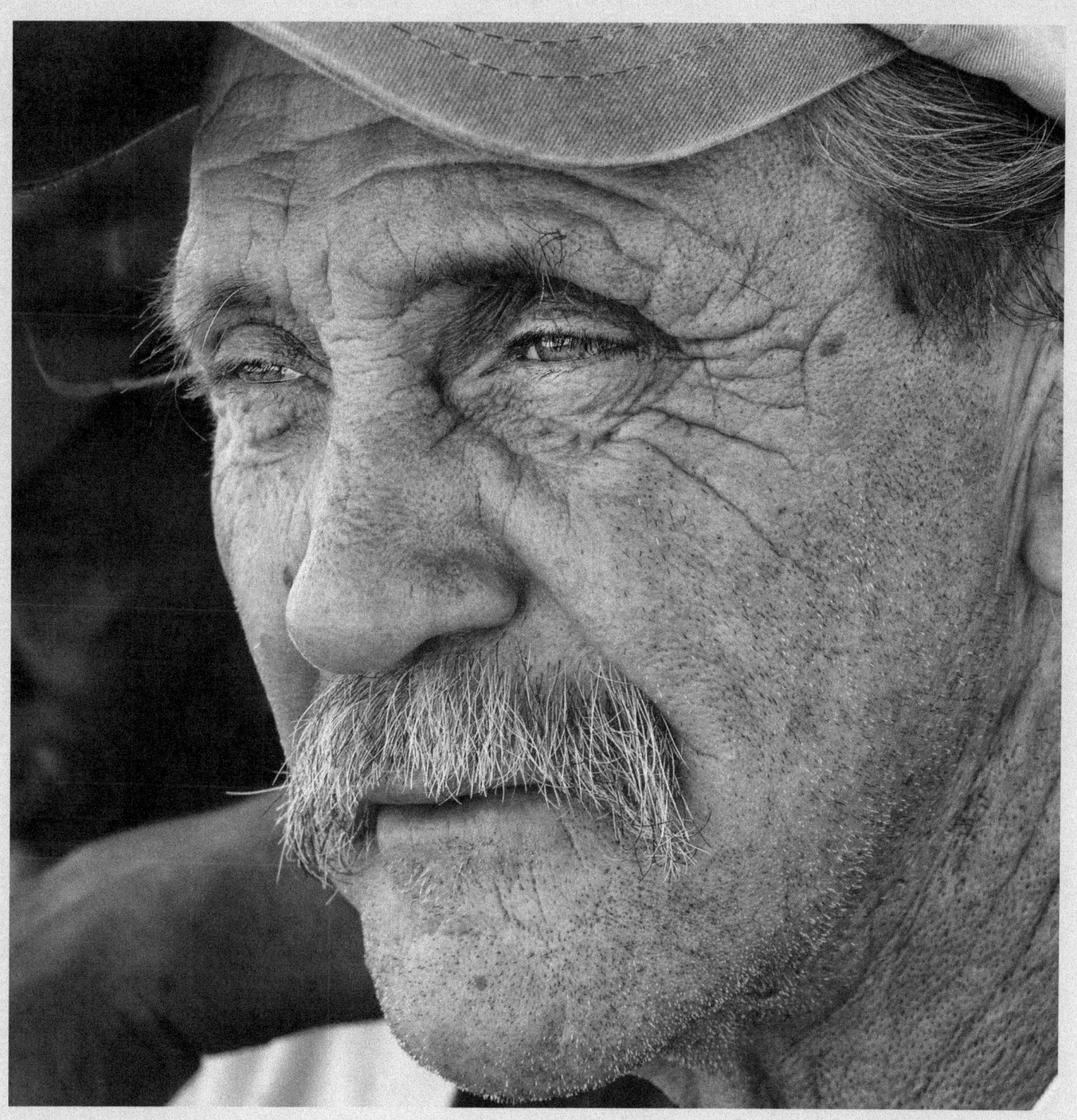

Dewey, visiting the docks; he is no longer shrimping, 2011.

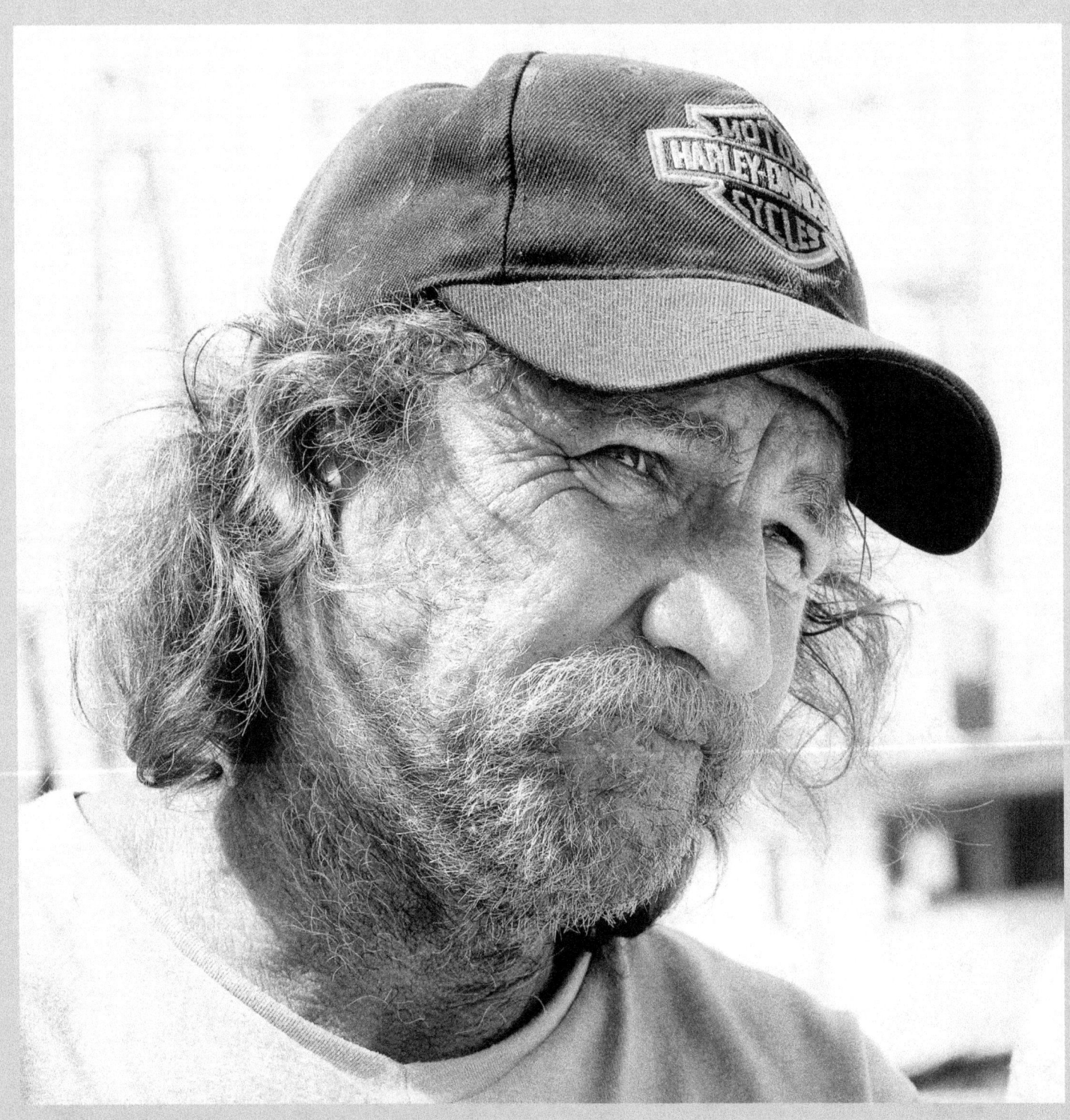

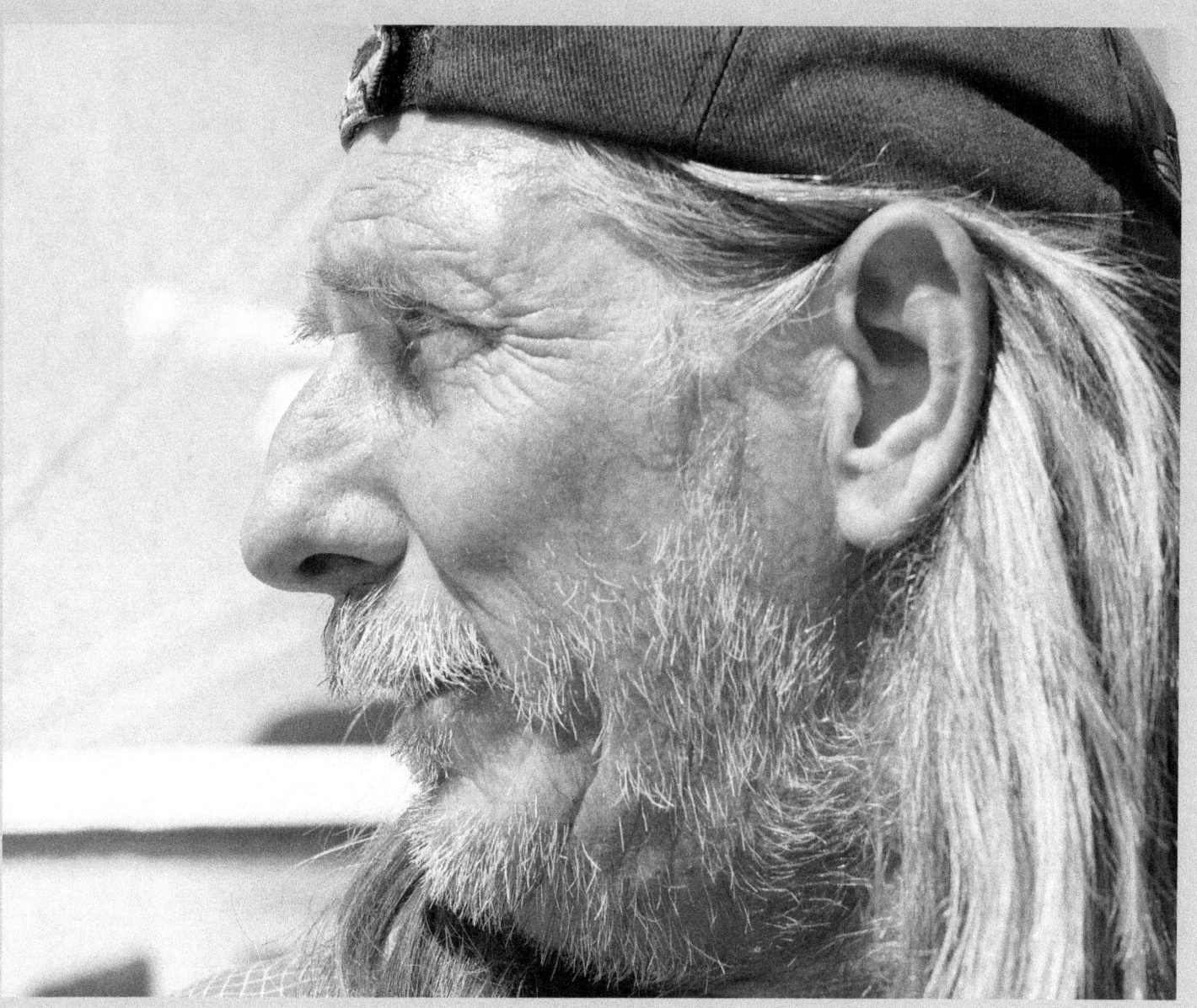

Opposite: Mark stopping at Stock Island on a shrimp boat out of Tampa after the *Lady-Danielle* was scrapped, 2011. Above: Pete, captain of the boat Mark is now working on.

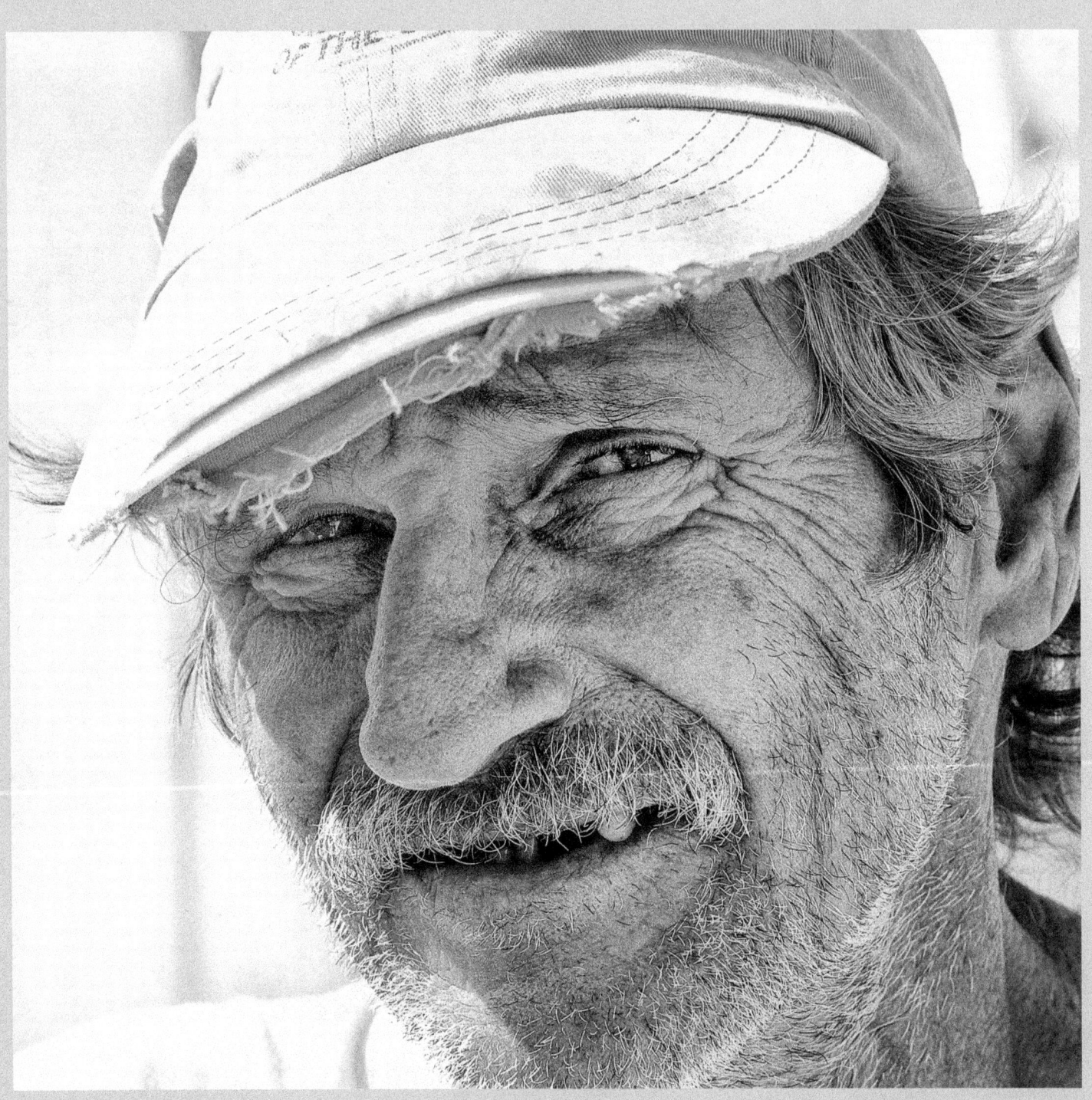

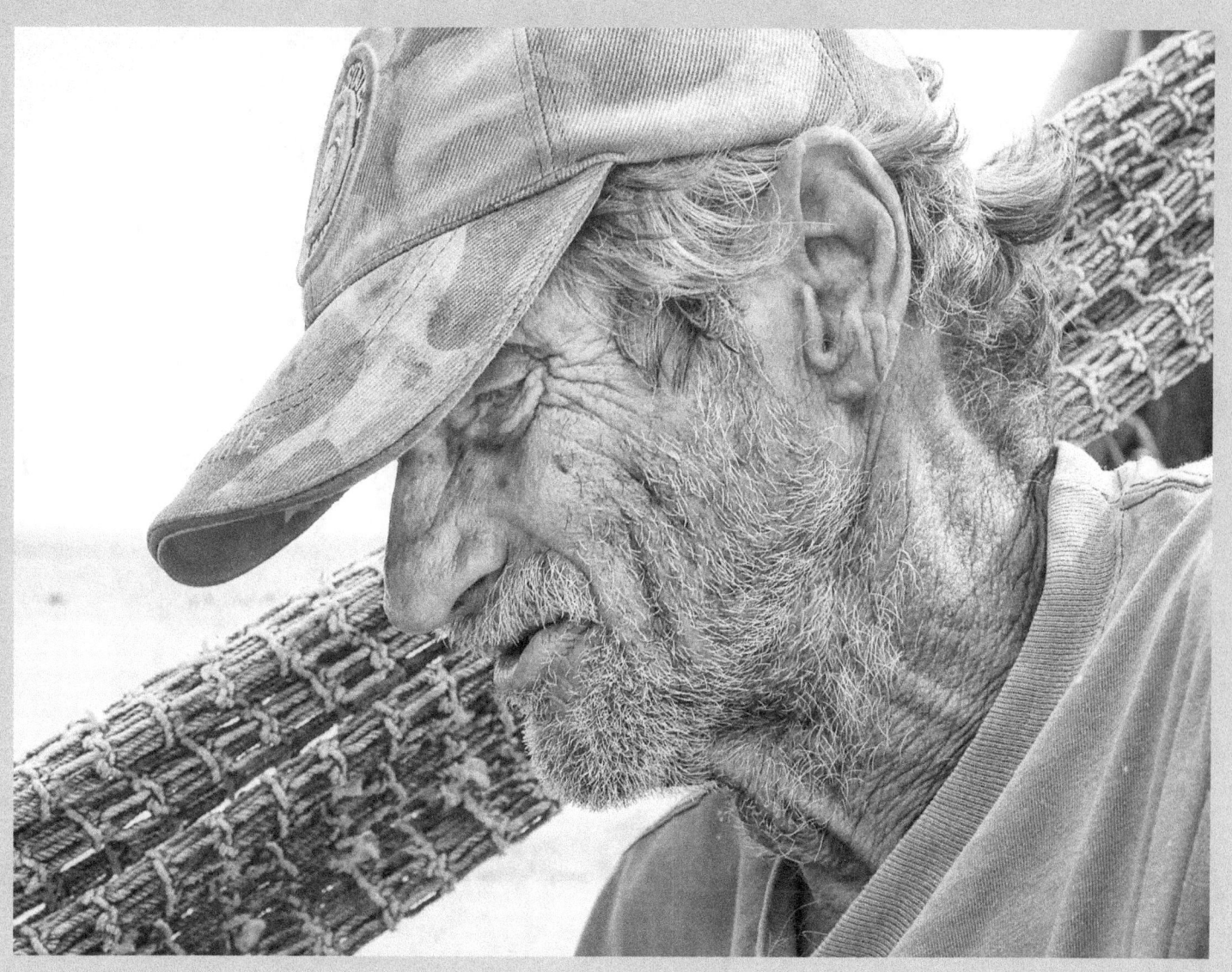

Wild Bill, shrimper and waterman, 2011-2012

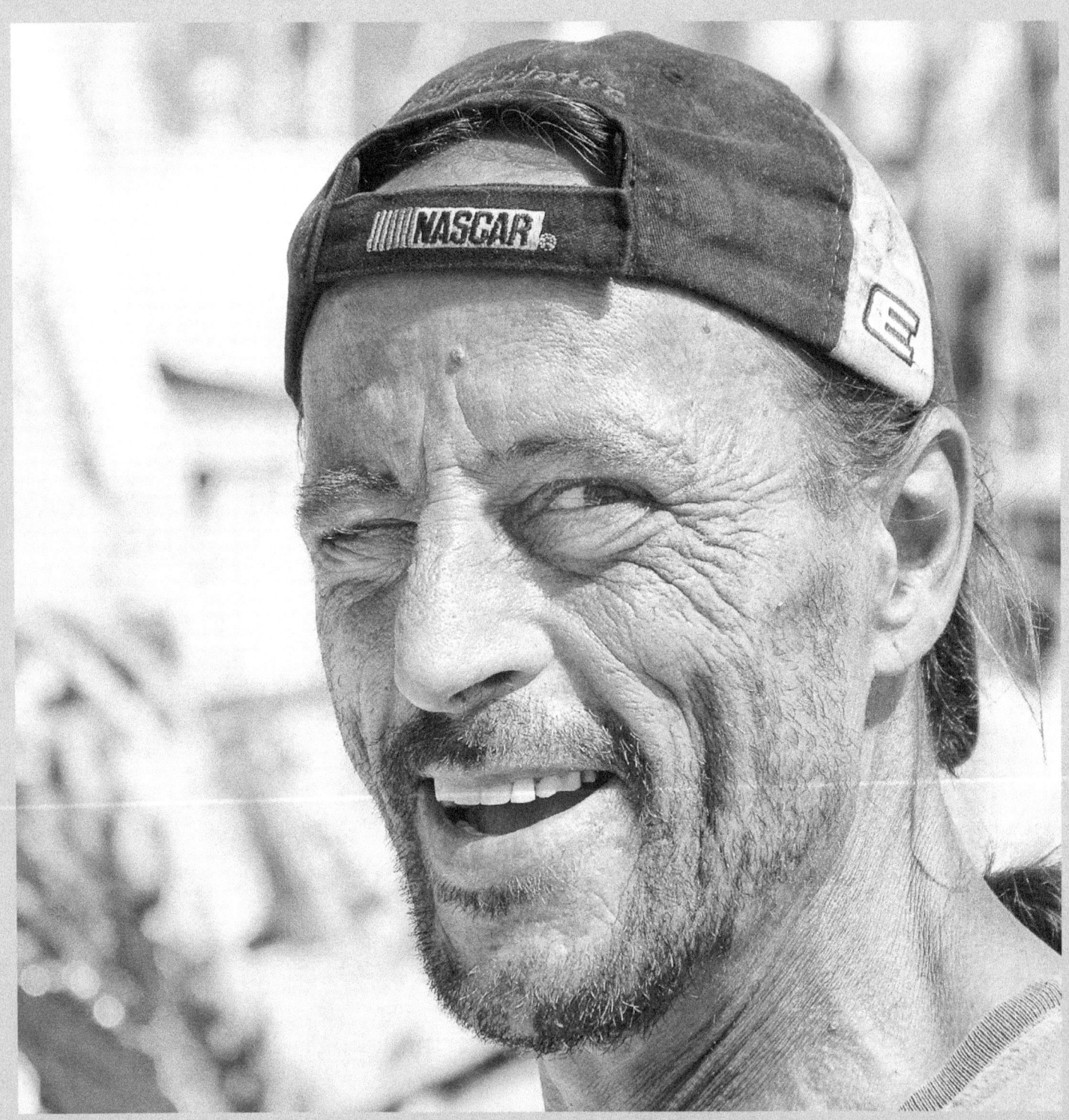

Captain Ron of the *Equalizer*, 2008.

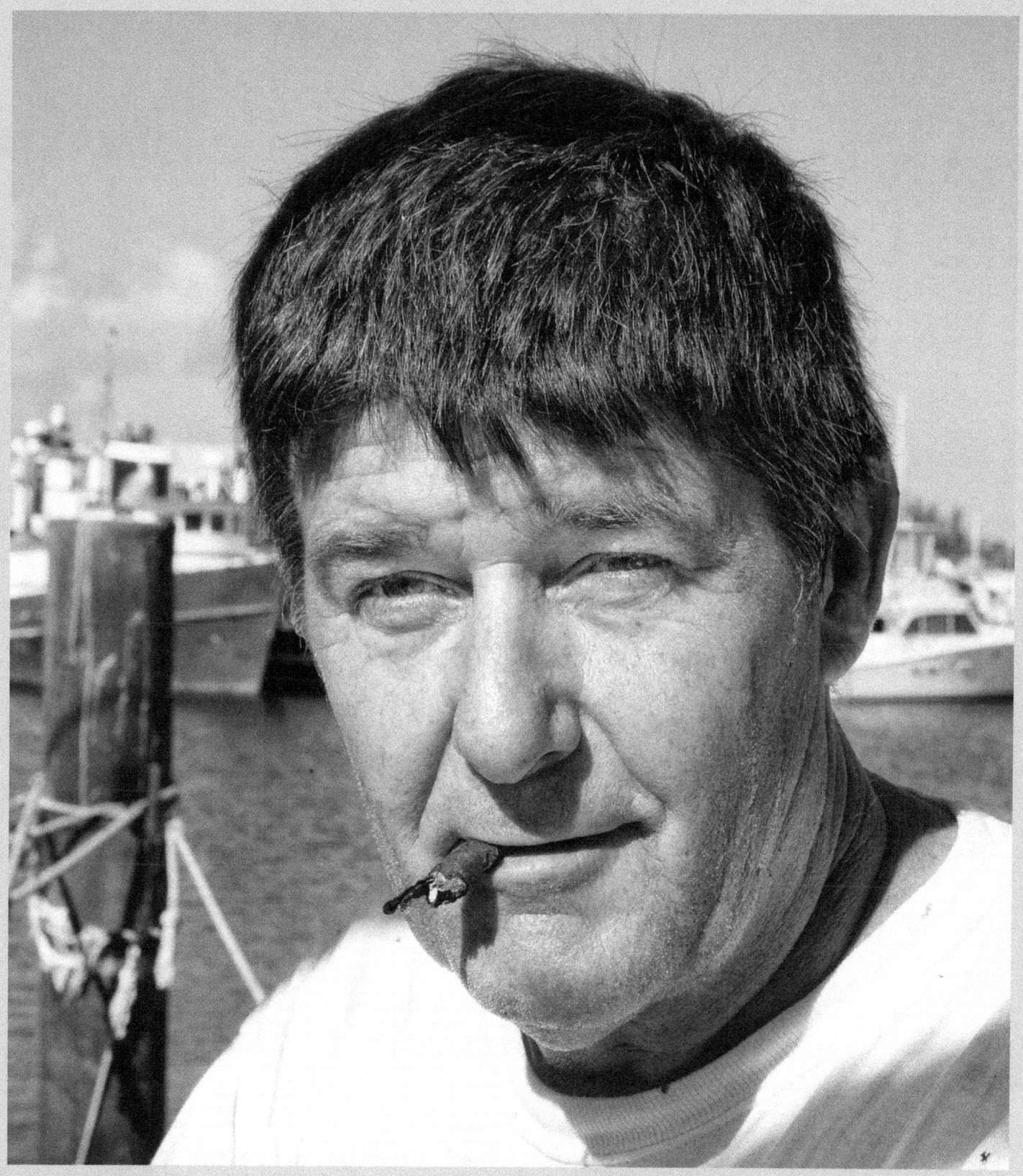

Captain Shep of the *Capt. Bud*, 2012.

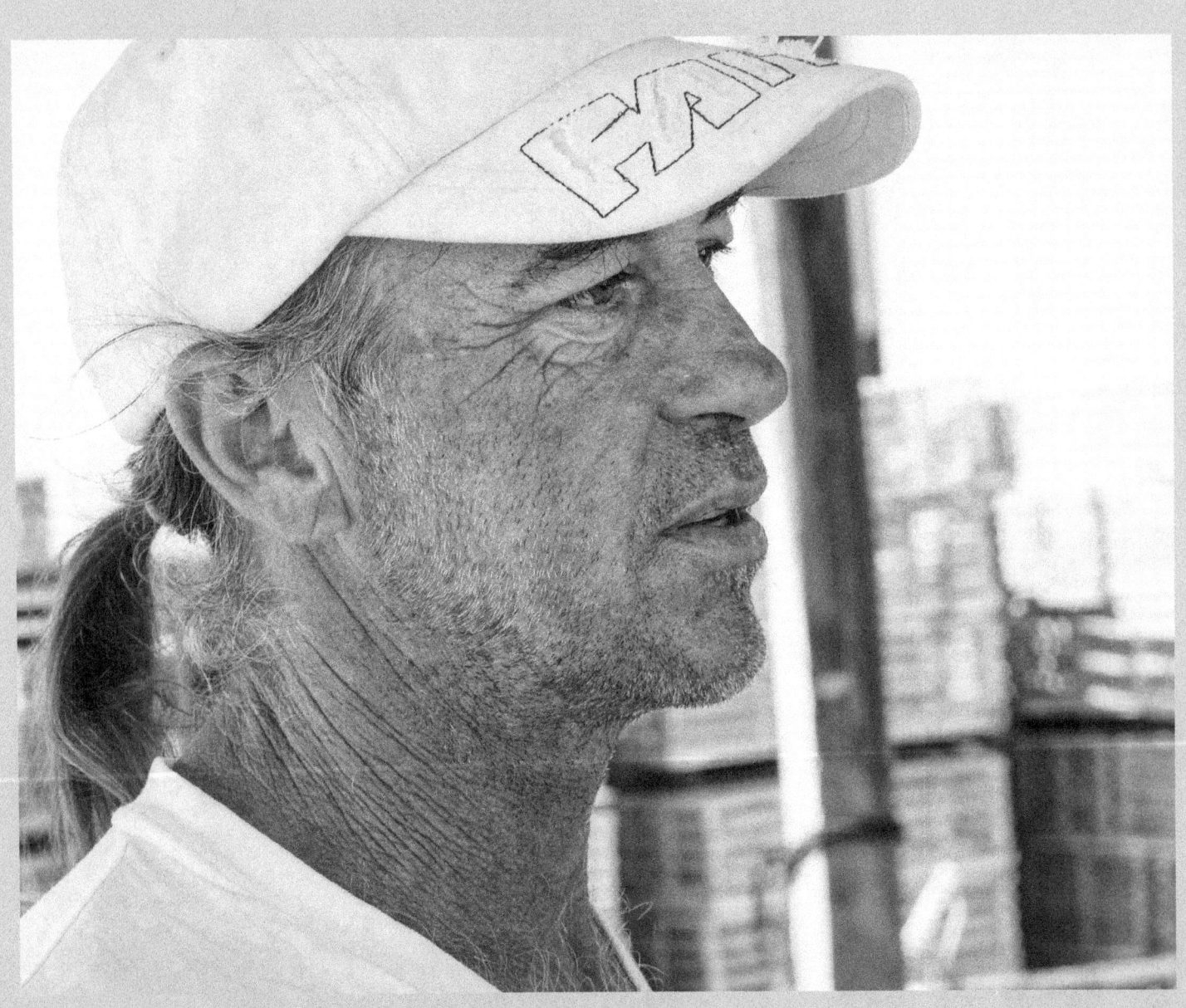

Curtis, formally of the *Michael James*, is now working on the crab boats, 2011.

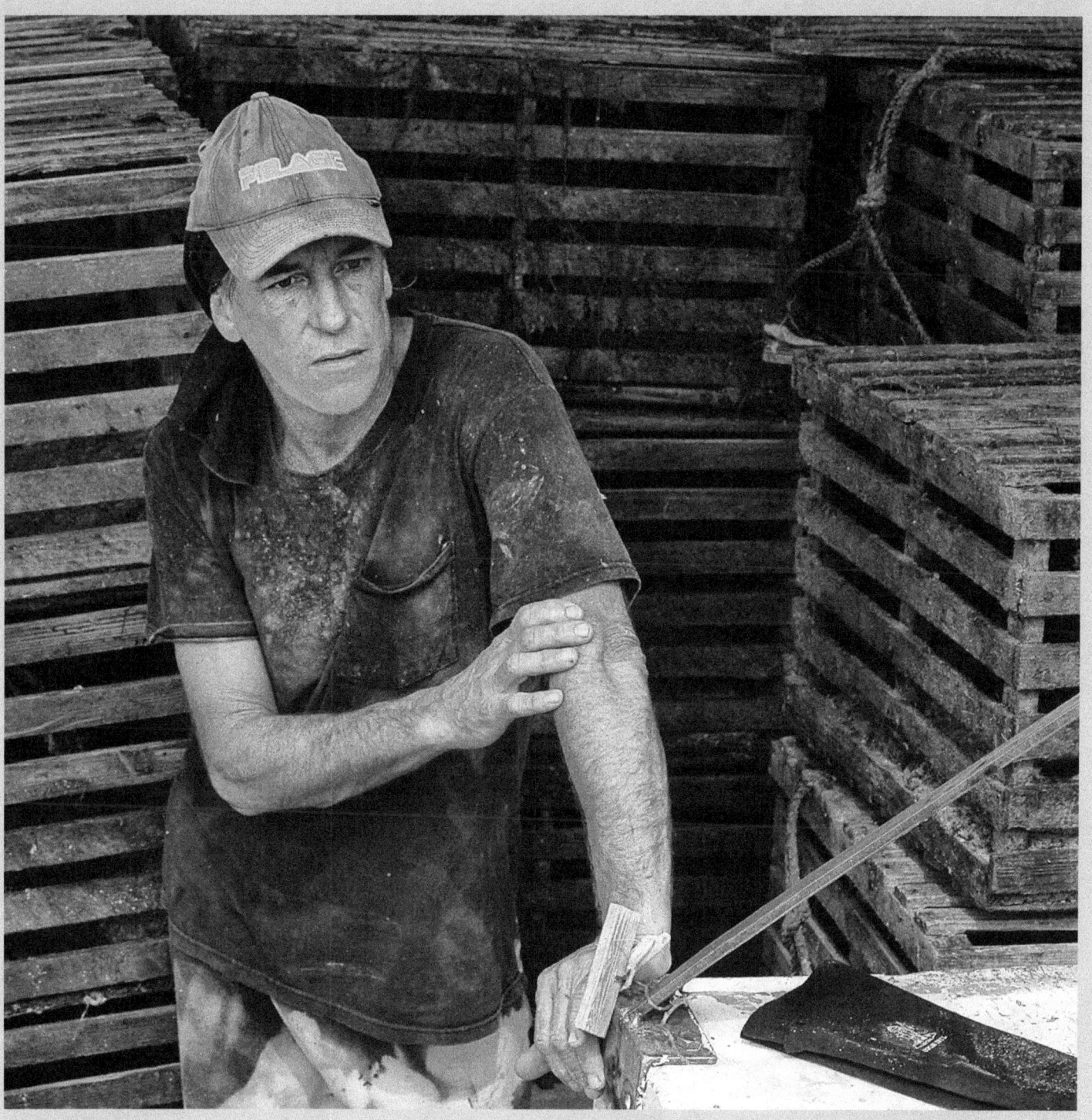

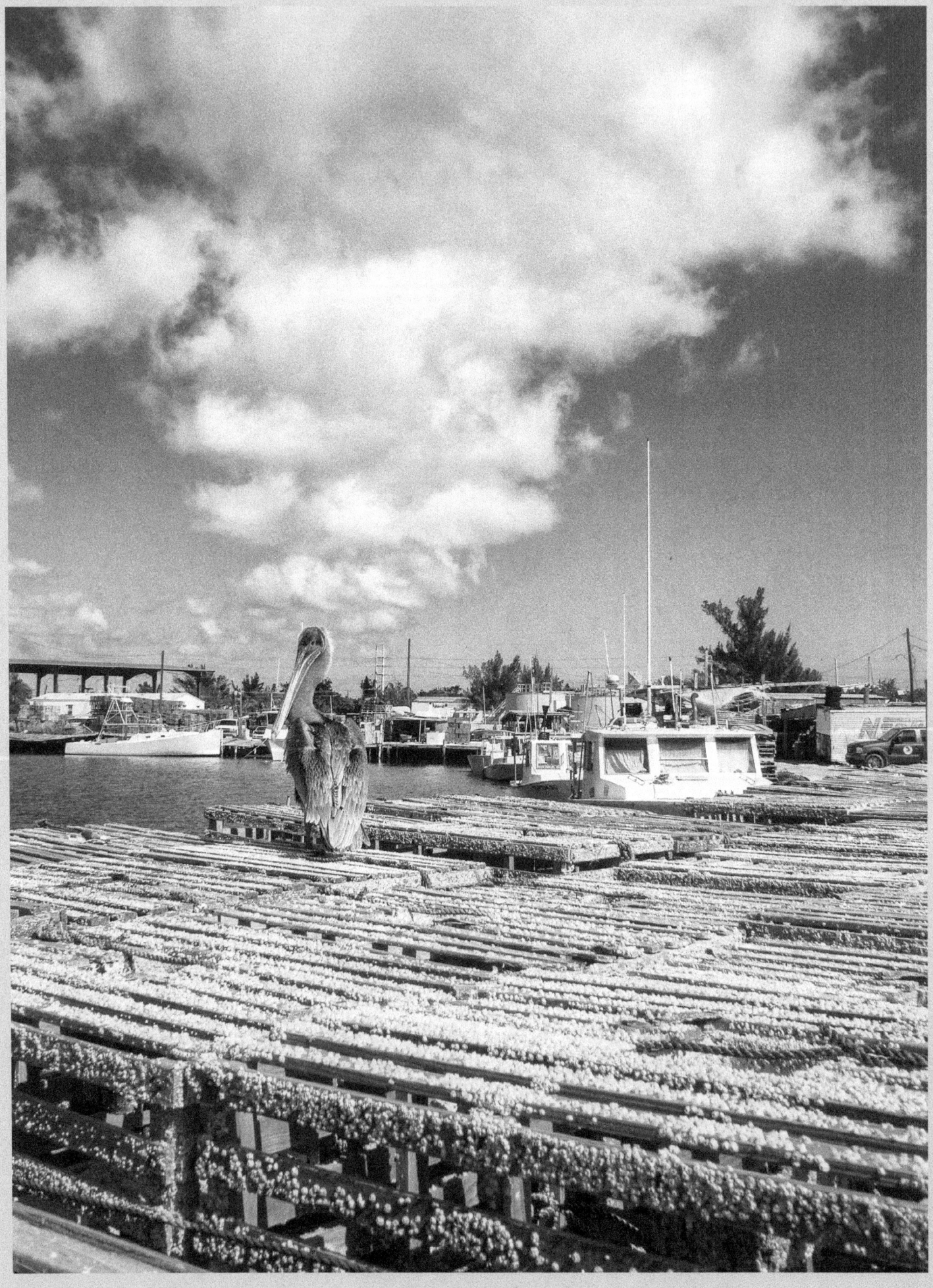

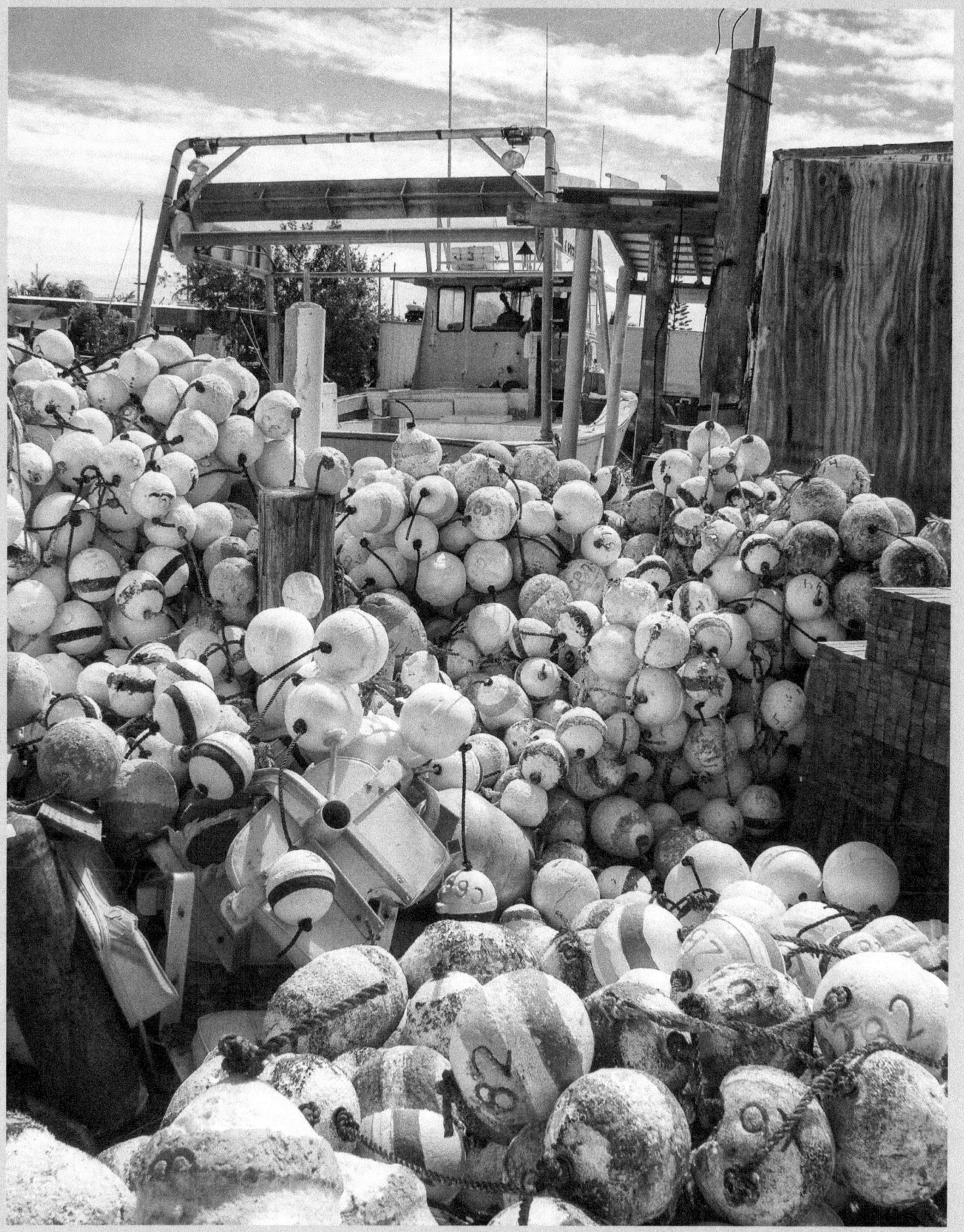

Crab pots and floats

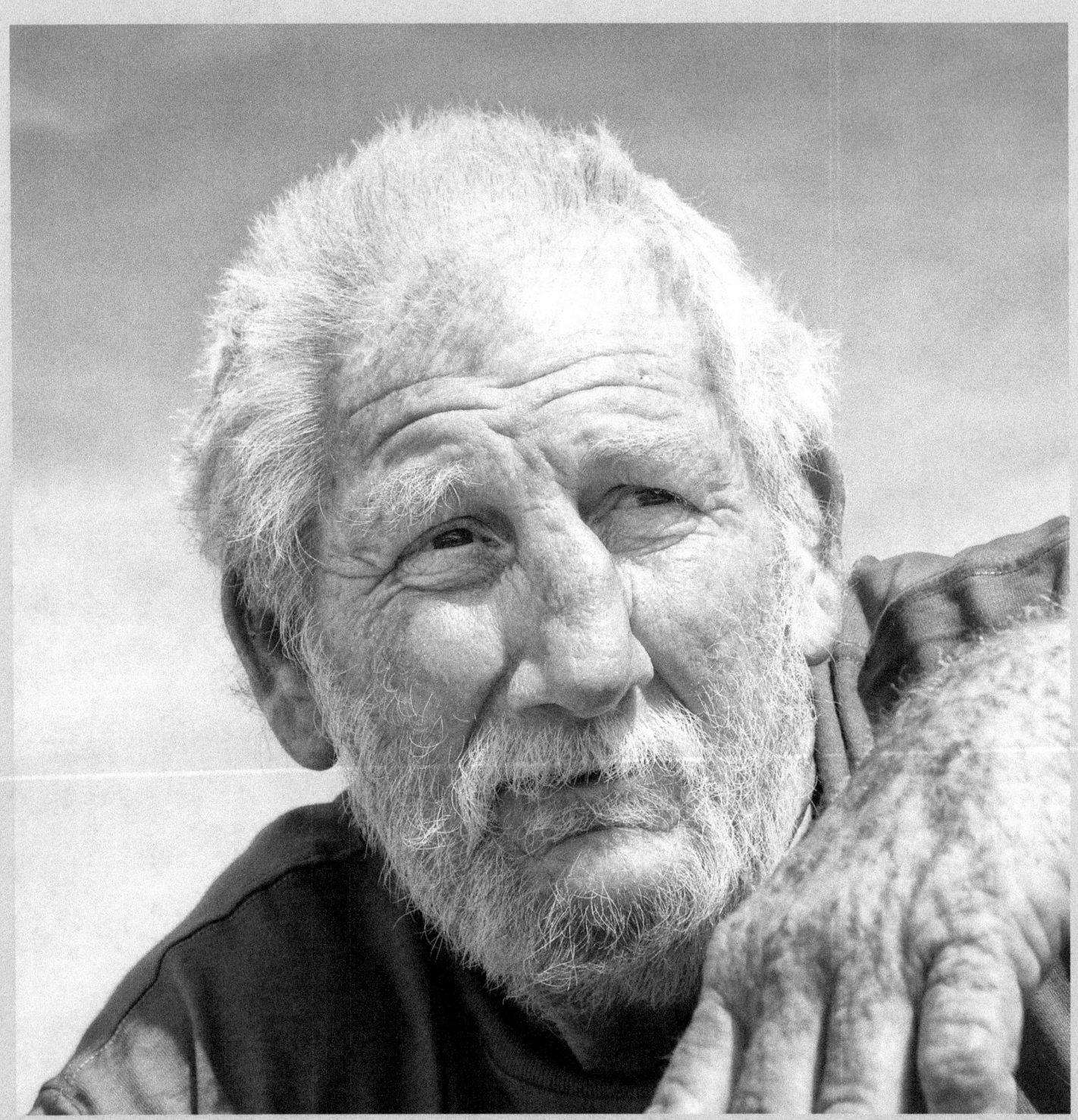

James, crewman on the crab boats.

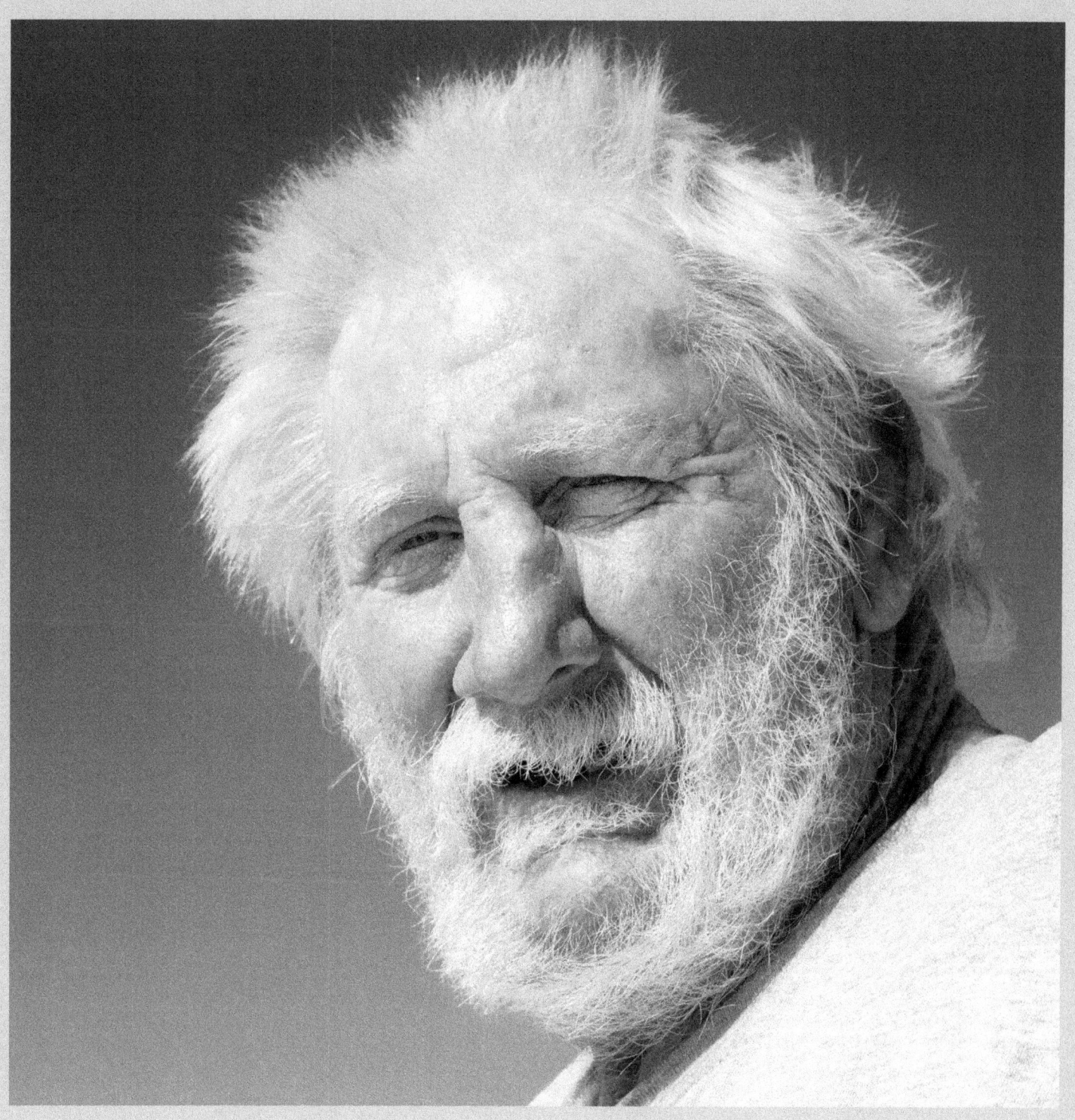

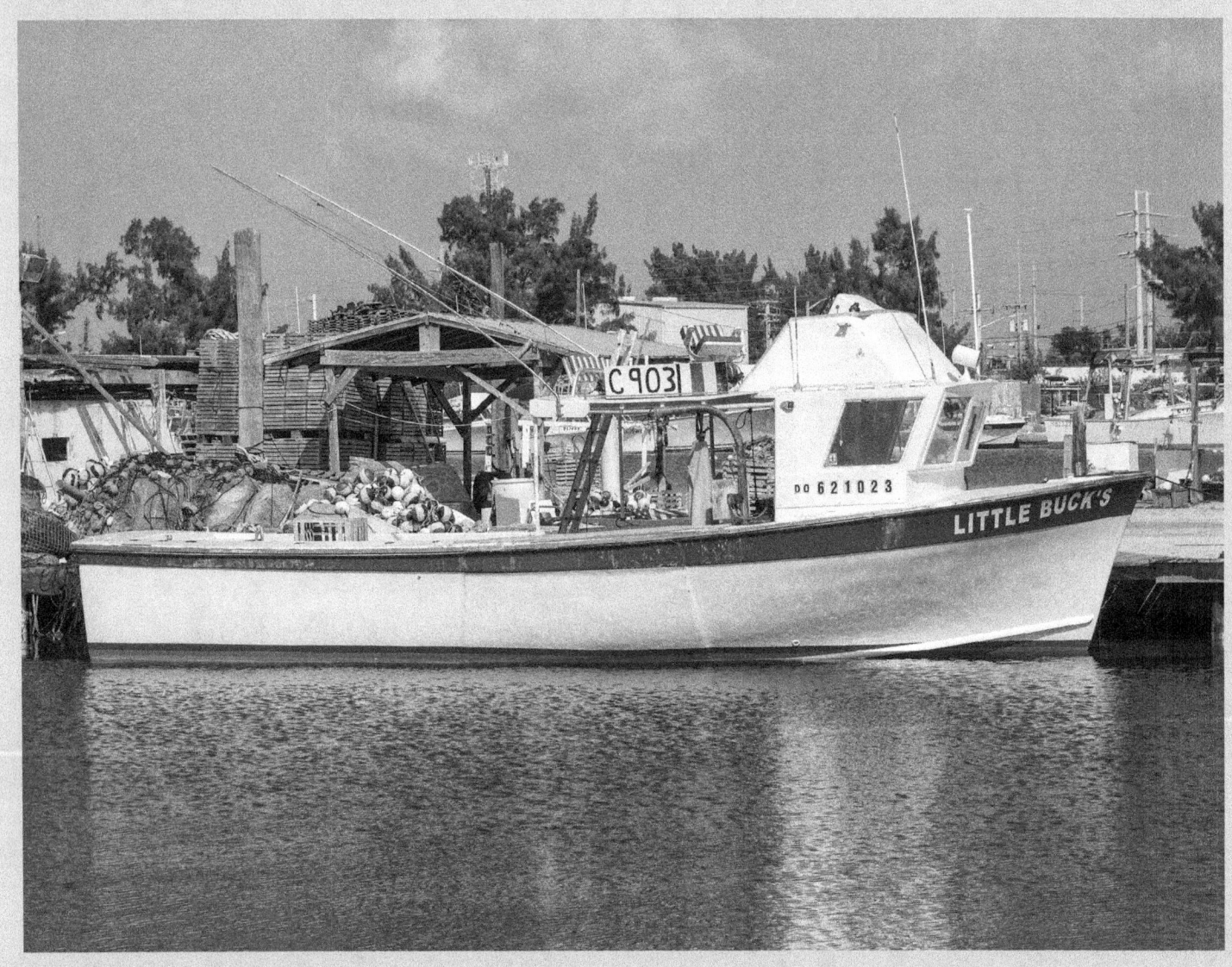

Crab boats: the well-kept . . . and the derelict. They are smaller than the shrimp boats and usually just go out for the day.

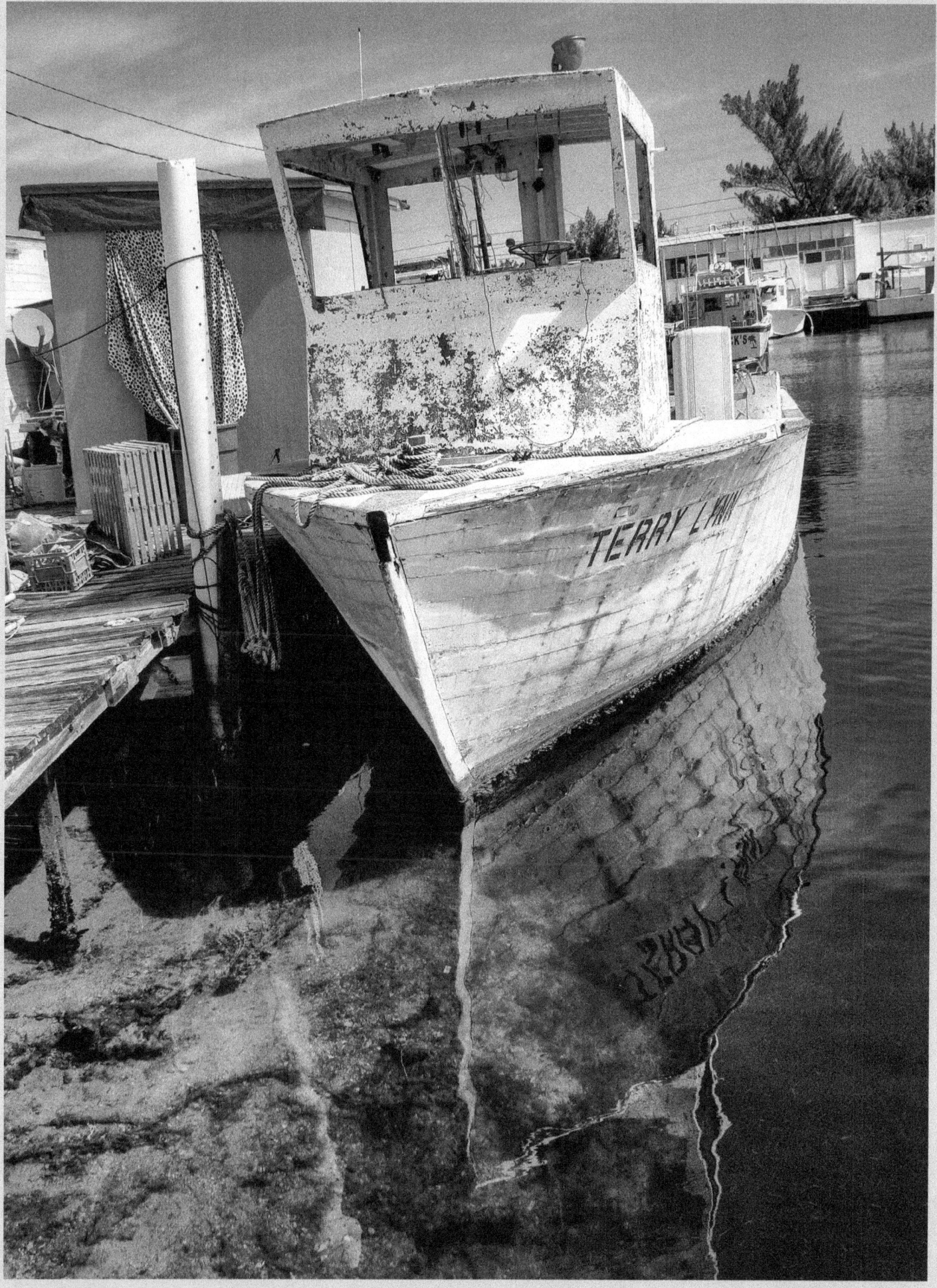

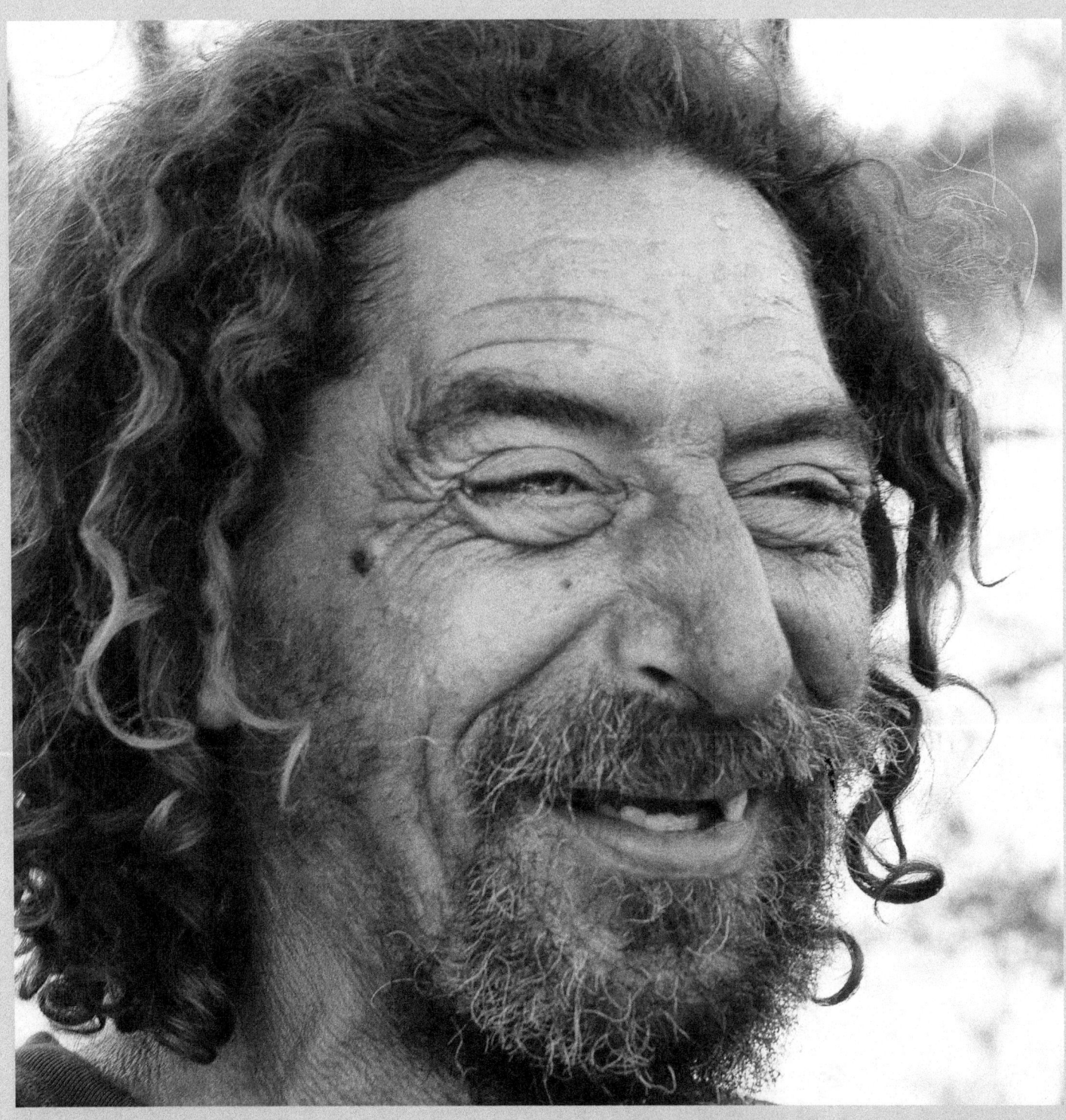

John on the crab docks--always a smile and
an entertaining personality.

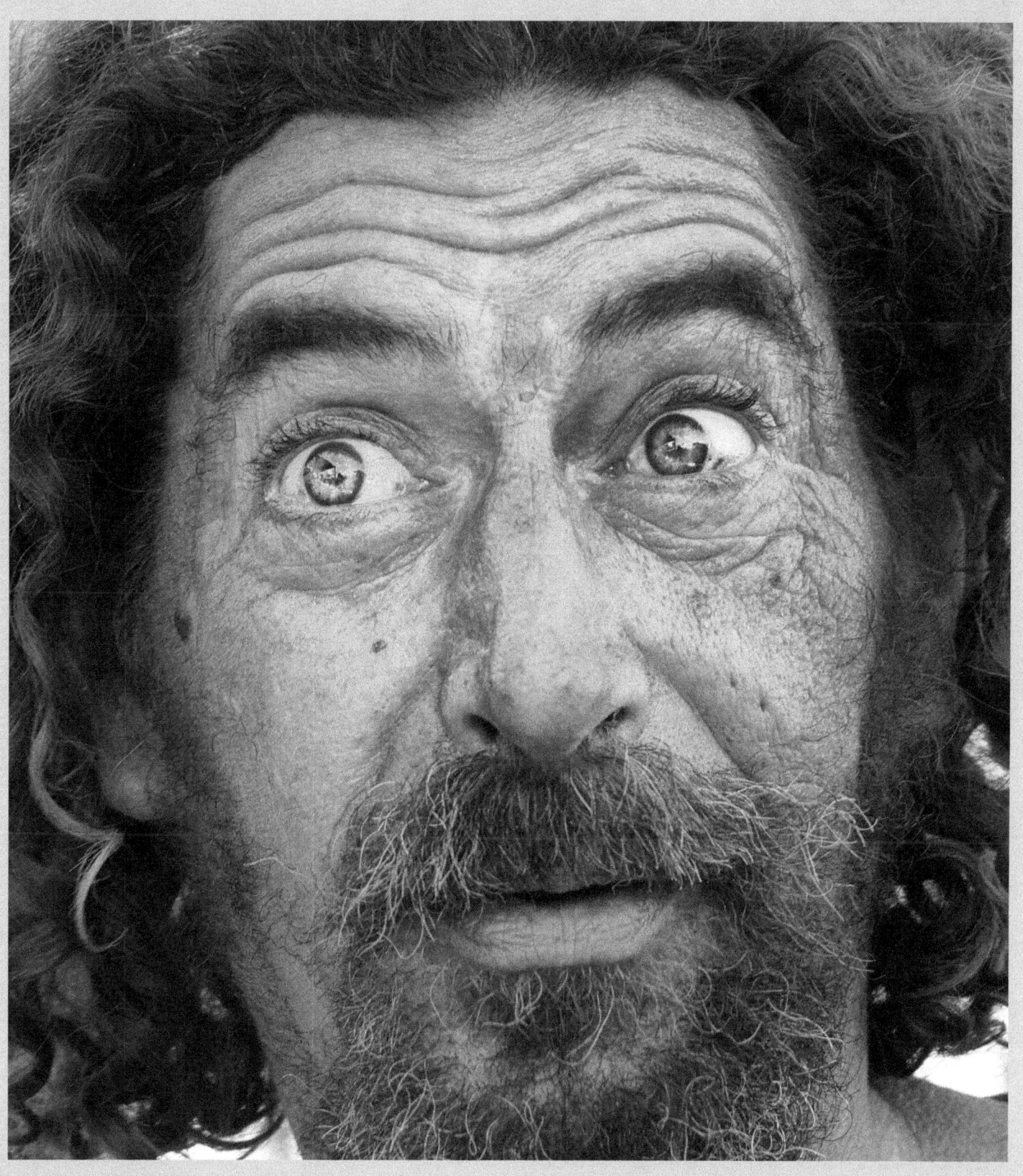

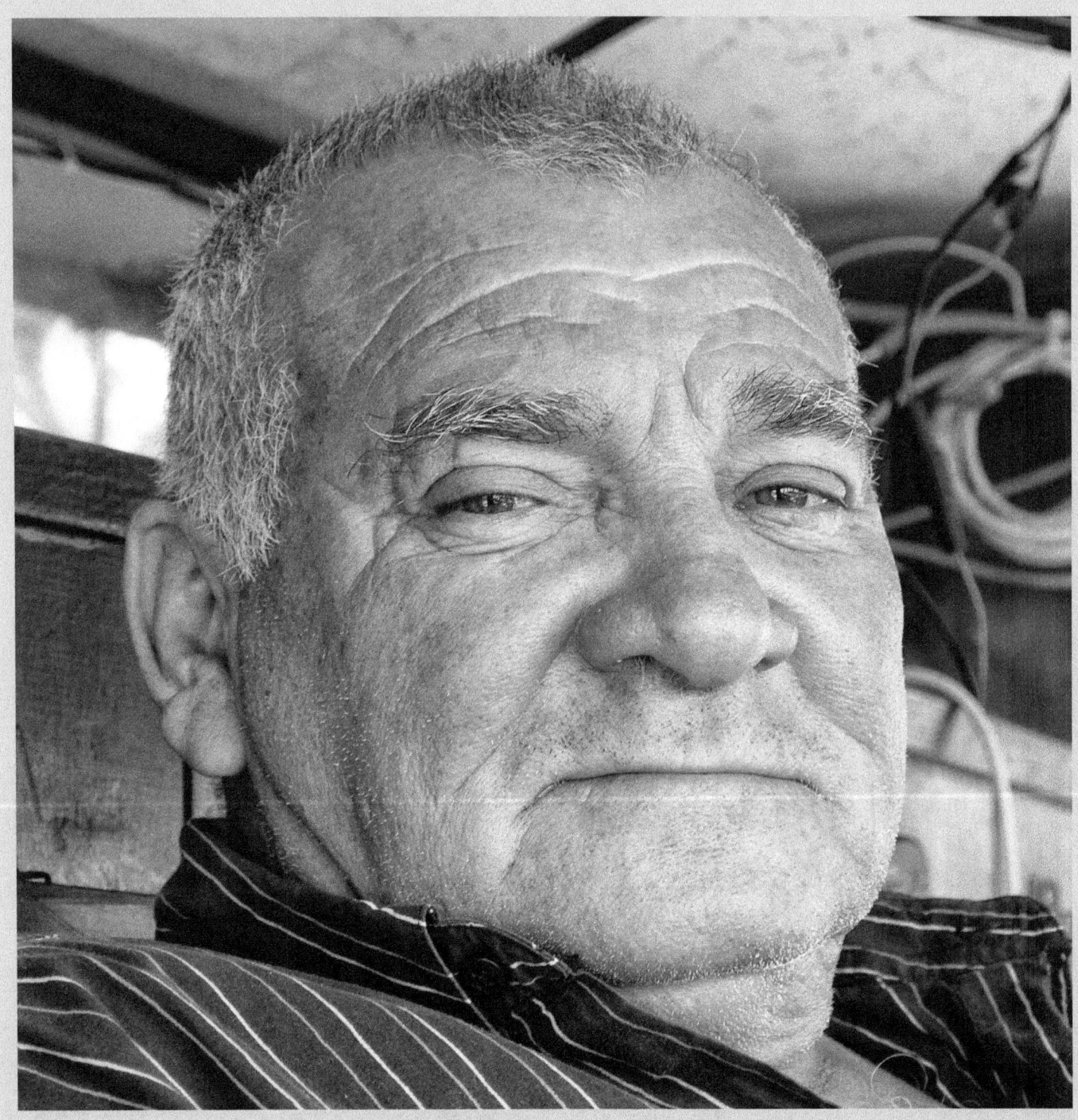

Juan stopped working on the *Princess Johana* and
bought the *Capt Eder*, 2012.

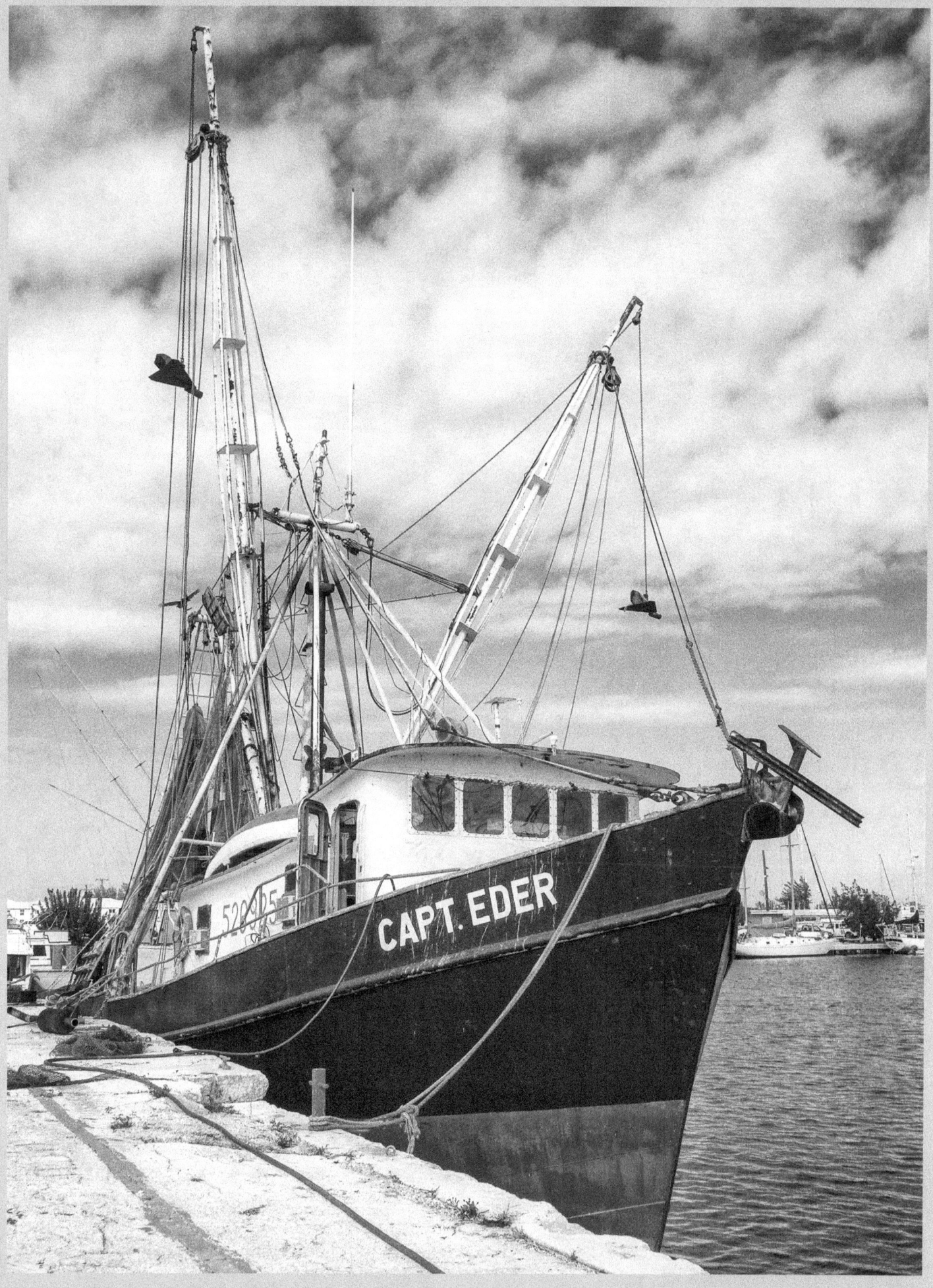

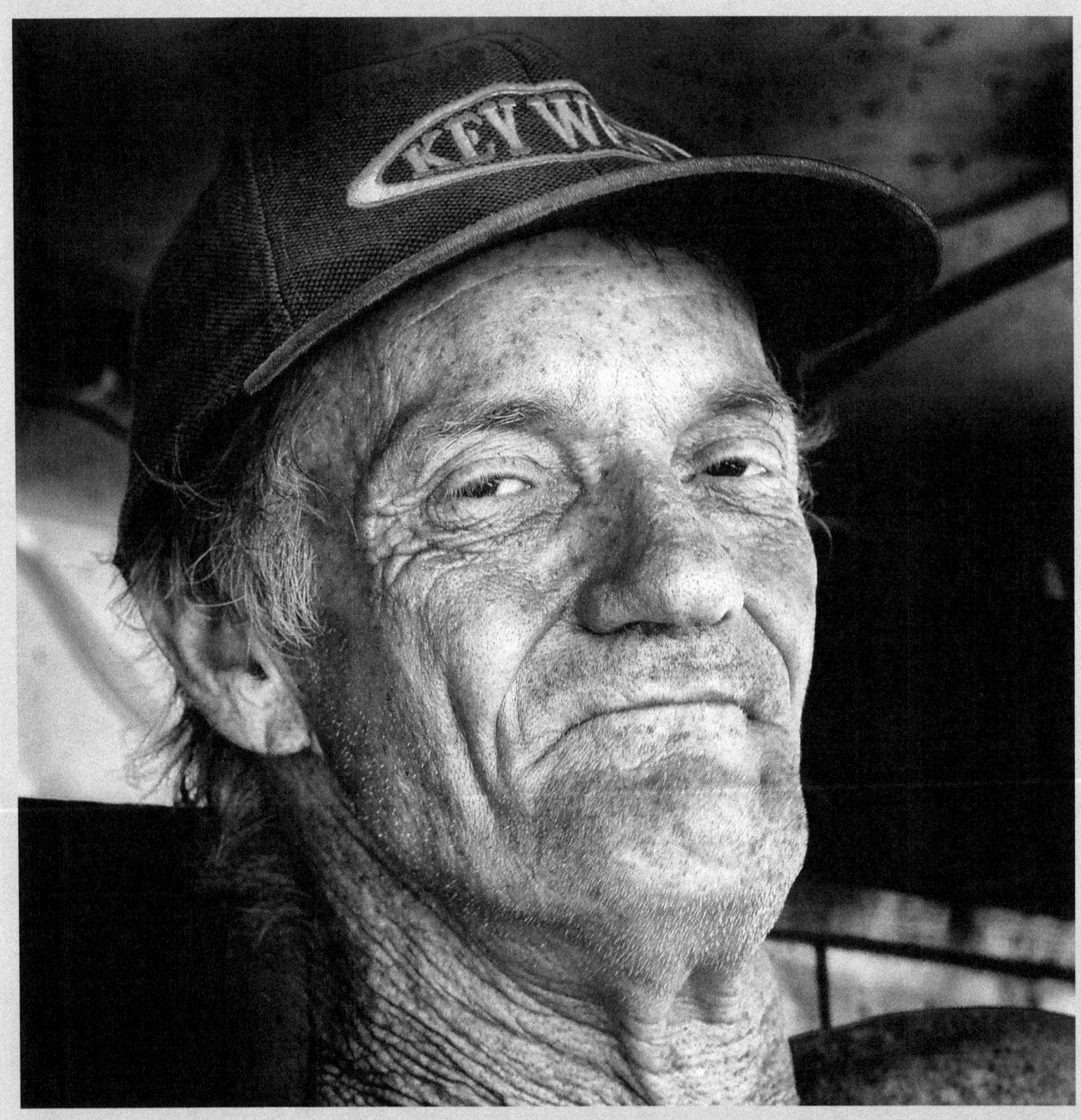

Key West Red followed Juan to the *Capt. Eder.*

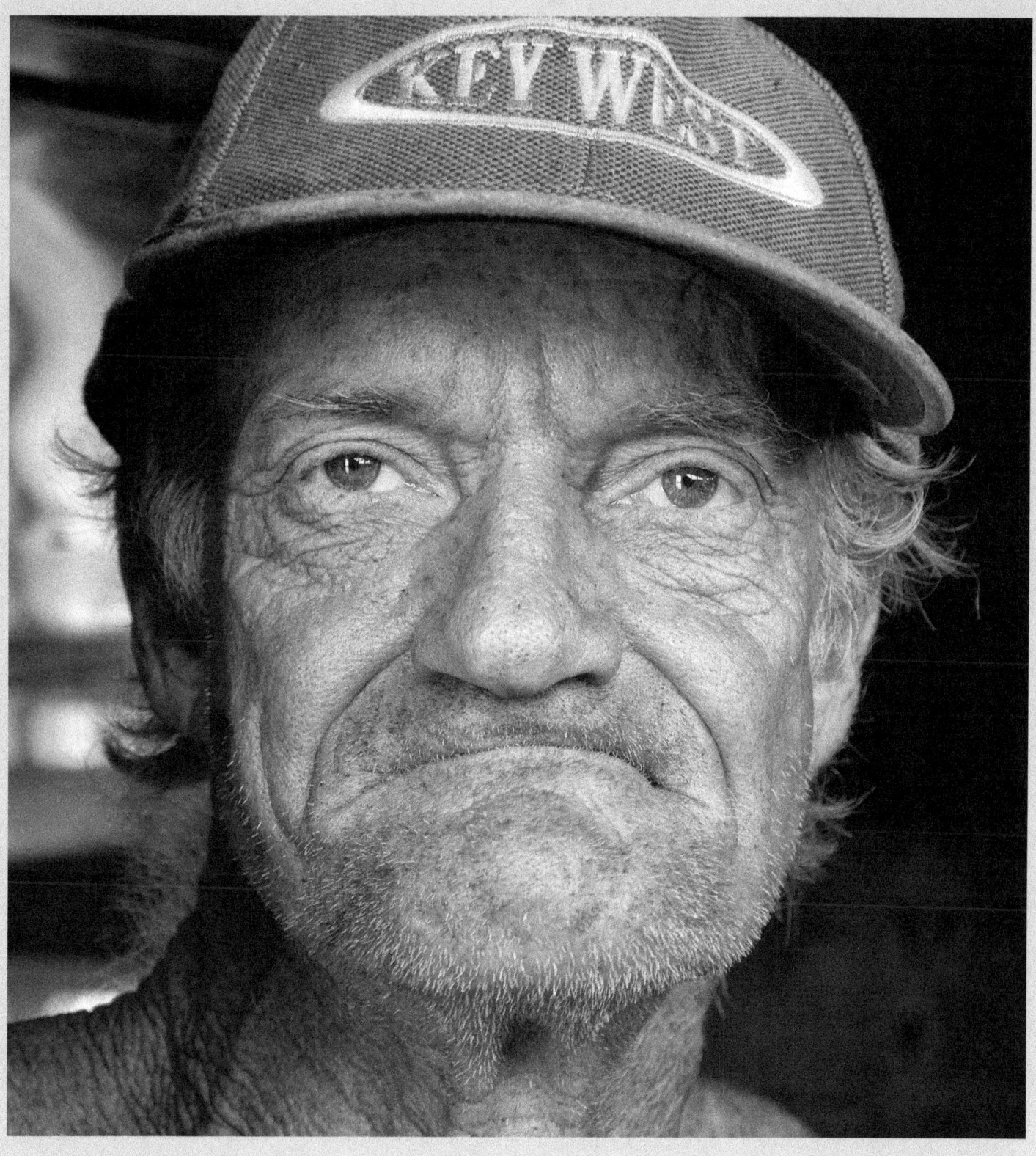

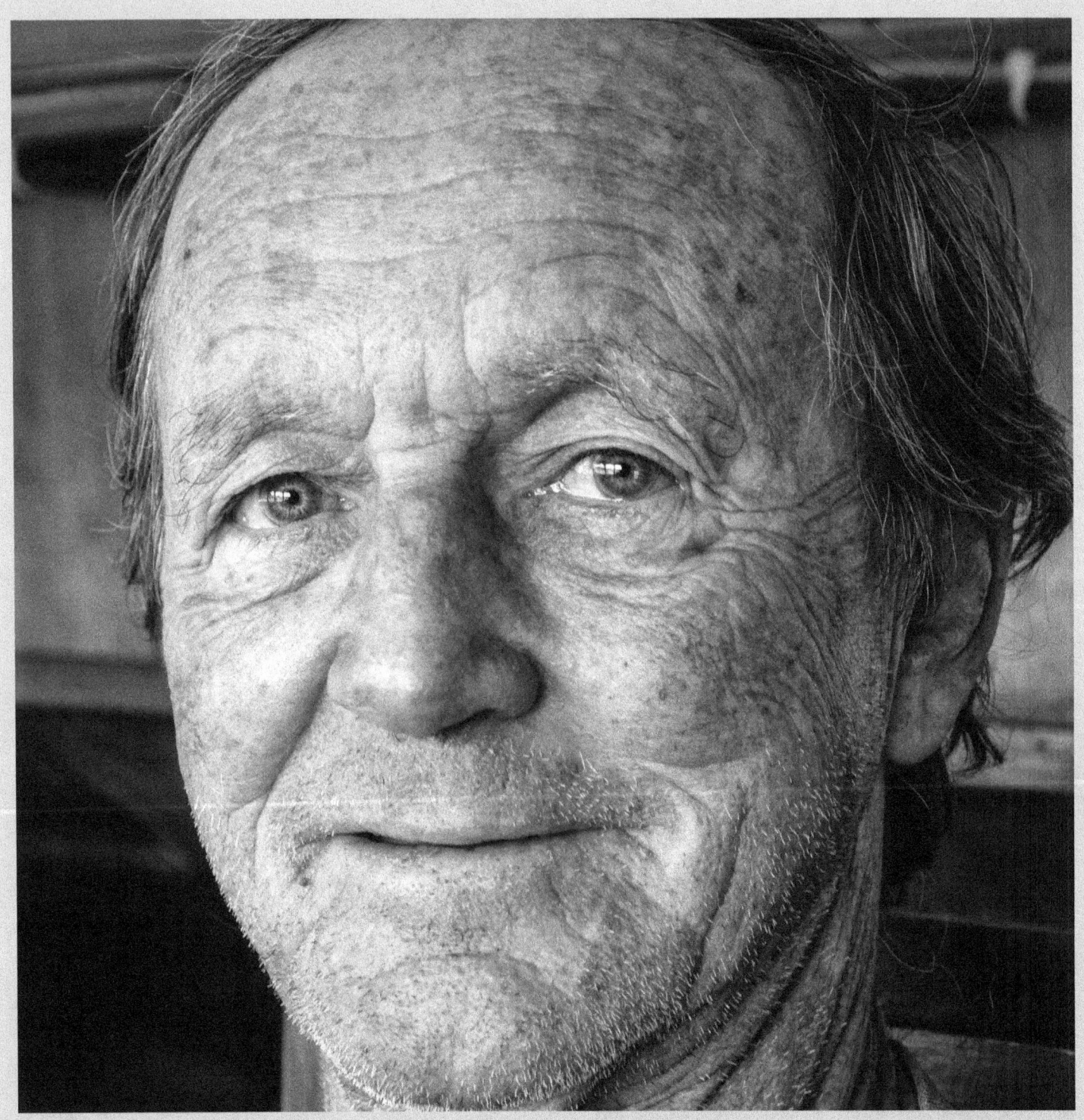

Cowboy also joined the crew of the *Capt. Eder*, 2013.

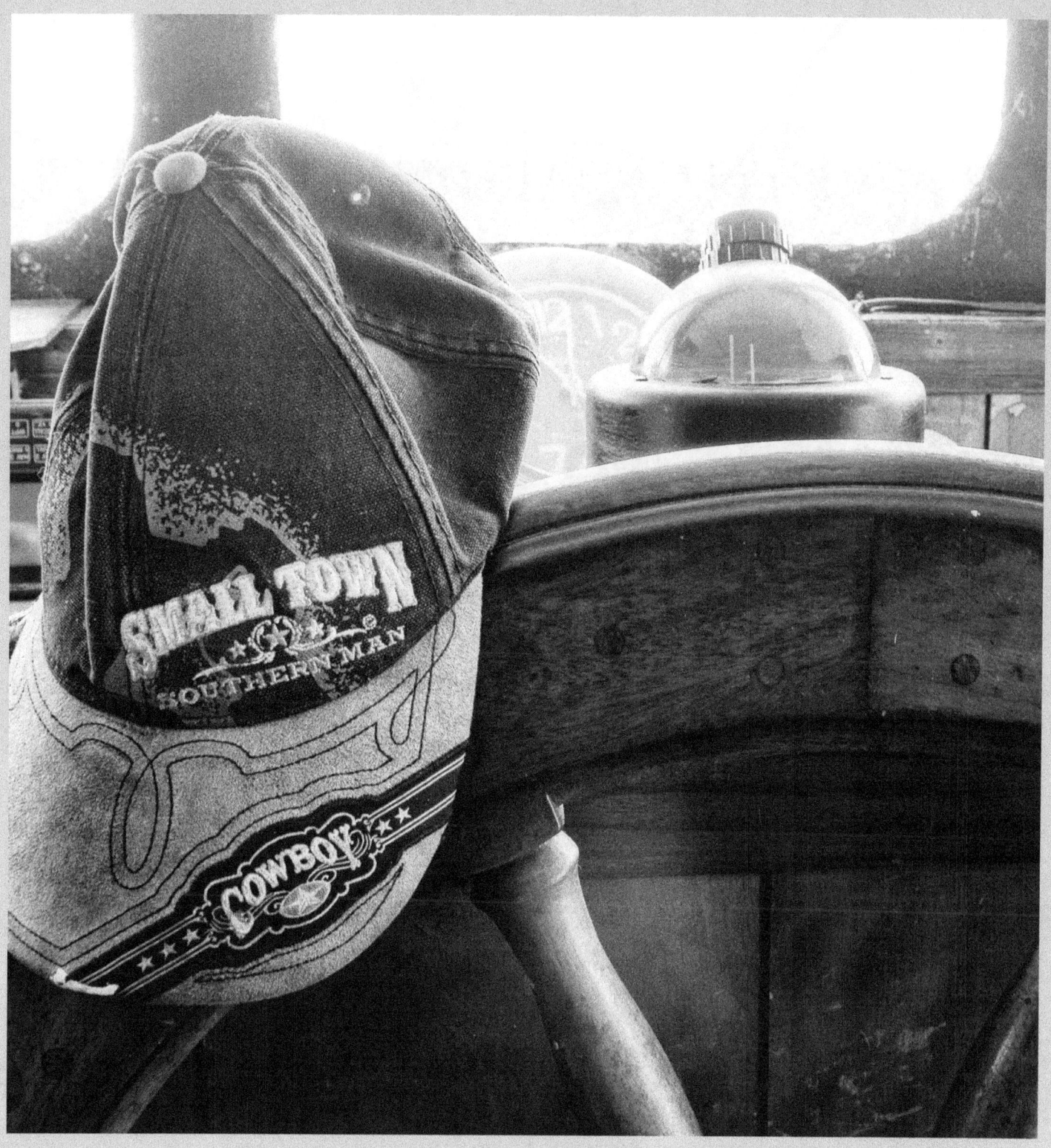

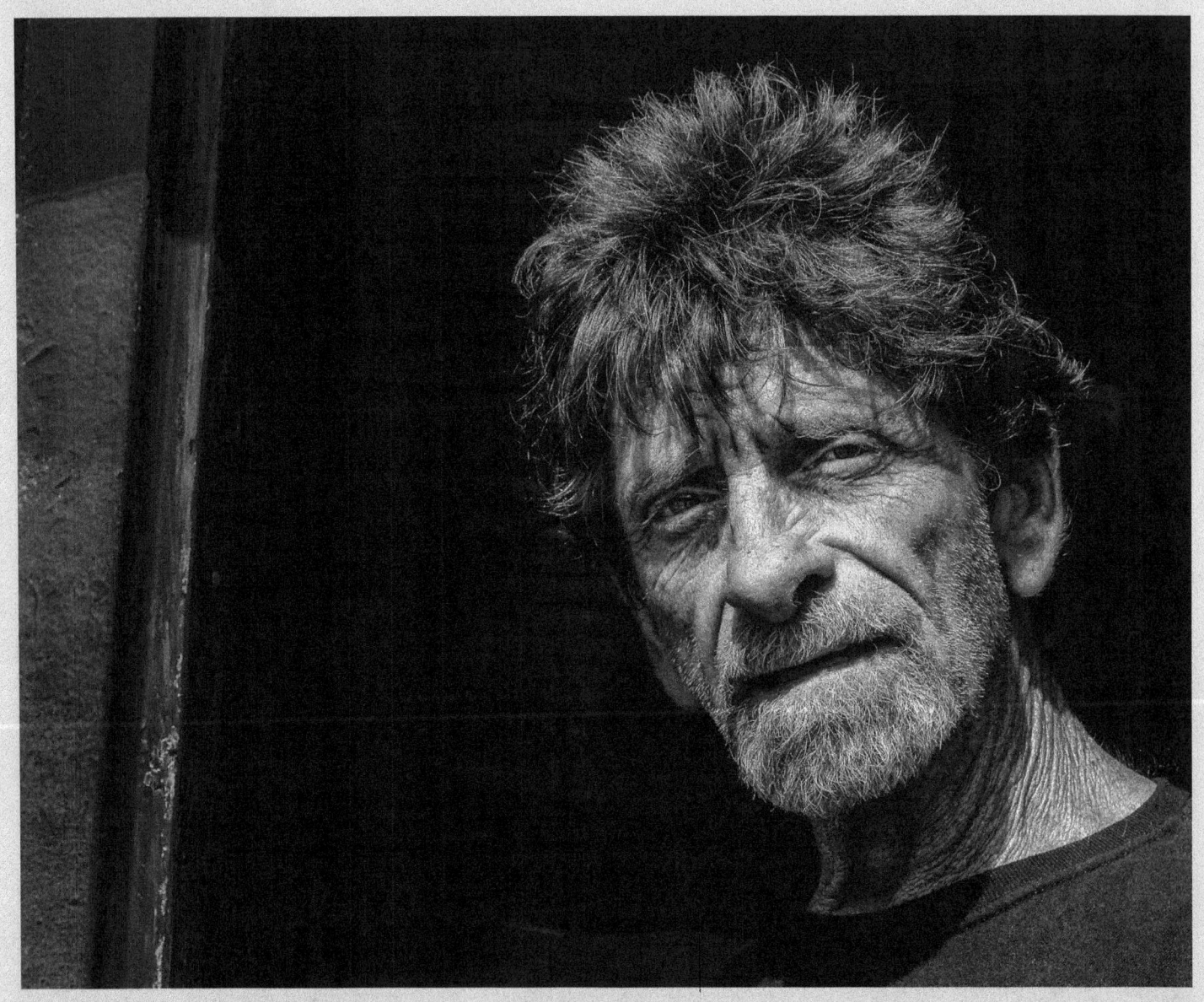

Tim's *Michael James* ended her life in Brunswick, Georgia with a broken keel. He is back on Stock Island as captain and owner of the *Russell Lee*, 2015.

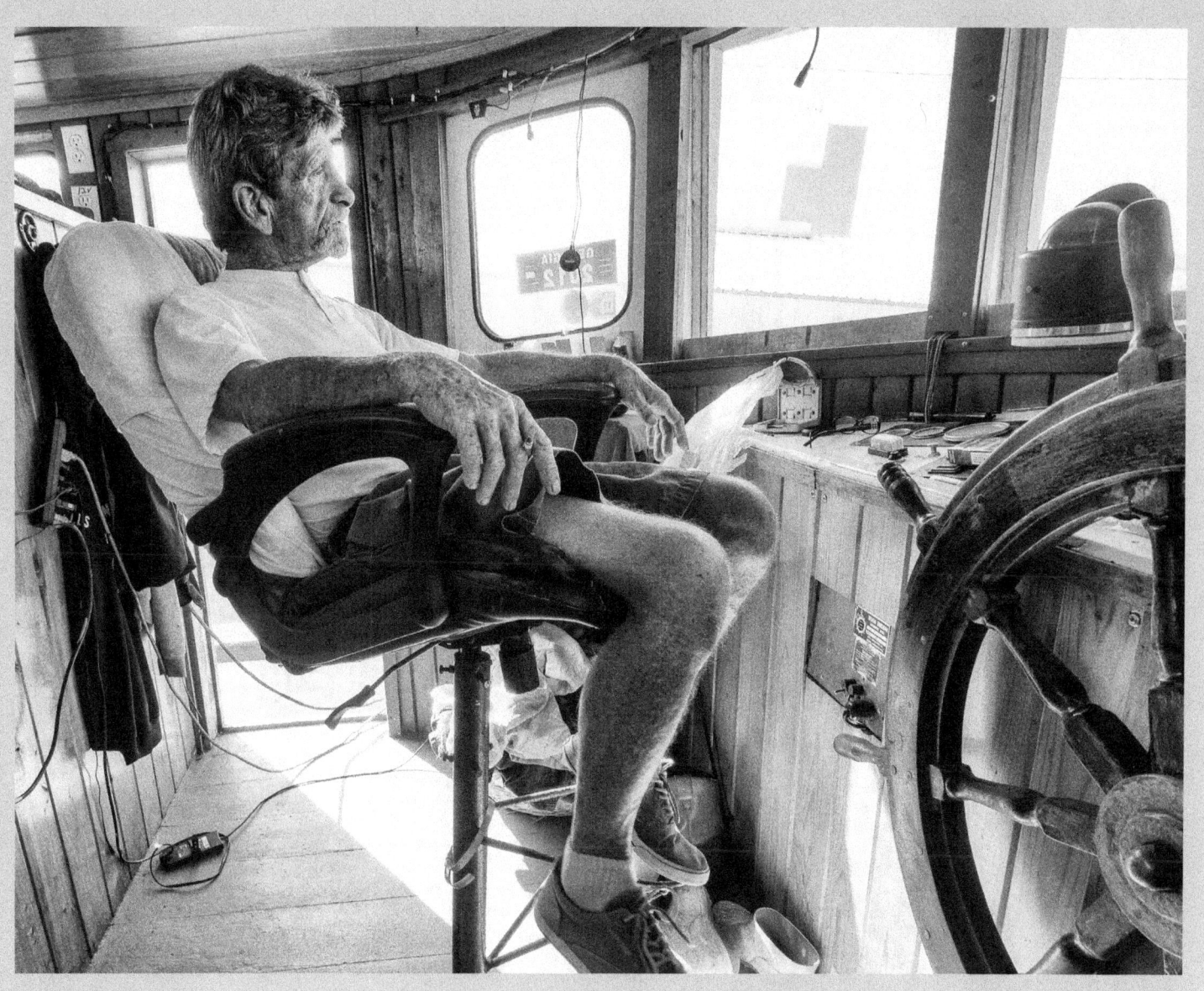

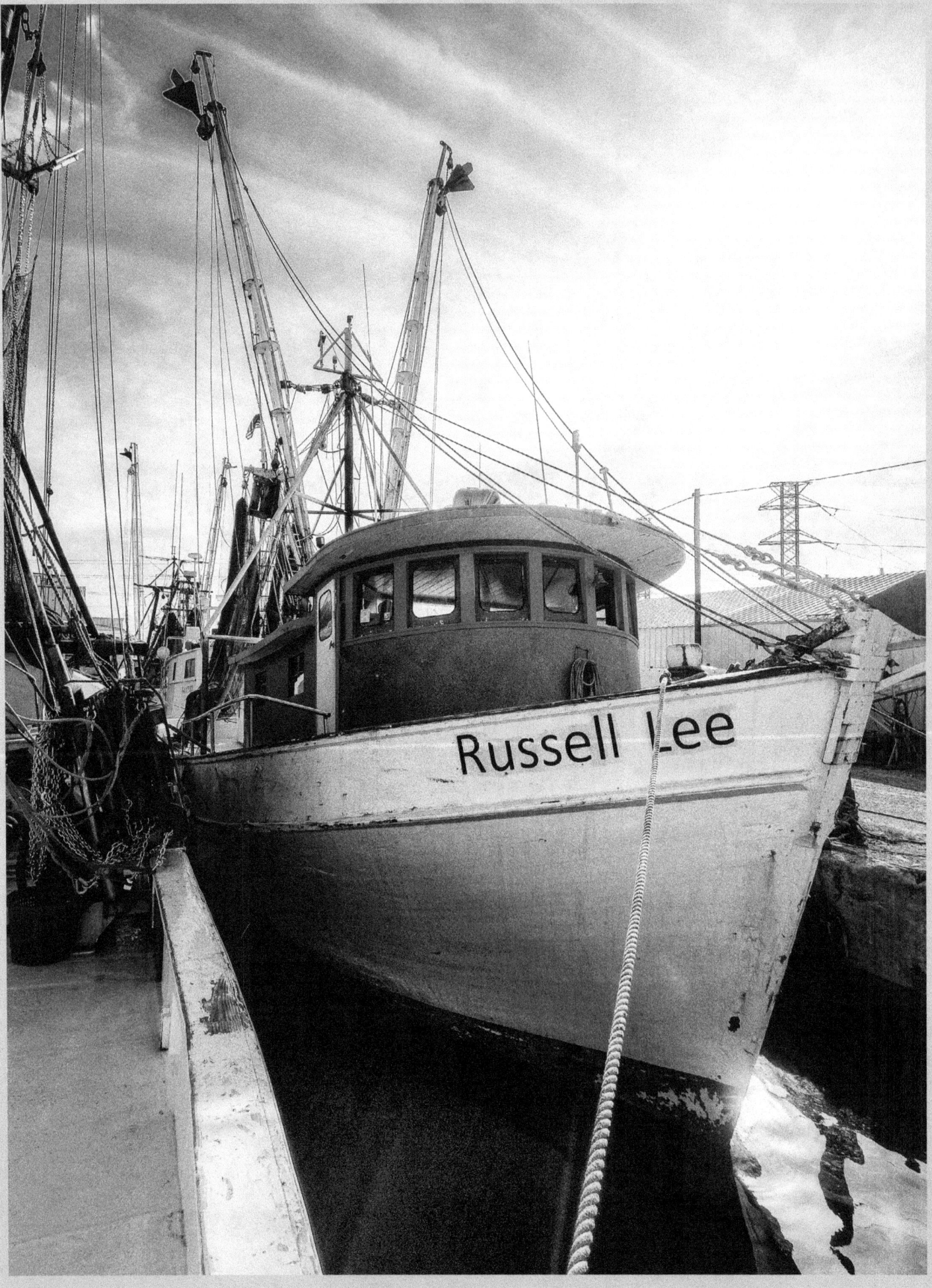

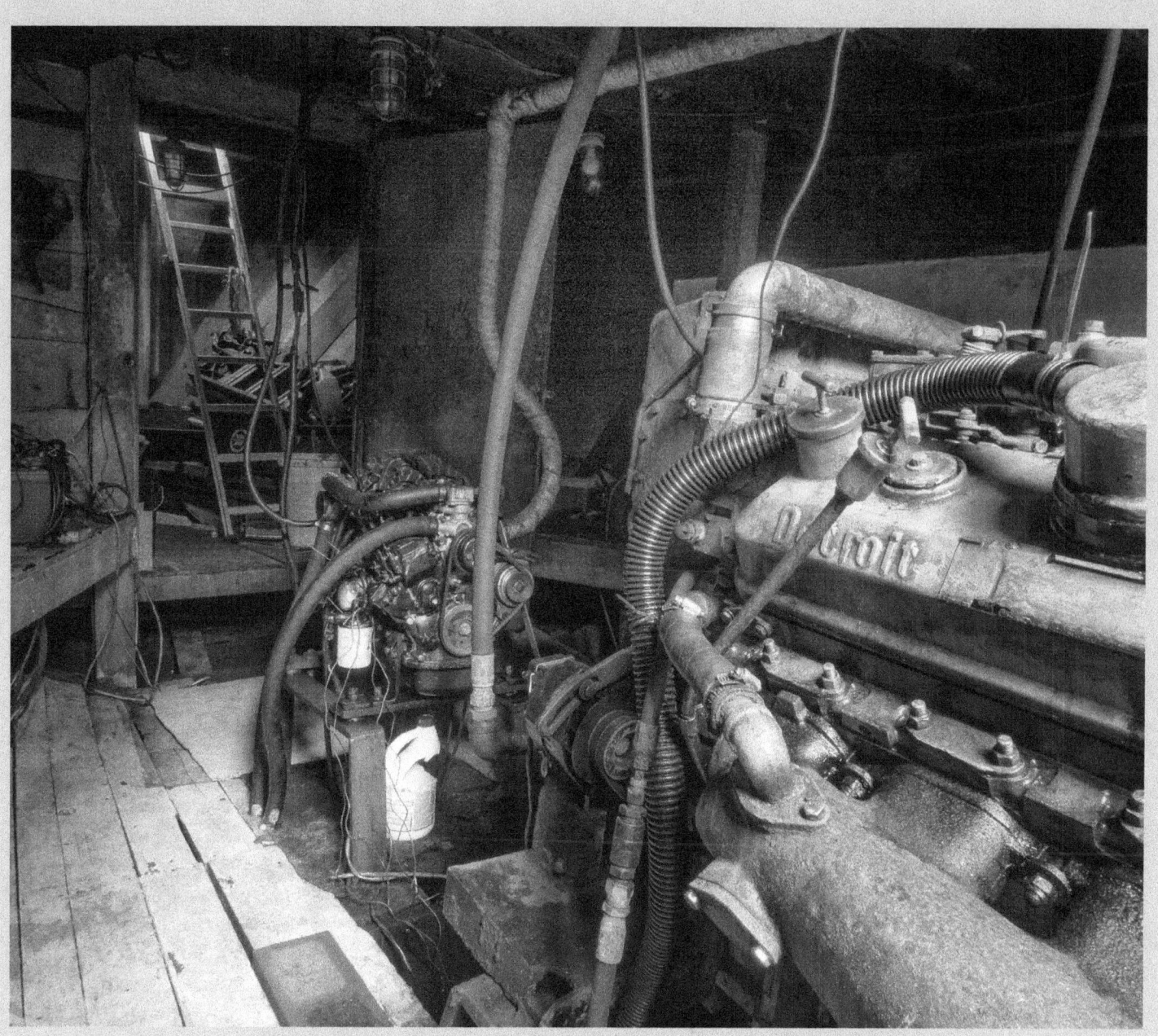

Opposite: *Russell Lee* tied up on Stock Island.
Above: *Russell Lee's* engine room.

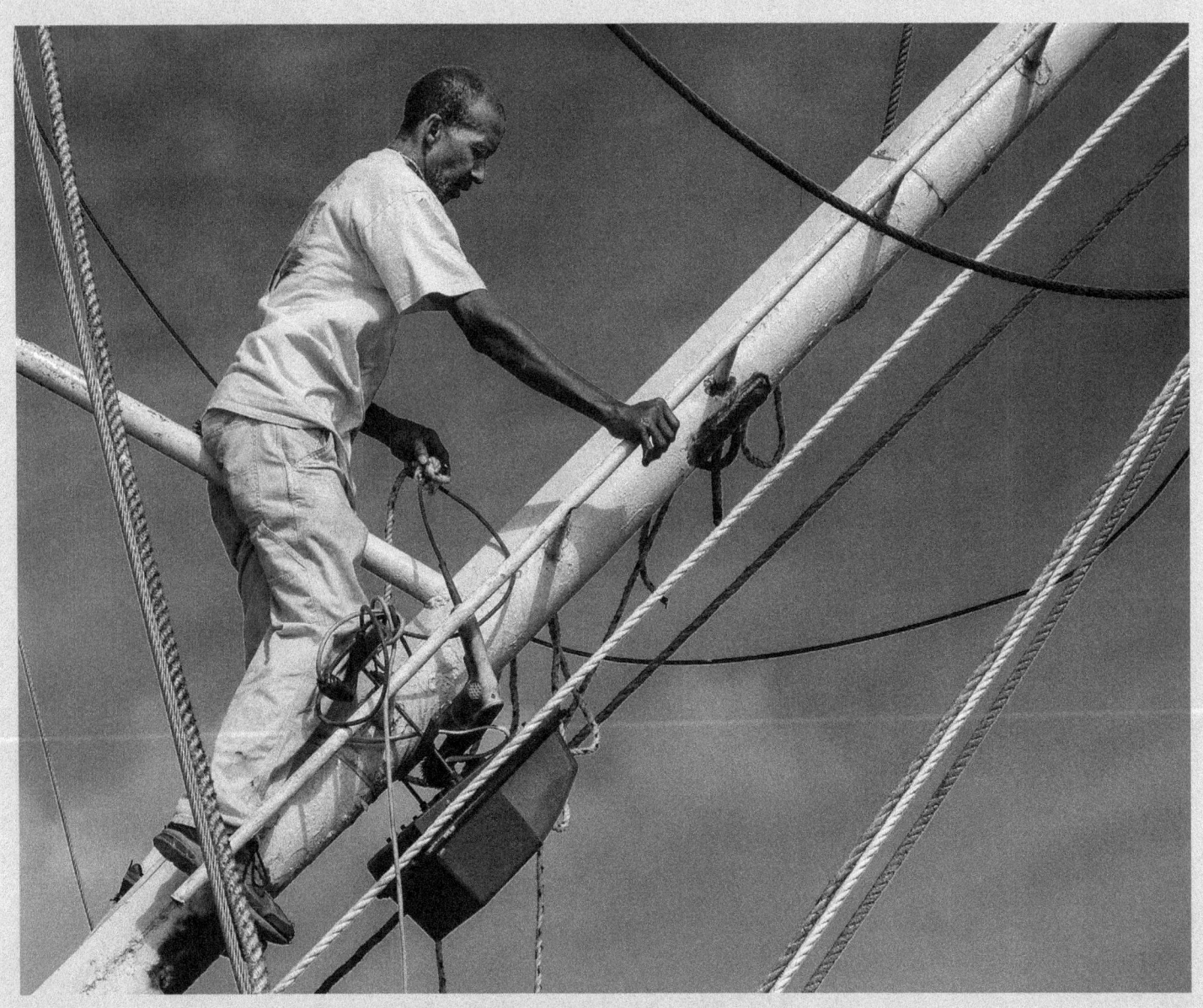

Billy, younger brother of
Red from Brunswick, and Randolph, helping out on
the *Russell Lee*.

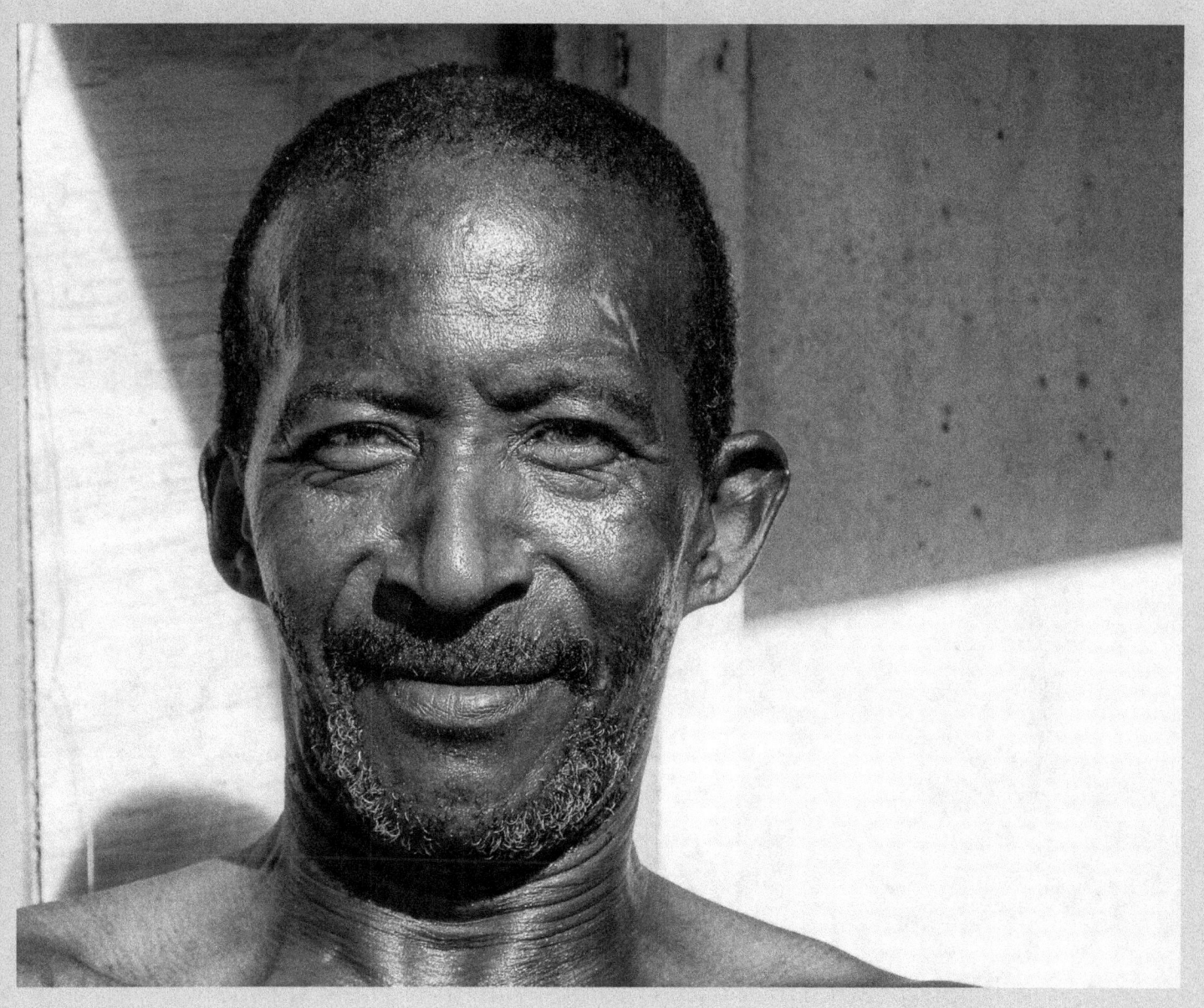

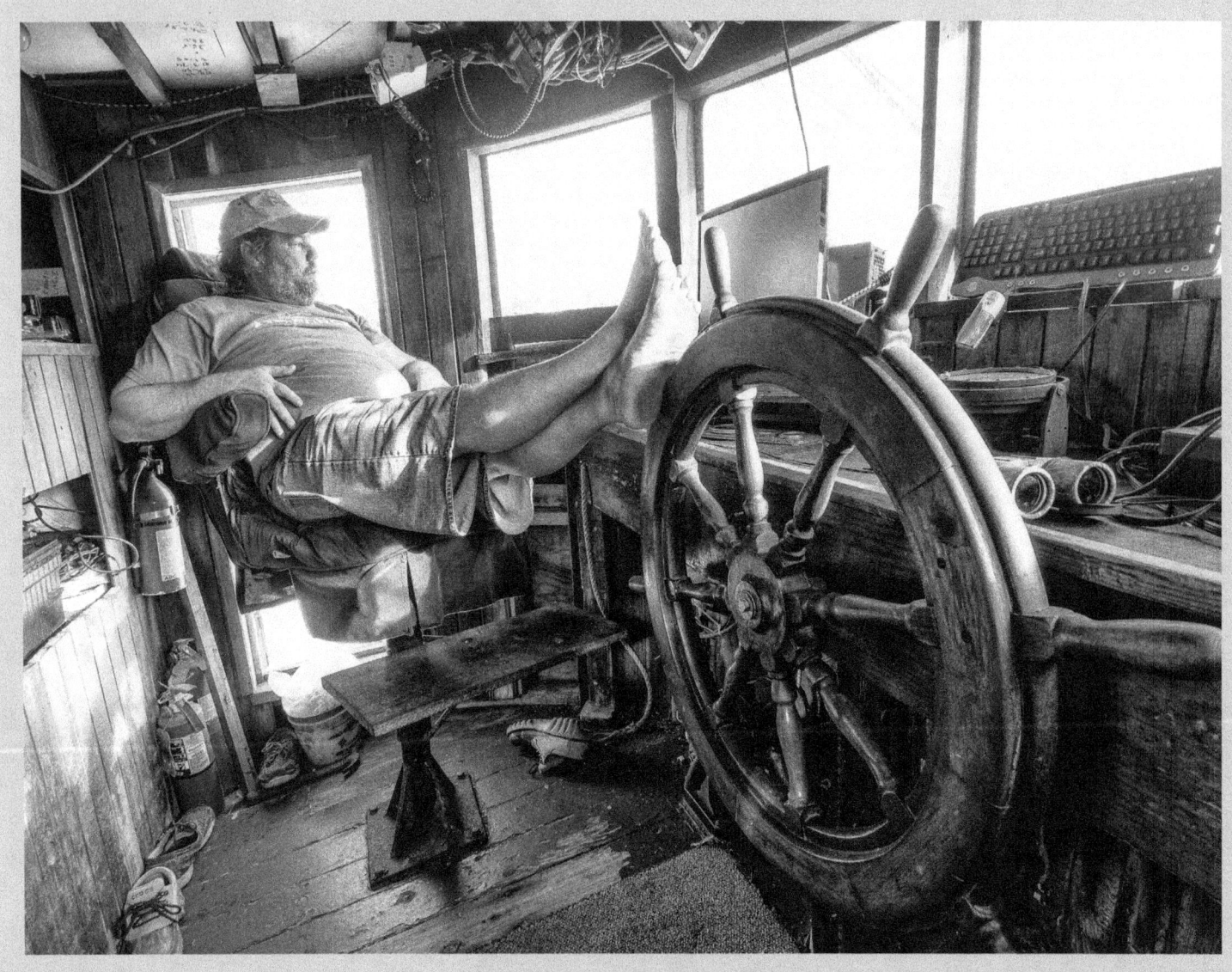

Bobby, captain of the *Ichiban*, waiting to cast off later
in the day to get back to shrimping, 2015.

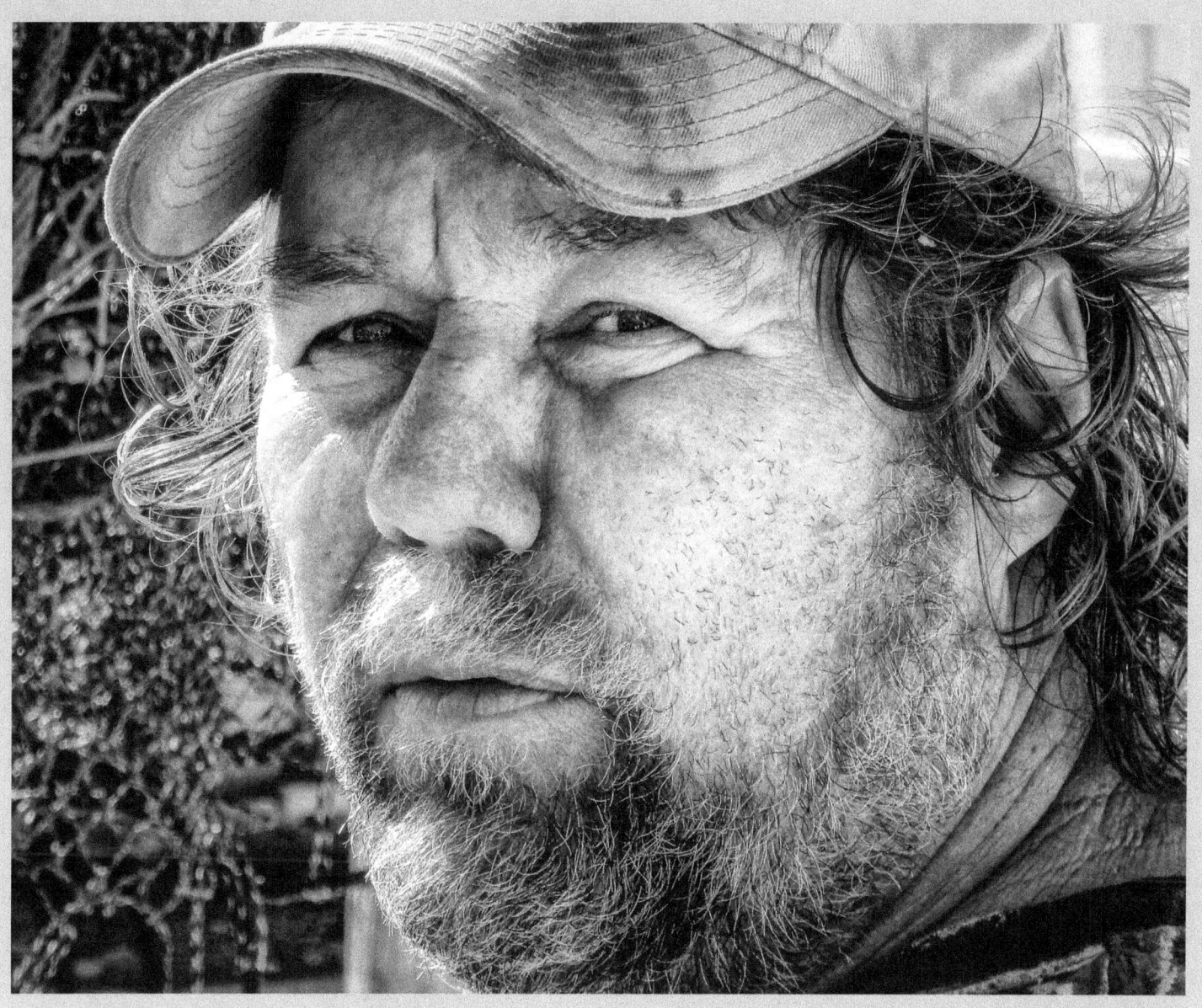

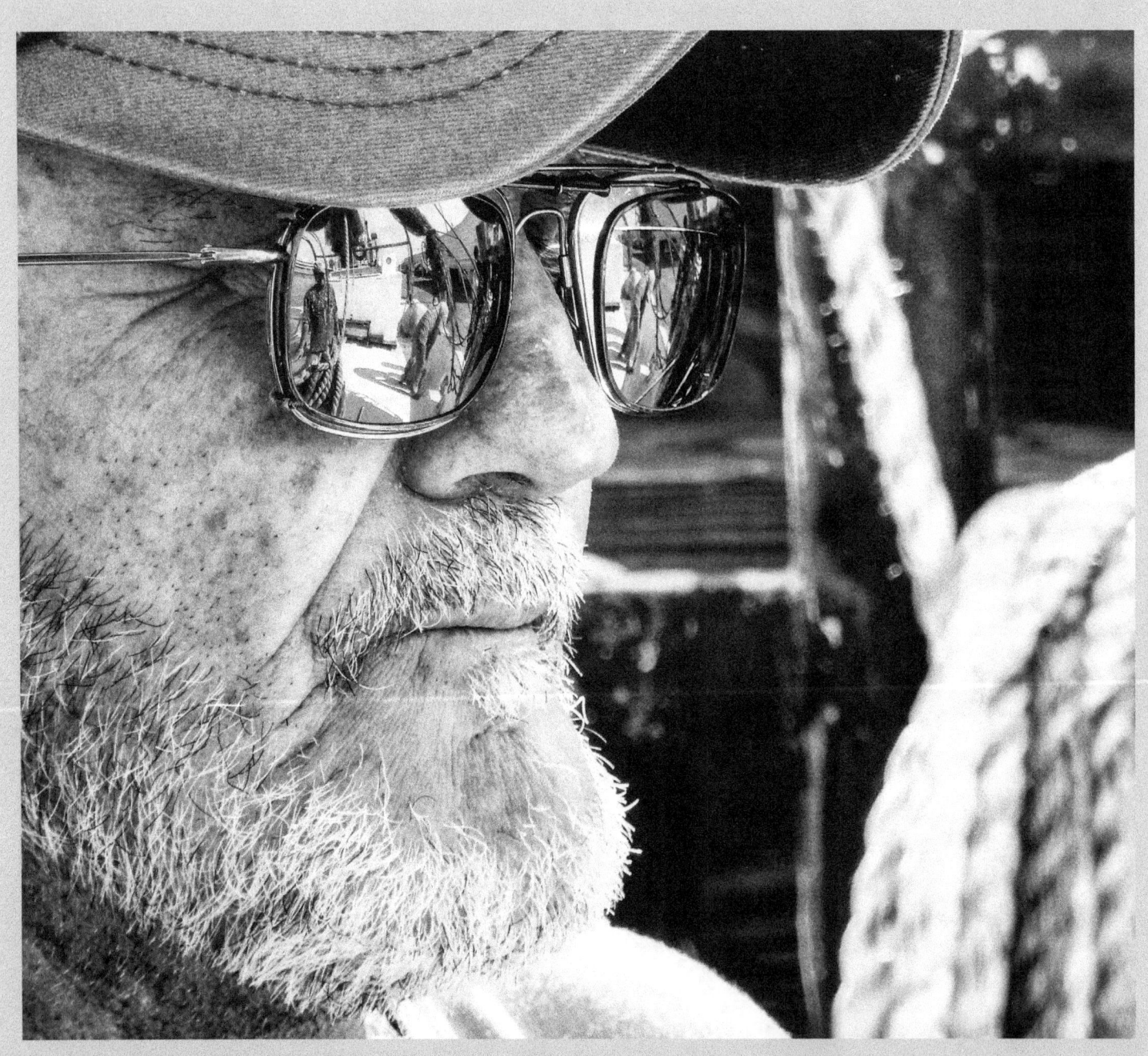

Gary, crewman on the *Ichiban*.

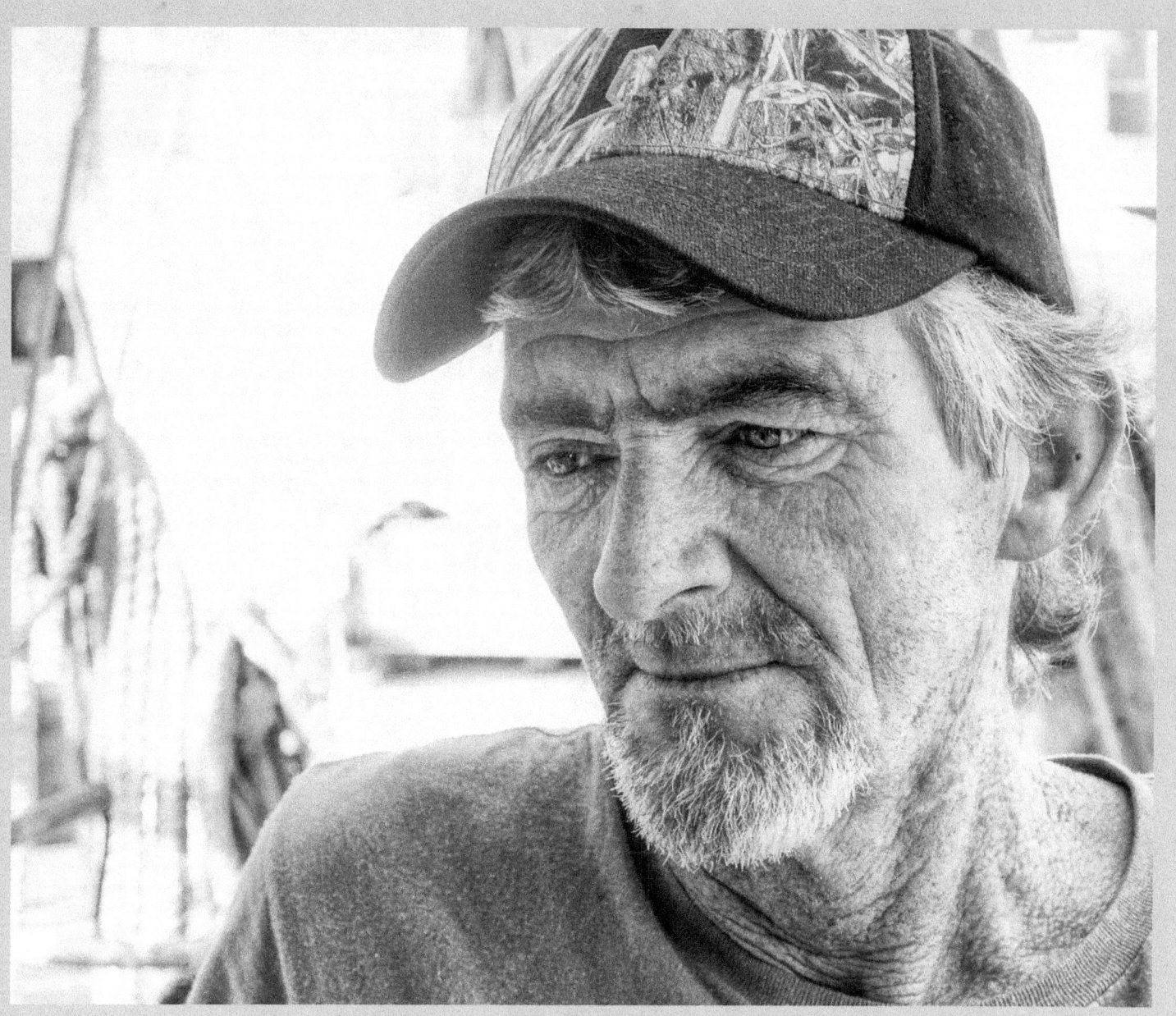

Clif, crewman on the *Ichiban*.

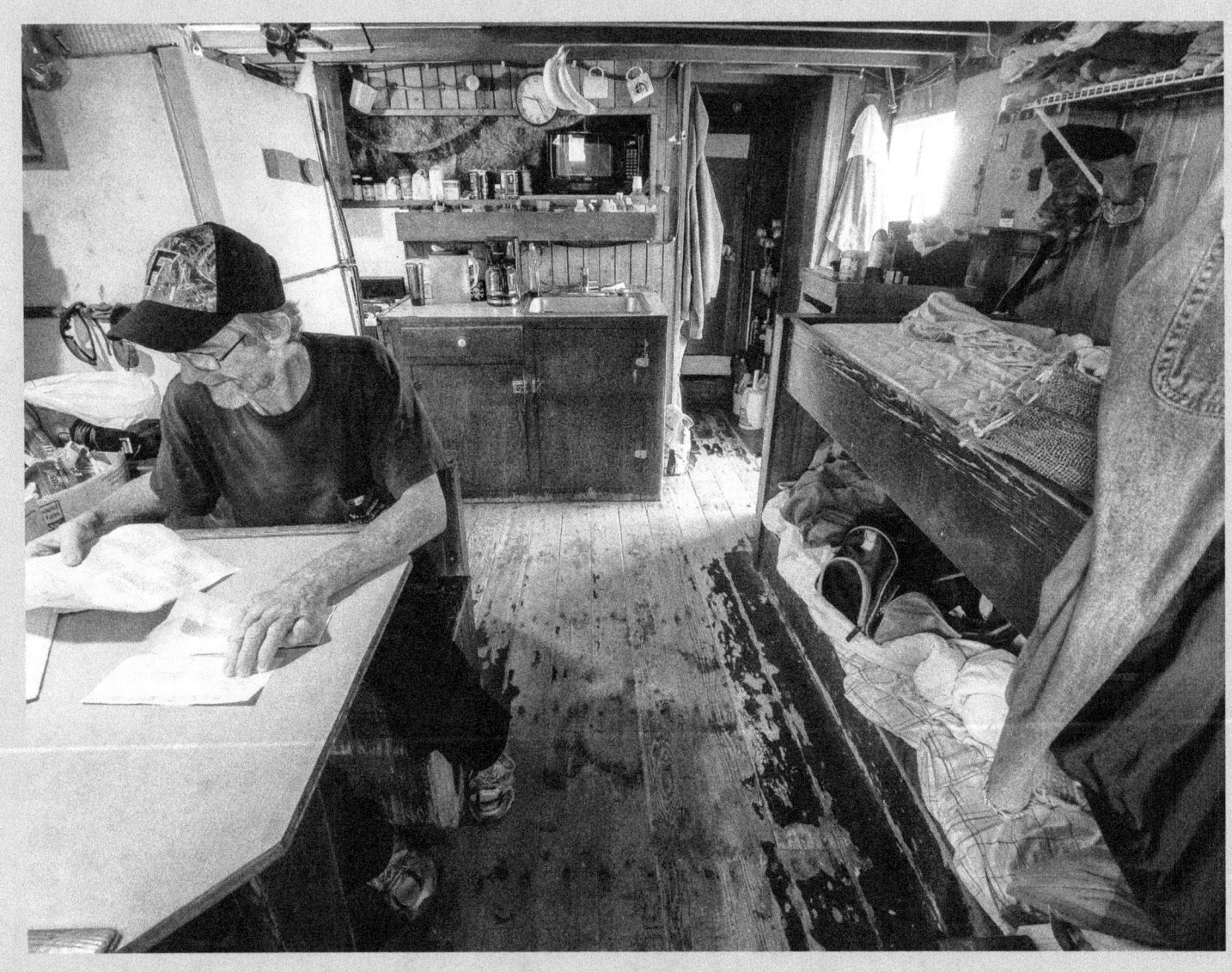

Above: Clif on the *Ichiban* taking care of some
paperwork while in port.
Opposite: The *Ichiban* taking on fuel.

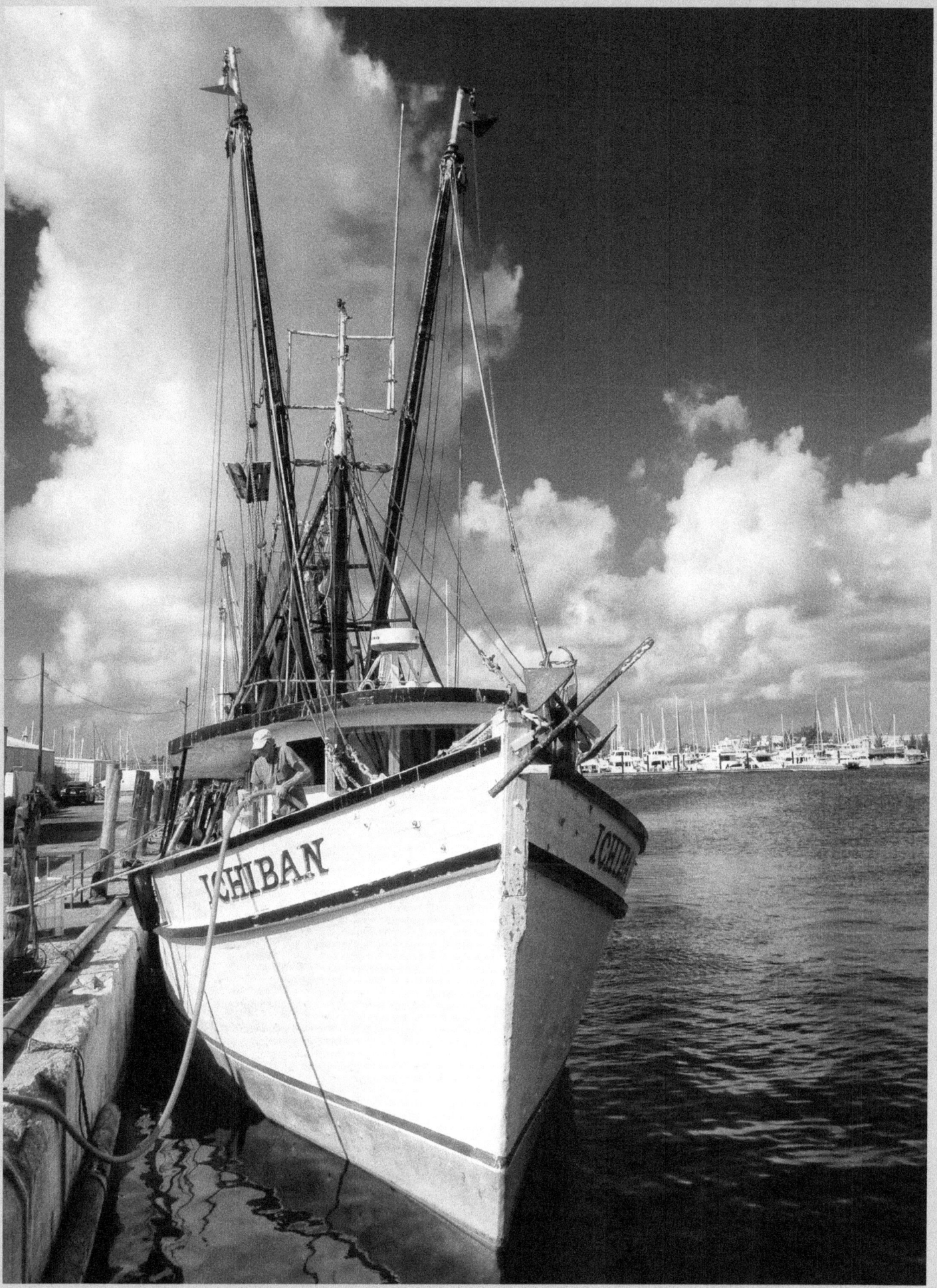

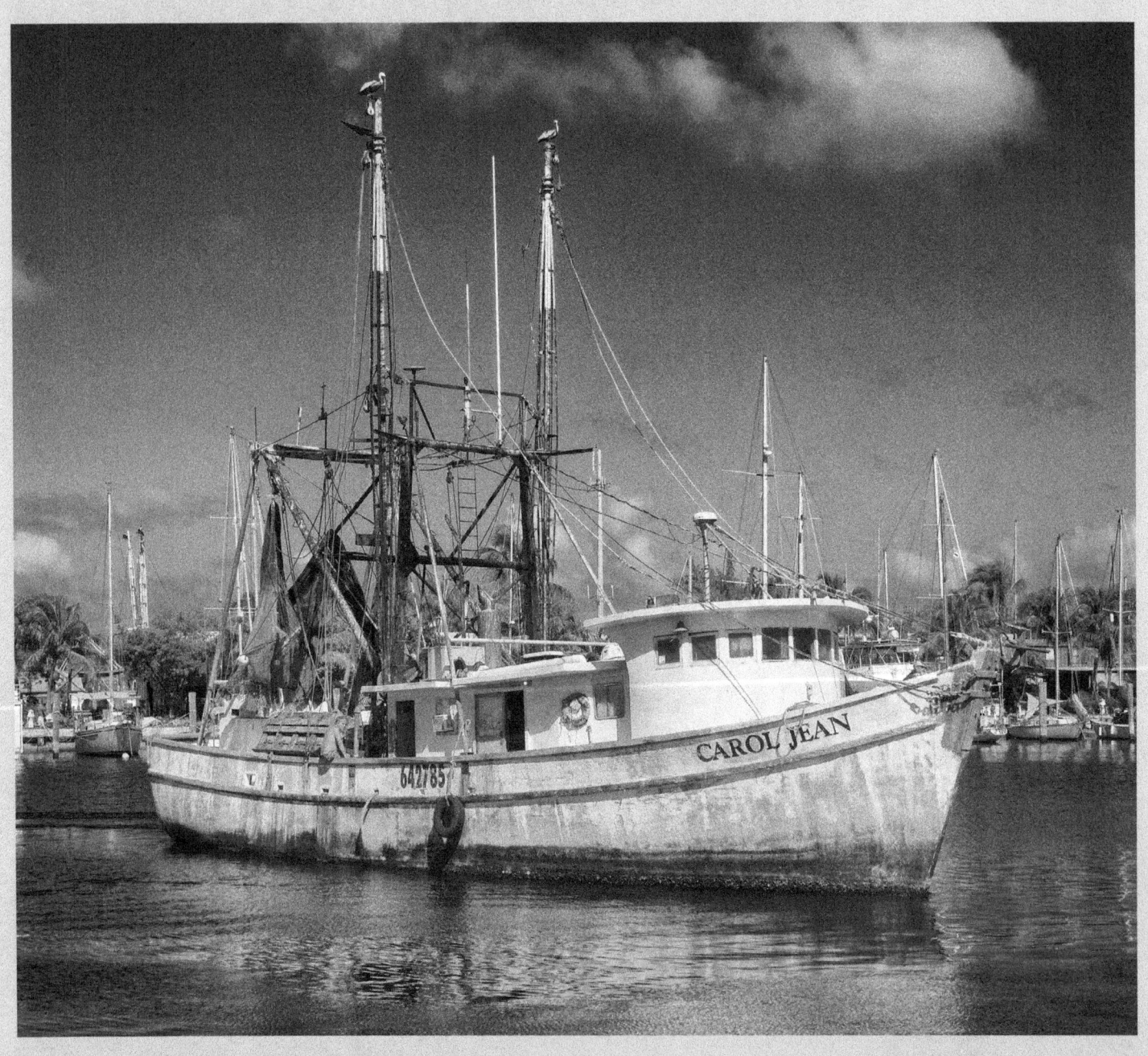

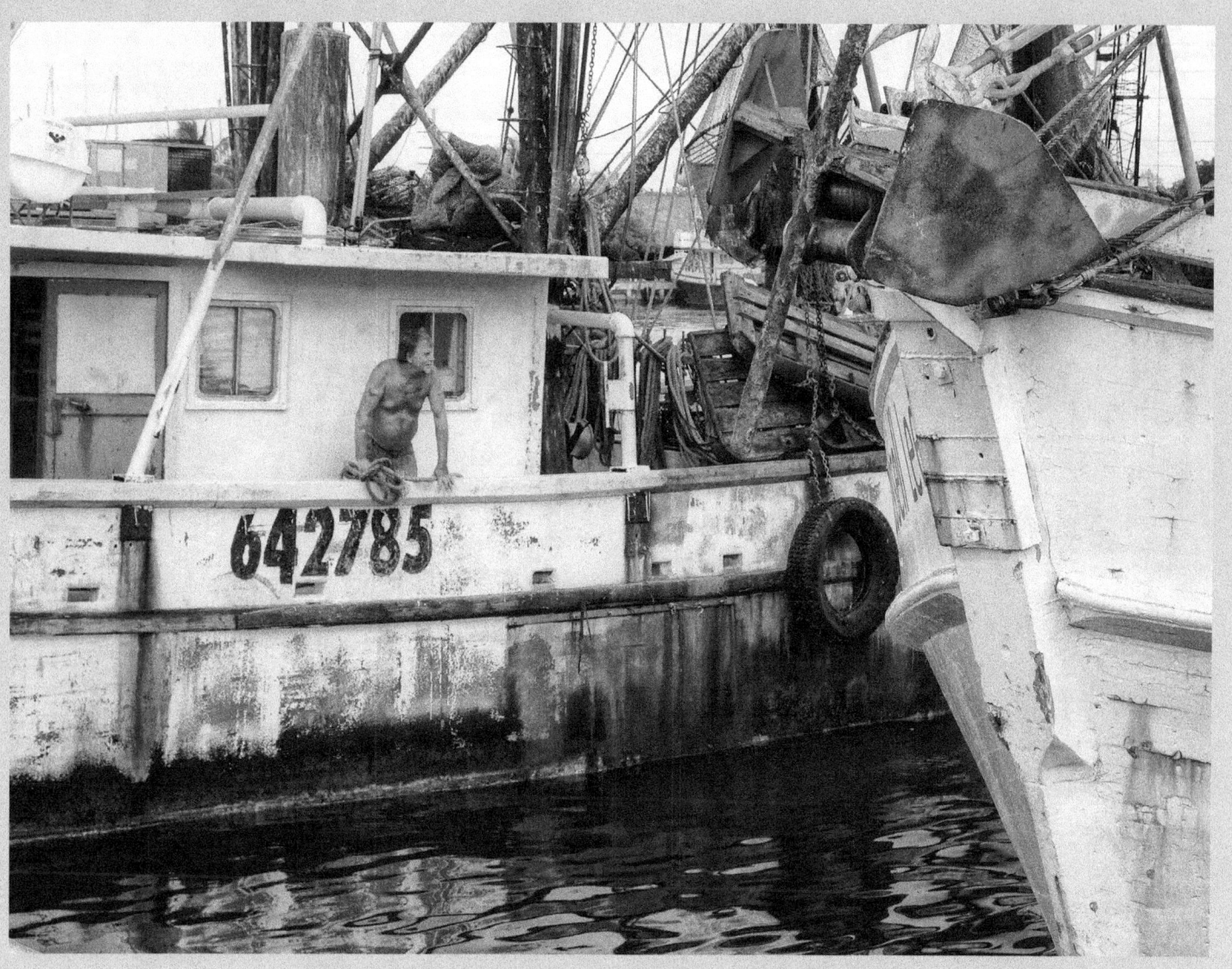

The *Carol Jean* arrives from Tampa, 2015.

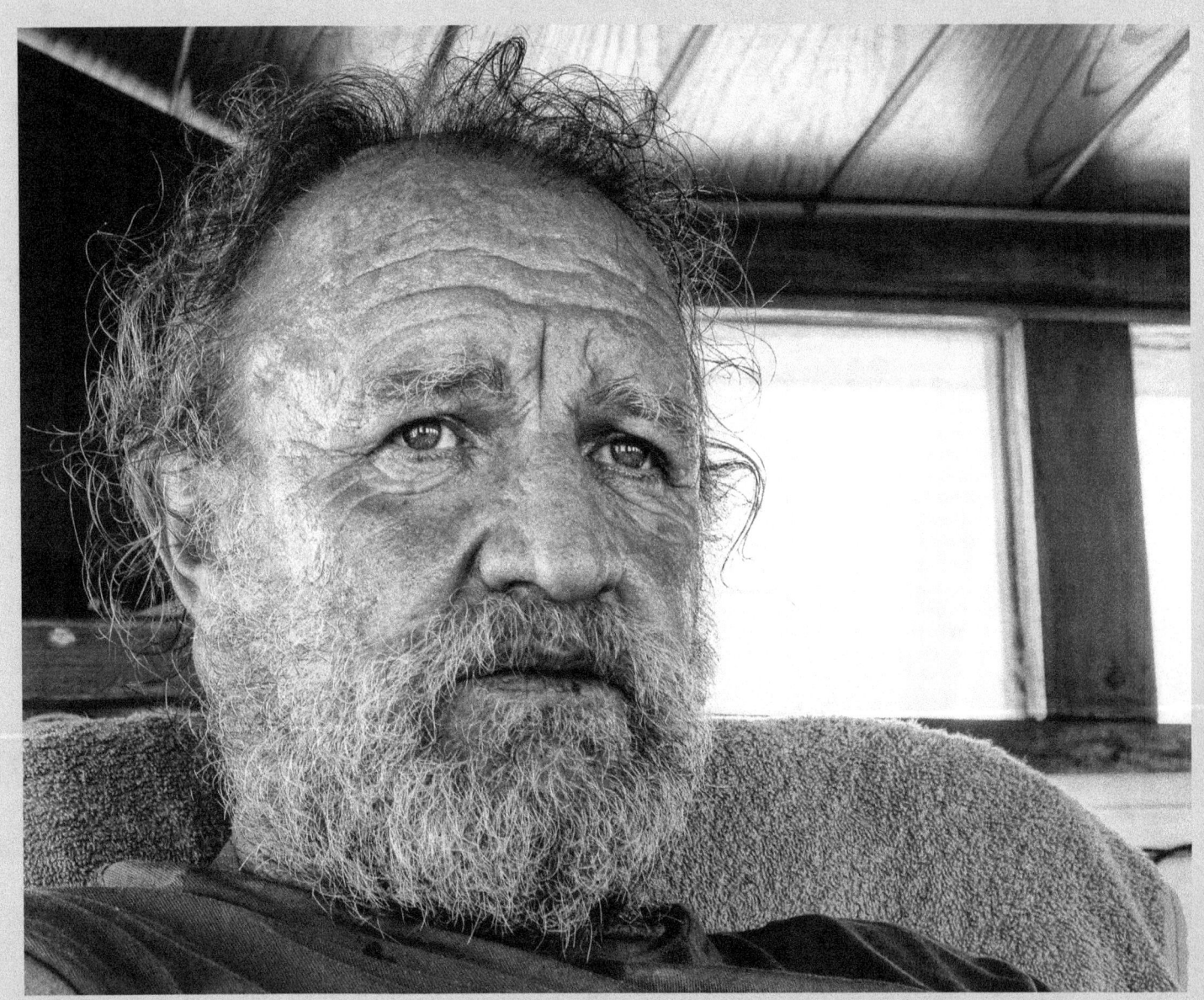

Mark, former owner and captain of the *Lady-Danielle*
is now Captain of the *Carol Jean*.

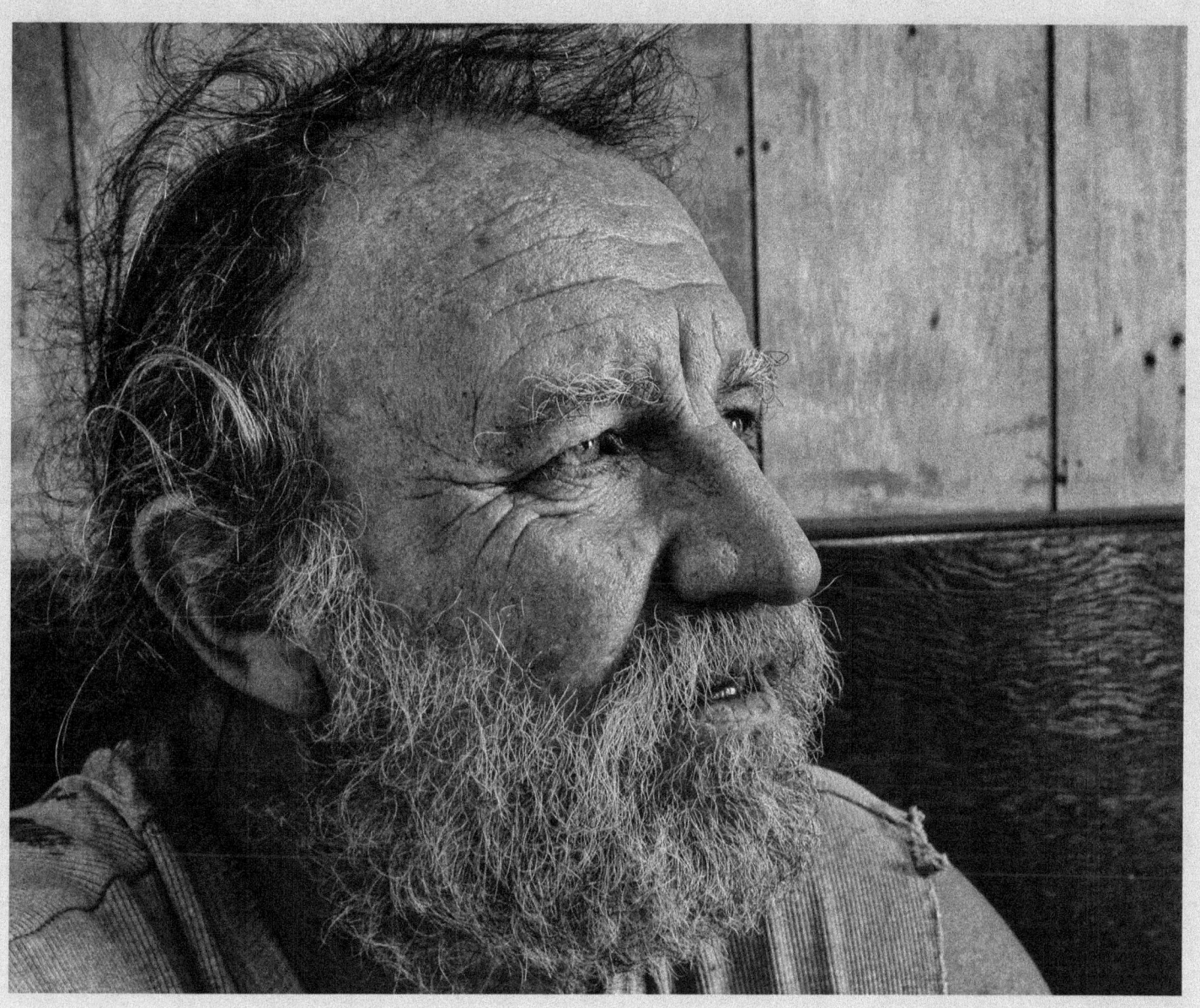

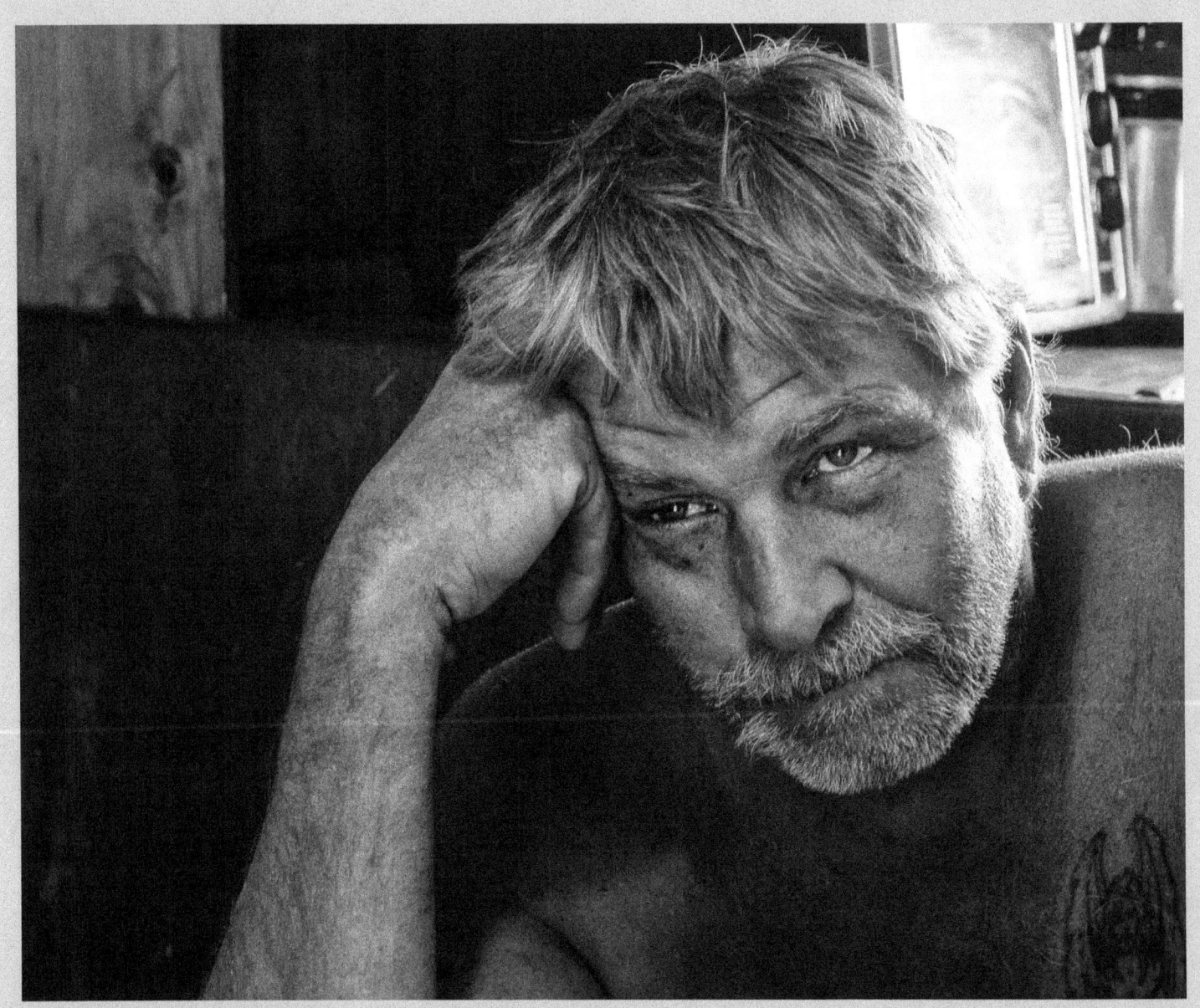

Warren on the *Carol Jean*, reflecting on life and shrimping.

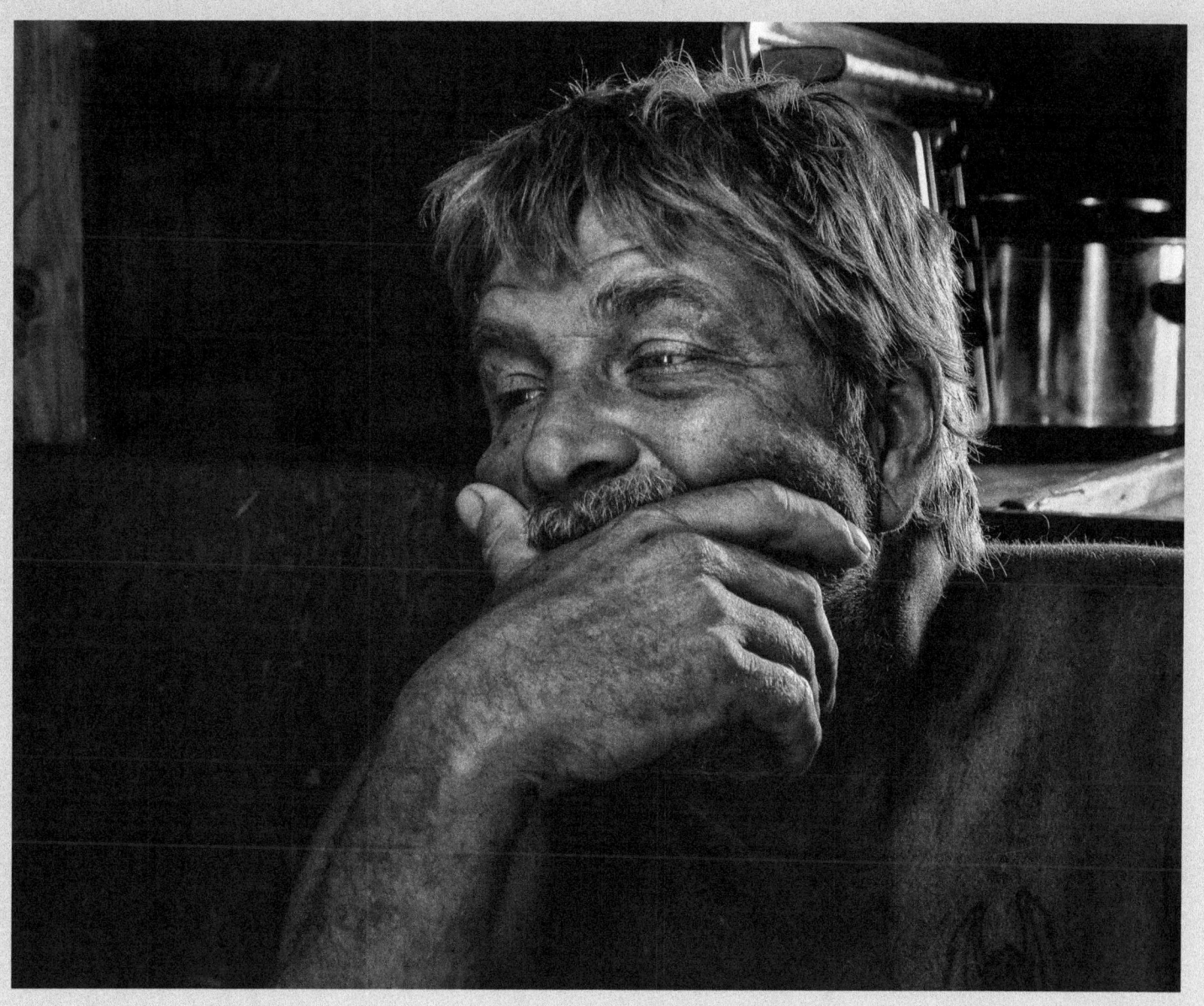

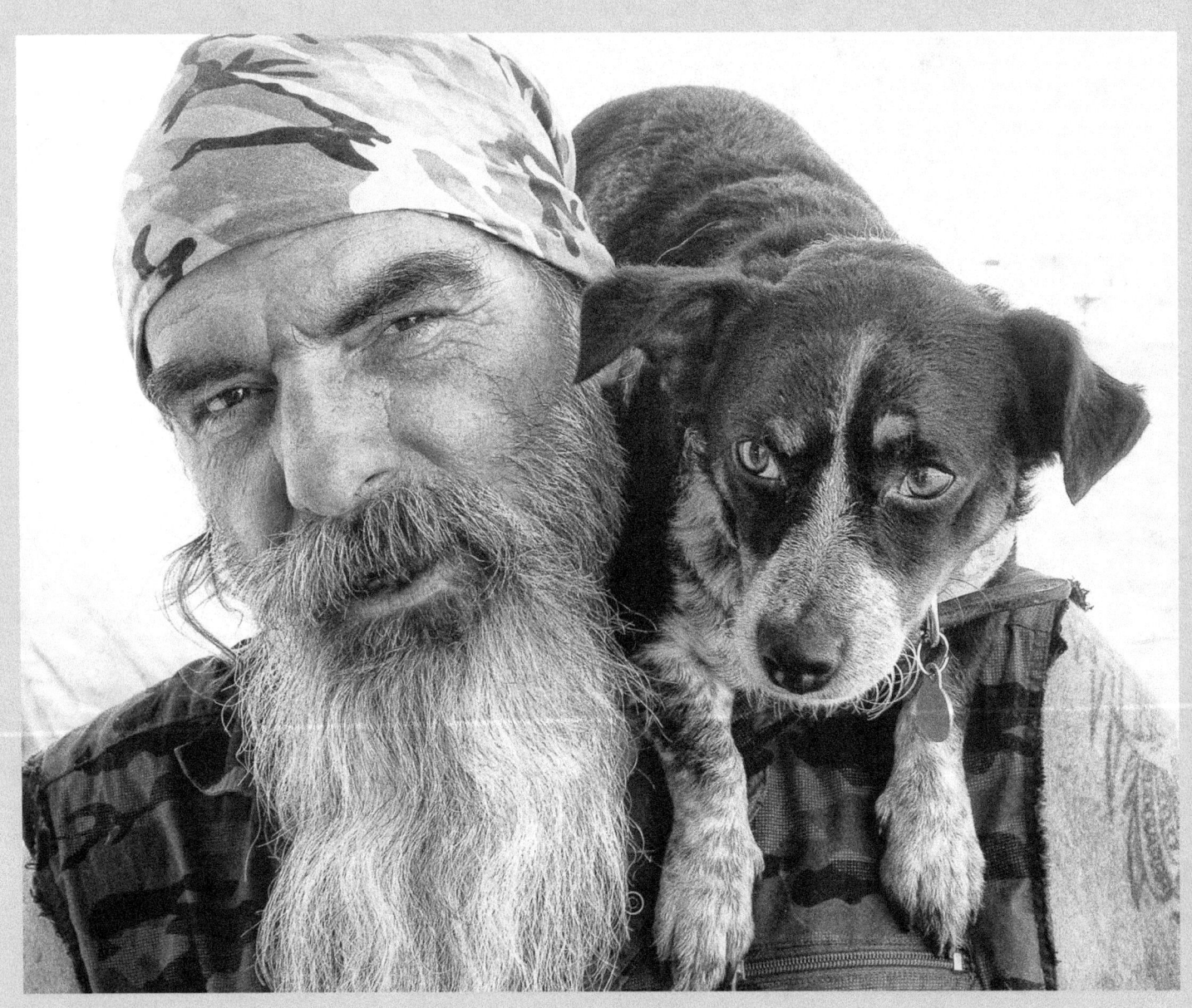

Art and his friend Short Dog visiting the *Carol Jean*.

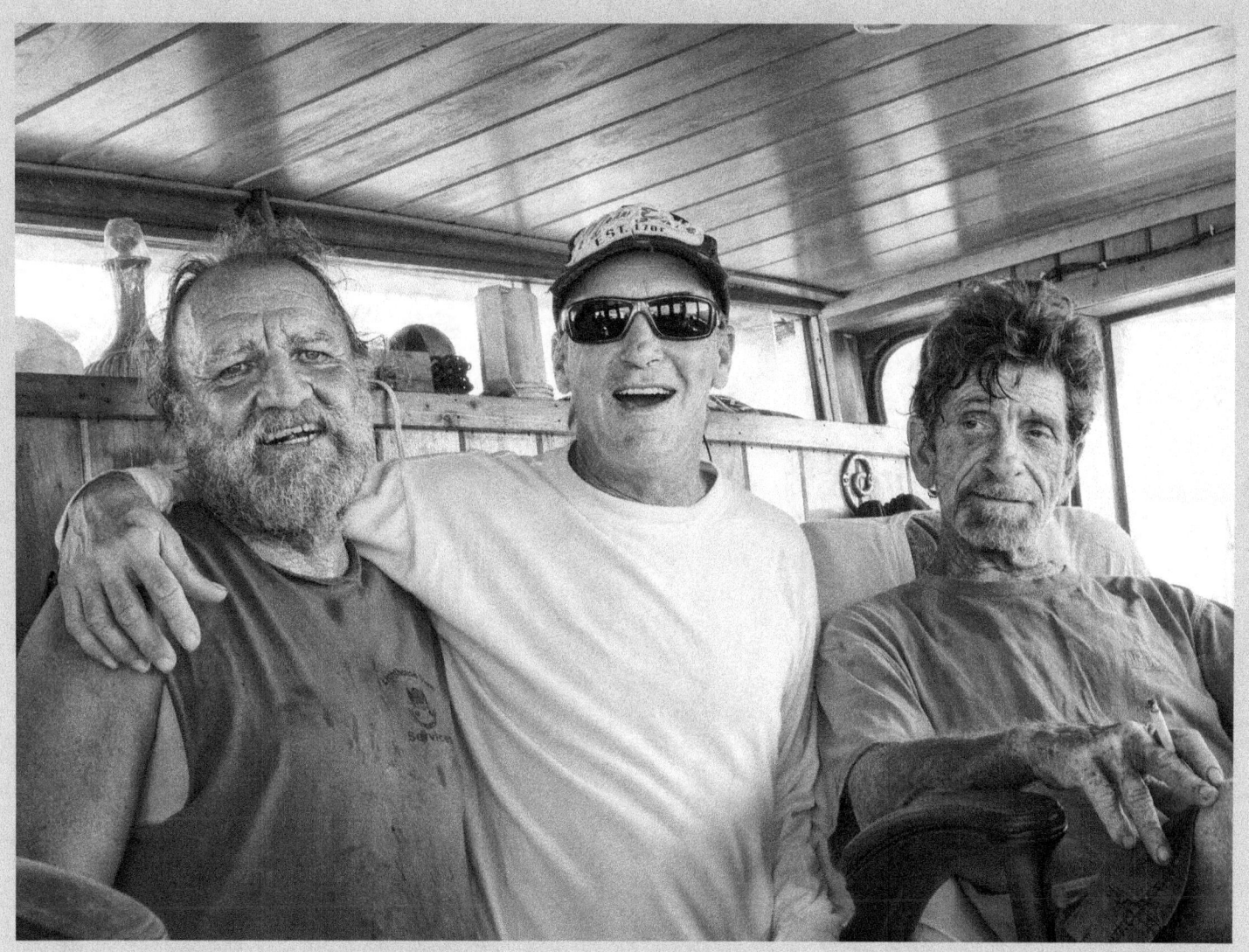

Reunion: Mark, Curtis and Tim, 2015.

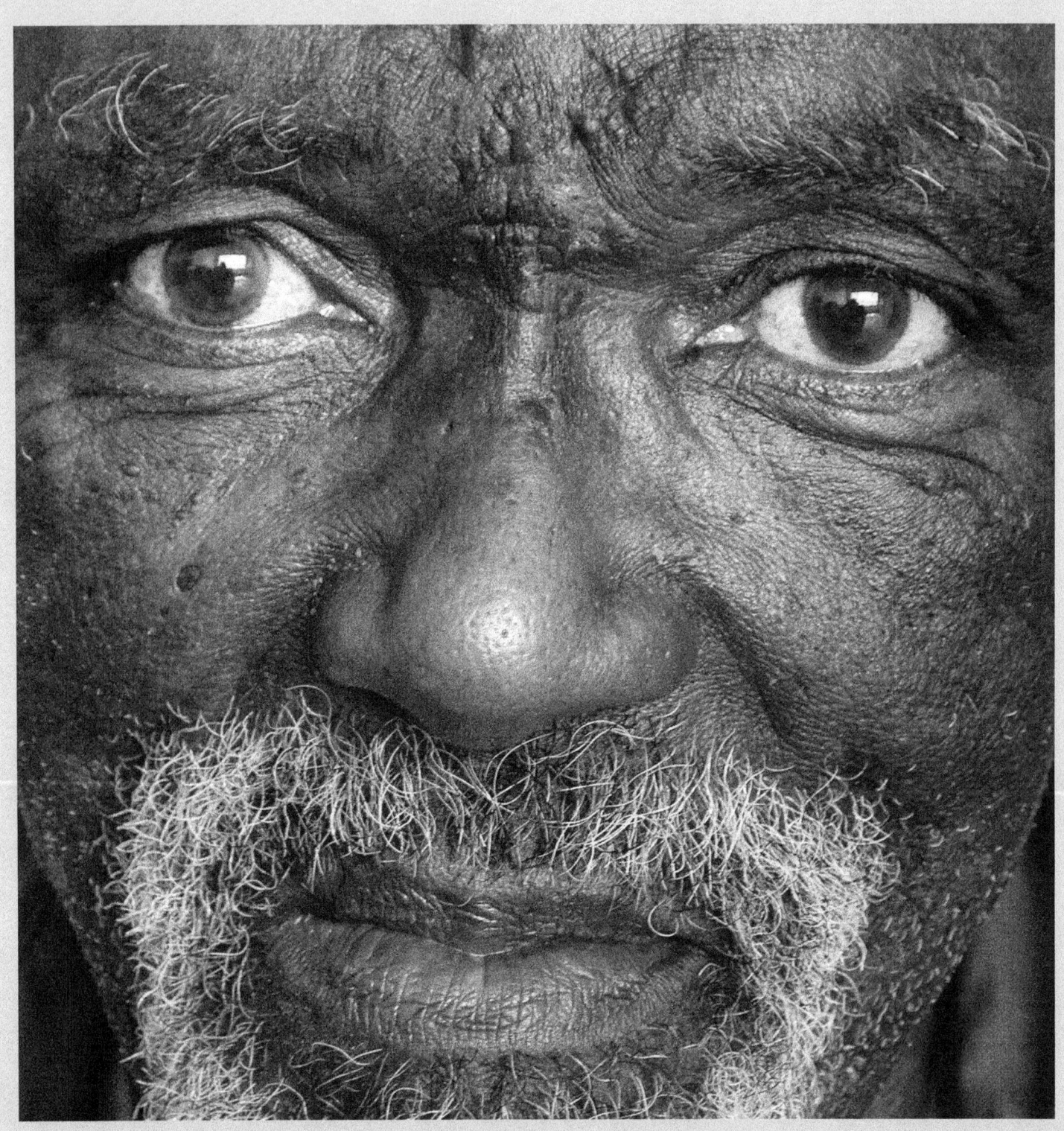

Charlie "Charlie Brown" Rose, Jr.
Died August 7, 2014 - Age 70

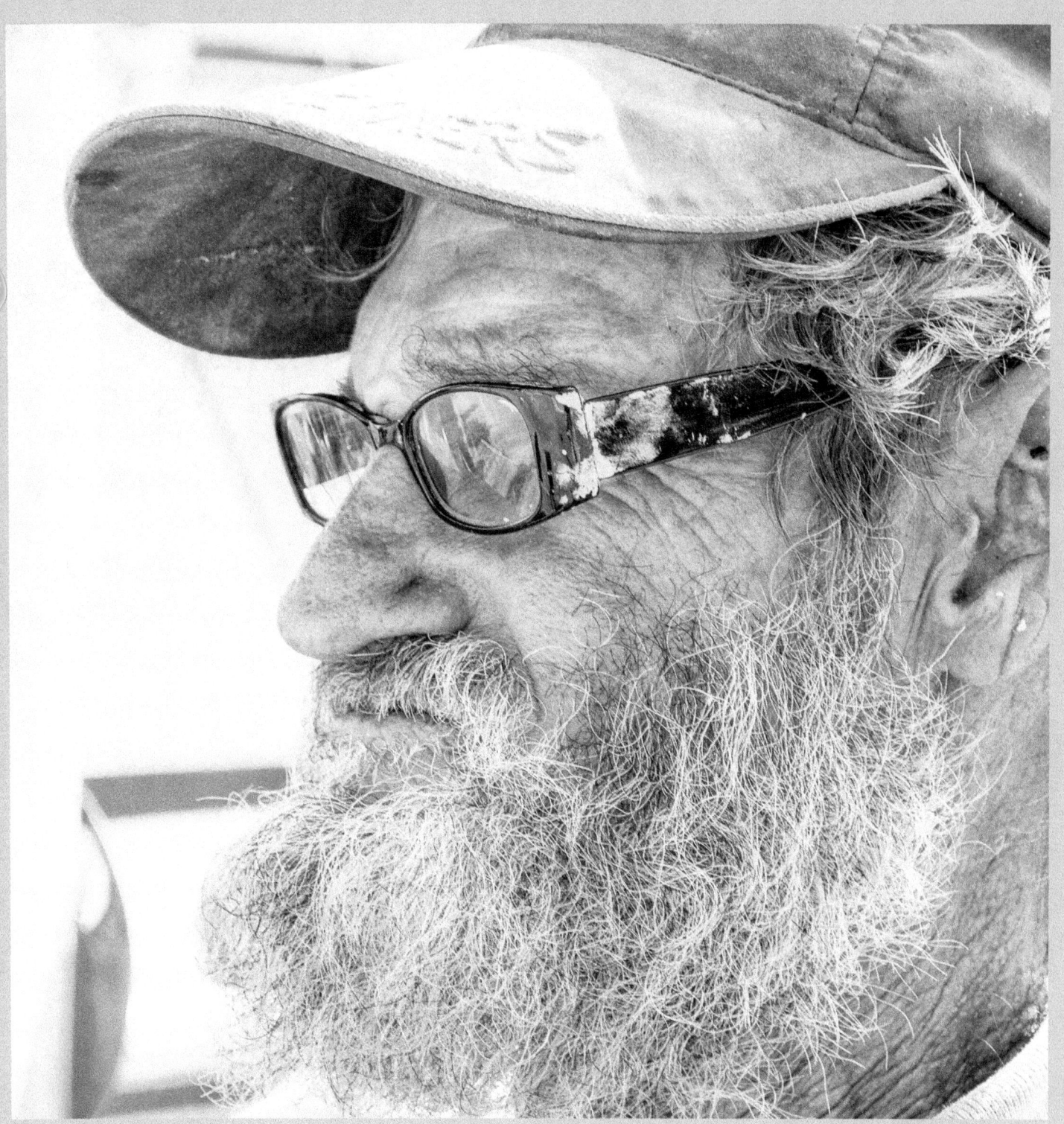

William R. "Wild Bill" Paglia, Jr.
Died January 25, 2014 - Age 61

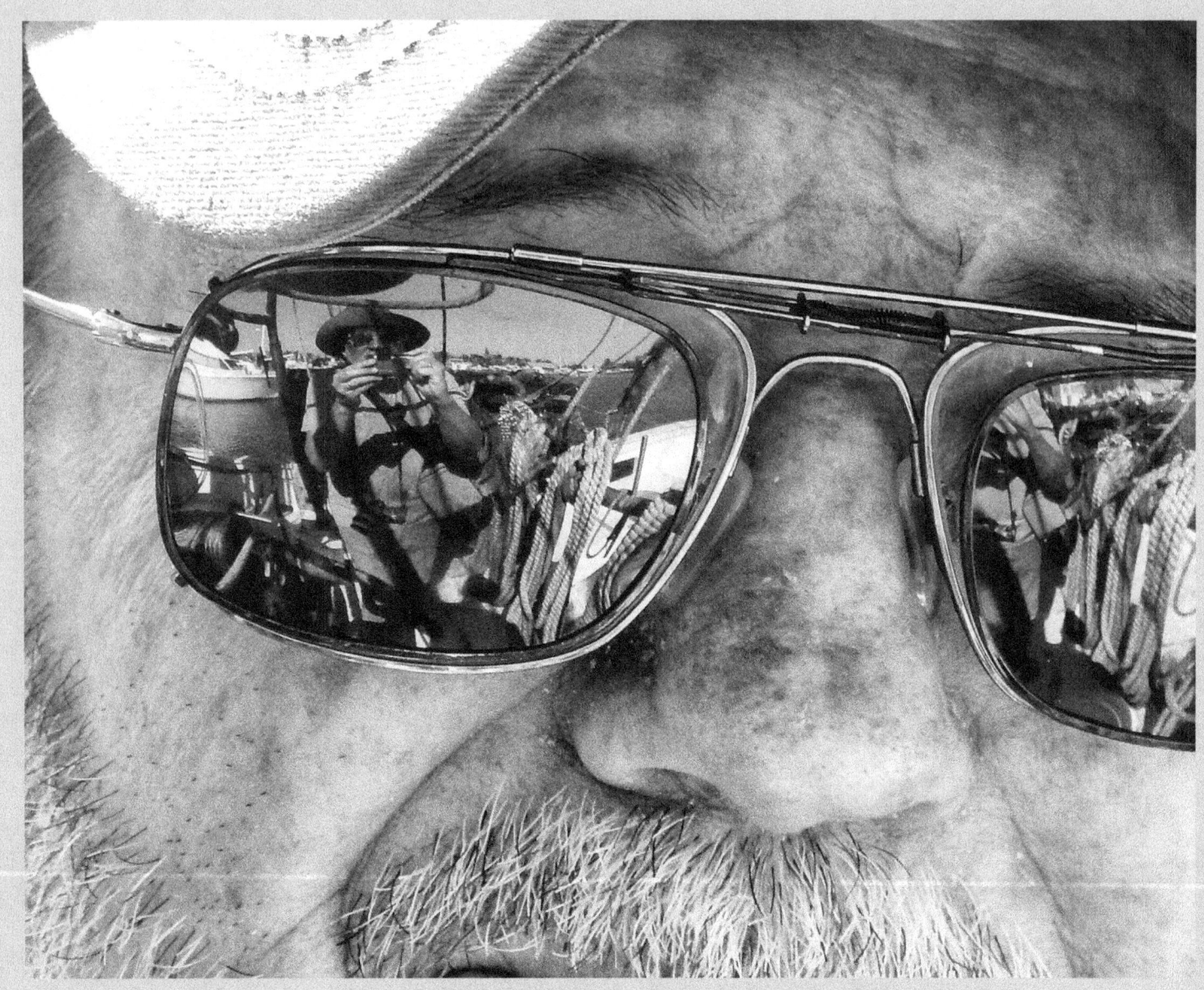

About the Author: John Van Horn is a writer and photographer residing in both South Carolina and Pennsylvania, which affords him a wide variety of subjects. His first novel, *The Tucson Phantom*, was published in 2016; he is presently working on his next novel, expected to be published this year. *Faces of the Sea* is John's fifth photo study, and there are several more in the works.